NEW IRISH WRITING

NEW IRISH WRITING

Edited by Colm Tóibín

BLOOMSBURY

First published 1993

This compilation © 1993 by Bloomsbury Publishing Ltd
The copyright of the individual contributions remains with the respective authors © 1993
This paperback edition published 1997
The moral right of the authors has been asserted

Bloomsbury Publishing Ltd, 38 Soho Square, London W1V 5DF

A CIP catalogue record for this book is available from the British Library

ISBN 0 7475 3205 2

10 9 8 7 6 5 4 3 2 1

Photographer

Tony O'Shea page 227–241

Typeset in Great Britain by Hewer Text Composition Services, Edinburgh
Printed in Great Britain by Cox & Wyman Ltd, Reading

CONTENTS

CONTENTS

CONTENTS

INTRODUCTION
Colm Tóibín

I remember when they came to the town. They were not like other traveller families of the time who would come to the door begging, the women wrapped in old rugs, often carrying a child. Unlike other travellers, this couple and their children wanted to settle, and they did not deal in horses or scrap, and they did not seem to have an extended family.

The woman's face was strong and open. There was a peculiar charm and kindness in the way she greeted you in the street, no matter who you were, even if you were a child. She smiled at you without wanting anything in return as she moved up and down John Street, Court Street, Rafter Street. She often had her children with her, and sometimes her husband. They drank a bit around the pubs and she wore a rug wrapped around her, and her hair long and straight. (At that time the Catholic women of the town all had perms.) I cannot remember whether she begged sometimes or not, but it did not affect her popularity. She was liked and admired for settling and for sending her children to school.

Years passed. I read a report in the paper and then I was told about it in the town. One of her sons, the eldest I think, had got into terrible trouble, had killed someone near a pub late on a Saturday night. Maybe it was an accident. Anyway, he was taken to Dublin and he started a jail sentence. I had been too long away from the town and I couldn't place him, but he must have been one of the small children who followed his mother through the streets.

More time passed and he was released. On a Saturday night/ Sunday morning soon after he came home he had a row with

2   his father, or so it was reported, and he ran through the town, breaking shop windows. He did not break the windows at random: he broke the windows of the big stores, and the more unpleasant, uppity shops. He spared the smaller shops, or the shops owned by pleasant, nice shopkeepers. He knew the town like a sociologist; he must have watched it as a small boy arriving with his mother and father and developed a sharp sense of which shopkeepers deserved to have their windows broken and which did not.

This is where the writer begins: the world of common knowledge. The town is life, society, language. Some have a sharper sense of these than others, but it does not make them writers. What then?

Let us pretend that there was one shop left unscathed which should have been attacked, if we followed the logic of the other attacks. Or one poor, innocent shopkeeper who was especially victimised. And this, then, is the stuff of speculation and gossip. Maybe there's a story there. And if there isn't a story, maybe we could make one up. Maybe that's the beginning.

But maybe there are other more important elements which spark off the imagination besides a peculiar twist in a tale. Maybe someone stood in front of that window, the one which should not have been broken, in the Market Square of that town and caught sight of a small piece of glass on the ground, and there was something in the shape, or the moment of looking, some grief, or beauty, something not deliberate and not easy to define, but nonetheless powerful, and it stayed with you for days until you could write it down. And then it was no longer a piece of glass, and you had anyway forgotten all about it, it was in words, and it was a story or a poem.

Or you turned in the afternoon light and saw the spire of Pugin's great cathedral, and a thought came into your mind for a moment, an insight, a conclusion you would draw if only you could hold it. And the other story, of the broken windows, which the whole town was talking about, had only been the beginning for something else, something you needed to say, to write down, if only you could get it right.

And as usual, someone stops to talk, and the story is gone over, the terrible deeds discovered first by people going to early Mass on Sunday morning, suddenly a word, a phrase, or a sound made by the tongue hits something in you, and you will never remember that this split-second was the first time an uncertain rhythm that you would use in a poem or a novel came to you, the word made flesh, and never left you again.

In the middle of the square the monument to *The Croppy Boy and 1798* by Oliver Shepherd stands greening with time. 'And since our knowledge is historical,' as Elizabeth Bishop has it in her poem 'At The Fishhouses', then we can make sudden, unforeseen connections between the recent act of defiance against the town's shop windows and echoes in the past. And we can move on to discover a year or two later that this first moment's thought in the square has led us elsewhere, has moved about in the imagination and been transformed and distilled.

And suddenly as you move up Cathedral Street, noting more broken windows, more hidden and unhidden motives, you think of elsewhere, the river at the bottom of Slaney Street, the new bridge, the flatness of Gorey town, the empty streets of Dublin on a summer's evening, the humid August air in Barcelona and you want to be away from this world which is so easily understood, in which so much is taken as given. And that longing to be away stays with you, and it, too, makes its way into words.

Let us call the town Ireland, and this book, then, is a sample of the reactions of forty writers and four photographers to the sights and sounds and the knowledge that inspired them. They have nothing in common except a beginning under the same sky, the same uncertain weather. And there is no collective consciousness, no conscience of our race, no responsibilities, no nation singing in unison. Instead, diversity, the single mind and the imagination making themselves heard.

Anthony Cronin

PRAGUE, MAY 1990

Imperial rhetoric adapted once
To comrades of the street or bed:
Tell them in England if they ask
What happened to your wits instead.
The two fires dust and damp ash, dead.

Nor banners elbowing as once along
The Ramblas like a river flow,
A transformation scene of wrong.
We see the puppet master smile
Hearing that open-throated song.

Analysis and learning led
To action which was always wrong.
No lodestar burning lone or high
Can show where faith was not misplaced;
The left is everywhere disgraced.

Nor logic, love, nor bombs, nor fire
Nor in that island of the west
Returns along the bloody gyre,
Desperate expressions of the letch
For the lost land of heart's desire

Will give us any other than
The state we're in. An honest man,
The noblest work of god, admits
That whether they were low or high
Those poor old dreams have lived their span.

The night shift with their sandwich tins,
Their faces lined and tired and grey,
At the last tram stop by the trees,
Dream also in this cloudy May
Of flats and cars and better pay.

So let it go then like a time
When beauty or a silly dream
Groundless of possibility
Lit up your days. Since what may seem
Selfless is often self-esteem;

And vanities the preacher said
Are at the root; since hindsight shows
The usual psychic masquerade;
Does that mean we must let things slide
Trust, like Lord Russell, to free trade

While millions die of interest rates
In Paraguay and Bangladesh;
The last brown trout turns belly up,
And acid, sent by corporate fates
Falls like soft dew on all twelve states;

And suffer the great spirit dearth,
The pointless agonies of birth
Whose issue is inanities,
Since no one now will ever see
The kingdom he proclaimed on earth?

6 'ON SEEING LORD TENNYSON'S NIGHTCAP
AT WESTPORT HOUSE'

And did he suddenly, while the little train clunked over the long
  stretch of brown bog outside Castlebar,
The farewell gaze of the younger Miss Browne still warming the
  impressionable cockles of his poet's heart,
The memory of her ladyship snoring through Maud last night
  becoming at last less painful,
Or while it clacked past the undrained fields between Claremorris
  and Ballyhaunis —
'They really are a feckless people, they never do anything except
  out of immediate need' —
Or perhaps as the Gothic spire of Roscommon topped a tangle
  of untended trees —
'They live in hovels but they spend thousands on churches' —
Did he suddenly remember
That he had not put in
The blasted nightcap?
And, seeing in his mind's eye the offending garment lying
  huddled on the bedside chair,
Hearing in his mind's ear how he had said to Lord Altamont's
  man, 'I'll pack the overnight bag myself',
And remembering how he had reminded himself, I must put
  that in,
Did he wonder in panic,
Would they send out for one from the Shelbourne?
Or would he have to go shopping in Dublin?
An appalling prospect, not to be entertained,
But he could not, he positively could not be without one on
  that draughty boat,
He would get his end.
And so, as the Byzantine mass of Athlone cathedral swung into
  the frame of the window,
Did he sit in gloom,

Becoming aware,
Once again,
Of
The heartache
At the heart of
Things?

REMINDER

The brain is protected by fragile shields a fraction of an inch
   thick,
The frontal, parietal and occipital bones,
Easily shattered, cracked or penetrated
By bullets, shrapnel, sticks, batons and heavy stones.

And if those eggshell shields of the skull are broken,
Because you are a target or happen, when the thing explodes, to
   be walking by,
In a casual second all that you are has vanished,
Your brain and the rest of you die.

Nothing then left where once was all in all,
Those delicate cells and fibrils now gone dead,
The lovely leaps of current and connection over
By which we hold a universe in the head.

We did not grow great scarps, the foreheads of mammoths,
But erect and lithe, with proportionate mind and face,
Depended on comity, compact each with the other,
From the moment one gripped a stone in some grey place;

And of course on imagination, reminding us that the other
Is also a consciousness, centre of cosmos and time,
Which weapons and blows can blot out: this tender reminder
Bringing home to our shrinking selves the finality of the crime.

THE CHURCH AND ITS SPIRE

John McGahern

I was born into Catholicism as I might have been born into
Buddhism or Protestantism or any of the other isms or sects,
and brought up as a Roman Catholic in the infancy of this small
state when the Church had almost total power: it was the
dominating force in my whole upbringing, education and early
working life.

I have nothing but gratitude for the spiritual remnants of that
upbringing, the sense of our origins beyond the bounds of
sense, an awareness of mystery and wonderment, grace and
sacrament, and the absolute equality of all women and men
underneath the sun of heaven. That is all that now remains.
Belief as such has long gone.

Over many years I keep returning to a letter Marcel Proust
wrote to George de Lauris in 1903 at the height of the
anticlerical wave that swept through France:

> I can tell you that at Illiers, the small community where
> two days ago my father presided at the awarding of the
> school prizes, the *curé* is no longer invited to the distribu-
> tion of the prizes since the passage of the Ferry laws. The
> pupils are trained to consider the people who associate
> with him as socially undesirable, and, in their way, quite as
> much as the other, they are working to split France in
> two. And when I remember this little village so subject to
> the miserly earth, itself the foster-mother of miserliness,
> when I remember the *curé* who taught me Latin and the
> names of the flowers in his garden; when, above all, I
> know the mentality of my father's brother-in-law – town

magistrate down there and anticlerical; when I think of all
this, it doesn't seem to me right that the old *curé* should no
longer be invited to the distribution of the prizes, as
representative to something in the village more difficult to
define than the social function symbolised by the phar-
macist, the retired tobacco-inspector, and the optician,
but something which is, nevertheless, not unworthy of
respect, were it only for the perception of the meaning of
the spiritualised beauty of the church spire − pointing
upward into the sunset where it loses itself so lovingly in
the rose-coloured clouds; and which, all the same, at first
sight, to a stranger alighting in the village, looks somehow
better, nobler, more dignified, with more meaning behind
it, and with, what we all need, more love than the other
buildings, however sanctioned they may be under the
latest laws.

Proust's plea is for tolerance and understanding that come from
a deep love, a love that is vigorous and watchful:

. . . let the anticlericals at least draw a few more distinc-
tions and at least visit the great social structures they want
to demolish before they wield the axe. I don't like the
Jesuit mind, but there is, nevertheless, a Jesuit philosophy,
a Jesuit art, a Jesuit pedagogy. Will there be an anticlerical
art? All this is much less simple than it appears.

The Church grows in the very process of change, Proust
asserts, and he argues that it had assumed an influence even
over those who were supposed to deny and combat it, which
could not have been foreseen in the previous century, a
century during which the Catholic Church was 'the refuge
of ignoramuses'. He names a number of great writers of the
time to show that the nineteenth century was not an anti-
religious century. Even Baudelaire was in touch with the
Church, Proust argues, if only through Sacrilege.

10   There is no danger, even today, of the parish priest being excluded from a school ceremony in Ireland. In any of the small towns it would be as much as a person's social life was worth to try to keep him away, which does not make Proust's truth less applicable. If the eighteenth-century church in France was 'the refuge of ignoramuses', my fear is that the Church in twentieth-century Ireland will come, in time, to be seen similarly, and my involvement was when it was at the height of its power.

My early grammar was made up of images. The first image was the sky; in that, at least, it is in harmony with the spire of Illiers. Heaven was in the sky, and beyond its mansions was the Garden of Paradise. House of Gold, Arc of the Covenant, Gate of Heaven, Morning Star were prayed to each night. One of my earliest memories is of looking up at the steep, poor rushy hill that rose behind our house and thinking that if I could climb the hill I would be able to step into the middle of the sky and walk all the way to the stars and to the very gate of heaven. I could not have understood then that it was necessary to pass through death to reach that gate.

If heaven was in the sky, hell was in the bowels of the earth, but not our earth, an earth that was elsewhere. A great dark river overhung with swirling mists flowed past an entrance screened by mountains and great boulders. Across a wide desolate plain came the souls of the damned from the seat of judgement, naked and weeping, bearing only a single coin to give to the boatman to take them across the river and into eternal fire.

Between this hell and heaven purgatory was placed. It had no entrance and descriptions of it were vague, probably because everybody expected to spend some time there before gaining heaven, as the saints alone went straight to God. The physical heat of the flames was as great as in hell but the suffering was leavened by the expectation of the eternal happiness to come, the sight of the face of God in heaven. Another part of purification was to relive transgressions committed in life in order to undo them. Yeats's play *Purgatory* revolves around this idea:

> She must live
> Through everything in exact detail
> Driven to it by remorse, and yet
> Can she renew the sexual act
> And find no pleasure in it and if not
> If pleasure and remorse must both be there
> Which is the greater?

More prosaically, I heard an old Guard, who had been a shoemaker before joining the police, complain good-naturedly as he stitched a football one Sunday (there was only one football in the village, it had burst before an important match, and all manual work was forbidden on Sundays) that we were asking a great deal of him because he'd have to undo each hempen stitch with his nose in purgatory.

Situated between earth and purgatory was limbo. Grave-faced children or infants with no stain but original sin had to wait there through all eternity, but without pain. Once we learned that limbo was no longer open to us after baptism and that we were faced with the likelihood of hell or, at best, certain purgatory, limbo appeared to be not such a bad place at all.

All this was learned in the home, through answers to ceaseless questioning, later through the catechism learned by rote in school, reinforced by constant images and daily rituals: the Pope's hand raised in blessing, the lamp that burned day and night before the Sacred Heart on the high mantelpiece, the silence that fell when the Angelus rang, the Rosary each night, the Grace before and after meals. We followed the life of Christ as a story that gave meaning to our lives through the great feasts of Christmas and Easter and Whitsun when it was dangerous to go out on water. There were even signs and manifestations. A boy in school was a seventh son, in a line unbroken by girls,

12   who had the power of healing; and we were told that the sun danced for joy in the heavens on Easter Sunday morning in remembrance of the Resurrection. When the sun did not appear on certain Easter Sunday mornings, hidden in the rainy skies of spring, we were told that it was dancing more carefree than ever behind the clouds. The contradiction inherent in the universe having a memory did not strike us then, even as we memorised that all that was past or present or to be was but an instant in the mind of God.

The time came when the religious centre moved from the home and school to the church. This was a natural, unconscious movement, and almost certainly began with the reception of the sacraments. All the doctrinal and ritual preparations for First Confession and First Communion took place in the school. The preparation for Confirmation was more elaborate because we were going to be examined by the Bishop. This took up much schooltime, but part of our instruction was given in the church by the old parish prist, Canon Glynn. On good evenings Canon Glynn would walk up and down the avenue of limes that ran between the presbytery and church reading his breviary while we played among the evergreens and headstones in the churchyard. At the time, people kept guinea fowl, and there was a boy in our class who had learned to imitate their call. So perfect was his imitation that when he climbed high up in the cypress by the gate he was answered by the fowl in the farmyards around. It was a terrible shriek. Mikey Flanagan was his name but all his life long he was never known as anything but the Guinea Flanagan. I remember little of Canon Glynn's instruction, other than the smallness of the class and overcoated priest in the empty vastness of the church, but I remember Guinea's call from high in the cypress branches with piercing clarity. The Bishop came that Easter. With his crozier and rich colours and tall hat he was the image of God the Father. At the altar rail he struck us lightly on the cheek. We were now soldiers of Christ. I became an altar boy, in scarlet and white, and began to take a more direct part in the ceremonies.

Before the printed word, churches were described as the Bibles of the poor, and they were my only Bible. I never found the church ceremonies tedious. They always gave me pleasure, and I miss them still. The movement of focus from the home and school to the church brought with it a certain lightness, a lifting of oppression, a going outwards, even a joy, that is caught in the very opening movement of the ordinary of the Mass:

Introibo ad alteri dei
Ad Deum qui laetificat juventutem meum

I will go unto the altar of God
To the God who giveth joy to my youth.

There were the great ceremonies of Christmas and Easter, but the ceremonies I remember best are the stations of the cross in Lent and the Corpus Christi processions. There were never more than a handful of people present at these Lenten Stations gathered beneath the organ loft. In the dimly lit church, rain and wind often beating at the windows, the church smelling of damp, the surpliced priest, three altar boys in scarlet and white, one with a cross in front, two bearing lighted candles, moved from Station to Station, the name of each echoing in the nearly empty church, 'Veronica Wipes the Face of Jesus', and the prayer:

O Jesus who for love of me didst bear Thy

cross

To Calvary in Thy sweet mercy grant to me

to suffer

And to die with Thee.

chanted at each Station.

Corpus Christi was summer. Rhododendron and lilac branches were taken by cart and small tractors from the

14 Oakport Woods and used to decorate the grass margins of the triangular field around the village. Coloured streamers and banners were strung across the road from poles. Altars with flowers and a cross on white linen were erected at Gilligan's, the post office and at Mrs Mullaney's. The Host was taken from the tabernacle and carried by the priests beneath a gold canopy all the way round the village, pausing for ceremonies at each wayside altar. Benediction was always at the post office. The congregation followed behind, some bearing the banners of their sodalities, and girls in white veils and dresses scattered rose petals from white boxes on the path before the Host. Jung remarks in his letters that the Gospels in themselves are such crude and naive documents that the myth of Jesus could not have taken root and expanded over centuries throughout the world if it didn't echo both current and older myths of a divine messenger taking on human form. Surely the simple Corpus Christi procession was a symbol of the divine leaving the tabernacle and visiting the ordinary human village for one mortal-immortal hour beneath the sky.

In contrast, there was the Mission. Every few years Redemptorists came to the village like a band of strolling players and thundered hell and damnation from the pulpits for a whole week. Stalls selling rosaries and medals and scapulars, prayerbooks and Stations were set up along the church wall for the macabre carnival. There was a blessing of holy objects on the closing night. The distinguished poet and translator, the late Eoin O Tuairisc, told me that on one such occasion an uncle of his, a keen fisherman, could find nothing but a wagtail in his pockets for the blessing and held it up with the scapulars and rosaries. That wagtail went on to catch more pike in the years that followed than any other bait that ever trawled the Suck.

These Redemptorists were brought in to purify through terror, but in my experience they were never taken seriously, though who can vouch for the effect they might have had on the sensitive or disturbed. They were evaluated as performers and appreciated like horror novels. 'He'd raise the hair on your head,' I heard often remarked with deep satisfaction. Poorer performances were described as 'watery'.

Some of the local priests were a match for these roaring boys, and while they were feared and accepted I don't think they were liked by the people, though they'd have a small court of pious flunkies. They were often big, powerfully built men. In those days it took considerable wealth to put a boy through Maynooth, and they looked and acted as if they came from a line of swaggering, confident men who dominated field and market and whose only culture was cunning, money and brute force. Though they could be violently generous and sentimental at times, in their hearts they despised their own people.

I remember a Canon Reilly well. He was so strong that he had once been able to lift railway gates off their hinges. The Canon was on his way to a sick call when halted by the closed gates. The railwayman had refused to open the gates because of the oncoming train. The Canon then lifted both gates from their hinges and drove across the railway track in front of the slow, puffing train. He ran little risk of collision. The narrow-gauged train had so little power that on steep slopes the second-class passengers sometimes had to get out and walk. Canon Reilly was also famous for the burnt-out clutches in his cars. He had never learned how to change gears, and when he met someone he wanted to talk to he would just put his foot on the clutch. It was known to be a delicate balancing act for his interlocutors to catch his words above the engine while staying clear of the car in case the clutch was forgotten in the heat of conversation. Also, the Canon carried a length of electric flex in a small suitcase round to the schools with which he chastised various delinquents, and every Sunday after second Mass he stood by the church gate ready to pounce on any boy attempting to escape Master Gannon's catechism class, which took place in a corner of the church at the end of Mass. Generally, the boys were hauled back into church by the ear.

16   The Canon also involved himself in an outing my father made each year to the Ulster Final in Clones. When one particular year he decided to take me with him to hear second Mass in Ballinamore before setting out, I warned him that I did not think it a good idea because of the Canon and that it'd be safer to attend Mass in some town closer to Clones. He laughed at my opposition and it seemed to make him even more determined to go to Ballinamore. I kept as close as I could to my father as we left the church, but I hadn't much hope once I saw the Canon's huge bulk at the gate. I was seized by the ear.

'He's with me,' my father said.

'I don't care who he's with. Like every other boy he's going to attend catechism class after Mass.'

'We are on our way to the Ulster Final and it is already late.'

'I don't care if you're on your way to Timbuctoo.'

'I ask you to let go of his ear.'

'He's going back into his class like every other boy.'

'If you refuse to release his ear, I'm taking hold of your ear.' My father, in plain clothes for the football match, was the sergeant in charge of a small barracks, but it was twenty miles away, and well outside the Canon's jurisdiction.

Even looking back on it across the years from a totally changed society it was an extraordinary act. The catechism declared it a sacrilege to touch or defile a holy person, place or thing. Some young priests played football and I had heard serious debates as to whether it was permissible or not to shoulder-charge an anointed priest within the rules of the game.

In this manner, under the sanctuary lamp before the high altar, my father, the Canon, and I stood, and after some verbal wrangling it was agreed that if I was allowed to join Master Gannon's class in the side chapel I would be asked one question, and if I answered it we could leave straight away for Clones. Ears were then released.

'Ask this fellow one question and if he answers it he can leave,' the Canon said to Master Gannon.

There was a twinkle of amusement in the teacher's eyes that did not reassure me till he asked, 'Who made the world?'

'God made the world.' I hadn't expected such an easy question. I stood in terror in case the question was difficult and I failed and was detained.

'Go. Both of yous go before I lose control of myself,' the Canon roared.

Another kind of priest was a Dr McLaughlin, who was thought to be a brilliant man, mostly, I suspect, because of his doctorate. He was, plainly, disturbed and remained a curate all his life. 'Great minds are close to madness,' was widely quoted. He was often seen driving around with his ancient mother, but on Sundays he would shout dire warnings against all feminine allurements. 'You may consider them visions of paradise when they are painted and powdered and dressed to kill on a Saturday night, but see them on Monday mornings when the powder and paint is taken off!' More strangely, he used to fulminate against those who had recourse to the Last Sacrament too frequently: 'There are some individuals in this parish who have enough oil on them to float a battleship!' On the eve of great feasts, when there were long queues outside all the other confession boxes, the queue outside his was either nonexistent or noticeably short. There was always the possibility of an eruption from within the darkness of his box: 'How dare you come into me with a soul like this!' and all eyes would fasten on the penitent's curtain to wait for the emergence of the disgraced sinner.

In contrast was a young and intelligent priest who took over for a few months when the Canon had to go into hospital. His sermons were short and simple and delivered quietly. They related Christianity to the lives of people and stated that quiet reflection on the mystery of life was in itself a form of prayer; and they dealt with character assassination, vindictive-ness, marital violence, child beating, dishonesty, and the primary place of love and charity of mind. Prominent people were furious, and some of the worthies in the front seats lifted up the

18   heavy kneelers and let them down with a bang while he spoke
to show their disapproval. They rejoiced when he left. Their
satisfaction took the form of a deep and troubled censorious-
ness. What they really wanted was hell and damnation, which
they could apply, like death, to other people: it is no accident
that funerals remain our most frequent and important carnivals.
Religion, like art and politics, can only safely reflect what is on
the ground.

Church and school and state worked hand in hand. Years
later when I was a national teacher I totted up the teaching
hours and discovered that slightly more than half the *clar* of that
particular day had gone on religious instruction and the
teaching of Irish. How the children received a rudimentary
education is difficult to imagine, and probably the truth is that
many of those less fortunate in the kind of homes they came
from did not.

I left national school to go to the Presentation College in
Carrick-on-Shannon. A few years earlier a Mrs Lynch opened
the Rosary High School in the town, which provided
secretarial training as well as secondary schooling. The Marist
Convent for girls had been long established. A woman in
charge of a school of adolescent boys and girls must have set off
all kinds of ecclesiastical alarms, and the Presentation Brothers
were brought in to close her down. They did not succeed, with
the result that the poor area around Carrick had one of the
most open and competitive secondary-school systems when
that kind of education was available only to the well-off or
scholastically brilliant.

The Brothers were remarkably liberal for that time, con-
centrating more on academic excellence and sport than on the
world to come, and the lay teachers they employed were in a
similar mould. I owe them nothing but gratitude. They
considered themselves somewhat superior. A Brother Damien
used to address us every summer before we went on holiday
with, 'My dear boys, you'll discover the more you enter into
life that this country has more than its surfeit of human

ignorance, and once it is learned you're attending the *Brothers* it'll be assumed to be the *Christian* Brothers. Now, inform these people from me that you are Christian in the sense that you are not pagan, but *in no other sense*.' When I came to teach for the Christian Brothers – I taught for a year in their school in Drogheda – I saw that the two Orders, in attitudes at least, were worlds apart.

All through this schooling there was the pressure to enter the priesthood, not from the decent Brothers but from within oneself. The whole of our general idea of life still came from the Church, clouded by all kinds of adolescent emotions heightened by the sacraments and prayers and ceremonies. Still at the centre was the idea: in my end is my beginning. The attraction was not joy or the joyous altar of God; it was dark, ominous, and mysterious, as befits adolescence and the taking up, voluntarily, of our future death at the very beginning of life, as if sacrificing it to a feared God in order to avert future retribution. There was, too, the comfort of giving all the turmoil and confusion of adolescence into the safekeeping of an idea.

The ordained priest's position could not have been easy either. No matter what their power and influence was they were at that time completely cut off from the people, both by training and their sacred office which placed them on a supernatural plane between the judgement seat and ordinary struggling mortals. Though they were granted power, they were also figures of sacrifice, and, often cynically, they were seen to be men who had been sacrificed.

I went from Carrick to train as a national teacher in St Patrick's, Drumcondra, Dublin. Teaching was known then as the second priesthood. Everything that happened during that training pointed to the fact that our function had been already defined by the Church. We were being trained to lead the young into the Church, as we had been led, and to act as a kind of non-commissioned officer to the priests in the running of the parish. In all things we would be second to the priest, including education. They gave us no education to speak of other than some teaching practice. What was under scrutiny at all times was our 'character', not in the true sense of the word but in the sense that we would be religious in observance, obedient and conventional, cogs in an organisational wheel. The scrutiny took place mostly in the first of the two years. *Ni beidh sibh arais* was the dreaded sentence, and every year a number of students were not *arais* to complete the second year of the course.

Each college day began with morning Mass and ended with evening Devotions in the chapel. Each meal was served by small boys from the orphanage in Artane in the huge refectory framed by public prayers of blessing and thanksgiving. All the societies in the college were religious. There wasn't a literary or historical or philosophical or, even more surprising, a Gaelic society. A few did attempt to start some kind of intellectual society, but they were hounded mercilessly by other students and dubbed *oideachas eireann*. They were seen, in the grand Irish phrase, as getting above themselves. Not to attend daily Mass or evening Devotions was to invite certain expulsion. Not to belong to a religious society in the first year was to put oneself in danger.

As soon as I could I joined the Society of St Vincent de Paul. (Ambrose Bierce's definition of a coward is one who in an emergency thinks with his heels.) I remember well visiting an old woman in a slum off Talbot Street. There was the unmistakable smell of poverty in her room, a photograph of a British soldier in uniform was on the peeling wallpaper. Myself and the other Brother were eighteen years of age. We sat and questioned the woman on the state of her soul. Her answers were properly hypocritical, she got her food tickets, and we solemnly reported on the visit to the Society.

We were allowed to go outside the college on Wednesday and Saturday afternoons and all day on Sundays, but even then we had to be back for meals. The gates were locked at

ten. Anybody late had to climb the high barbed-wired wall or
enter through the president's house. That required serious
explanations. Any whiff of alcohol was guaranteed disgrace
and freedom in the morning.

After the Presentation Brothers in Carrick I found the
college half-barbaric and hid behind a kind of clowning. It
is only fair to add that those students who came from the
Diocesan seminaries found the place quite agreeable by
comparison. Seminaries at that time were pointed firmly
towards Maynooth, and as ours was the second priesthood
it could afford to be less rigorous.

When we left the college, the dean, a Father Johnston, a
strange figure known as 'the Bat', gave us all a little packet of
salt, very like promotional packets of breakfast cereals that are
pushed through letter boxes nowadays. I think it was called
Cerberus. The Bat informed us that while we had our own
Catholic country now, nearly all the wealth of the country was
controlled by Protestants or Jews. This salt was the one brand
owned by a Catholic company. Saxa, the best-selling salt, was
in the hands of the Protestants. As we were sent out to lead the
little children unto God, we were given the little packets of
Cerberus to promote Catholic salt and all things Catholic. At
the time when I had acquired the sky above the rushy hill as the
image of heaven and all eternity, we were told that if we could
manage to place a pinch of salt on a bird's tail we could capture
the bird, even in flight, and we threw salt time and time again
towards branches where birds sat. The little packets of Cerberus, I am happy to report, proved as ineffectual as the other
grains of salt we had scattered so hopefully on the swift birds.

In *The Human Condition* Hannah Arendt describes how
Christianity displaced the ancient order:

> For the Christian, glad tidings of the immortality of the
> individual human life had reversed the ancient relation-
> ship between man and world and promoted the most

mortal thing, human life, to the position of immortality, which up to then the cosmos held.

In doing so, it made this world subservient to the world to come. The fear of God displaced the fear of death, and this solid world of ours became no more than a testing ground or place of trial for our position in the eternal world to come. Arendt points out that this intrinsic value given to life still remains unchallenged in purely secular modern states long after the reason for it has been lost:

> If modern egoism were the ruthless search for pleasure (called happiness) it pretends to be, it would not lack what in all truly hedonistic systems is an indispensable element or argumentation – a radical justification of suicide. This lack alone indicates that in fact we deal here with life philosophy in its most vulgar and least critical form. In the last resort, it is always life itself which is the supreme standard to which everything else is referred, and the interests of the individual as well as the interests of mankind are always equated with individual life or the life of the species as though it were a matter of course that life is the highest good.

In the older civilizations suicide was thought preferable to an intolerable life. Unwanted new-born infants were left by the wayside. A slave would want to commit suicide if he realised his condition.

The spirit of Proust's spire pointing upwards into the sunset 'where it loses itself so lovingly in the rose-coloured clouds, and which, at first sight, to a stranger alighting in the village, looks somehow better, nobler, more dignified, with more meaning behind it, and with, what we all need, more love' than the other buildings – was the spirit of the Christianity to which the Gothic cathedrals gave such extraordinary architectural expression. The religion was the same for the earlier Romanesque cathedrals, but the preoccupation with sin and the consequence of sin had been transformed into an elevation and emancipation of the soul, of love and light, height and openness.

In Ireland we were left the Romanesque spirit – the low roof, the fortress, the fundamentalists' pulpit-pounding zeal, the darkly ominous and fearful warnings to transgressors. To some extent this can be explained by history, but it was further emphasised when the Church was re-established by Great Britain as a tool of colonial order. The huge nineteenth-century presbyteries all over Ireland for celibates are touching examples of British benevolence.

After Independence, Church and State became inseparable, with unhealthy consequences for both. The Church grew even more powerful and authoritarian: it controlled all of education, and, through its control of the hospitals, practically all of health-care too. The right to divorce was taken away from minorities. The special position of the Church was even inserted into the Constitution. Childishness was nurtured and encouraged to last a whole life long. Foolish pedantry took the place of thought and feeling. (When I was young I heard a conversation between a priest and teacher on whether Einstein or de Valera was the greater mathematician. They came down firmly on the side of de Valera.) Faith and obedience were demanded, mostly taking the form of empty outward observances and a busy interest that other people do likewise, which cannot be described as other than coercive.

A kind of utopia was created in the national psyche. It was as if suddenly the heavenly world of all eternity had been placed down on the twenty-six counties, administered by the Church and the new class which had done well out of Independence. Those who managed to stay in this utopia – many of them deep in all kinds of poverty – even managed to think of themselves as superior to those unfortunates who were forced to emigrate into foreign unholiness. Few of our writers would have any truck with this state of grace, and the Church had even less truck with them.

24   The copy of *Ulysses* which I still possess was bought from under the counter in Brown & Nolan's Bookshop and wrapped in brown paper before it was handed to me. Since I knew it hadn't been banned I enquired why it wasn't on the shelves. The assistant told me courteously that putting it on the shelves would offend the priests from the colleges. School textbooks were the shop's bread and butter.

As well as the substitution of empty observances for reflection, thought or judgement, there was an obsession with morality, especially sexual, which resulted in an almost complete exclusion of the spiritual. I believe that religion and morals are two separate things. Religion is our relationship with our total environment; morals, our relationship with others.

When I came back to Ireland to live as a small farmer in the countryside I discovered that most of the people there had no belief, and they looked cynically on both Church and State. 'Oh, sure,' I was told as if it explained everything and how nothing under the sun is new, 'we had the auld Druids once and now we have this crowd on our backs.' 'Why don't you go to Mass, John?' I was asked by a dear friend and neighbour once. 'I'd like to but I'd feel a hypocrite.' 'Why would you feel that?' 'Because I don't believe.' 'But, sure, none of us believe.' 'Why do *you* go, then?' 'We go for the old performance. To see the girls, to see the whole show.' He was completely unfazed by my question, even mimicking the pious prancing of a fashionable woman as she approached and left the communion rail, and laughed out loud: 'We go to see all the other hypocrites!'

Given such a climate, when change happened it was certain to be rapid, and much of the power that the Church had in my youth has now gone in the South. In the North the power and structures have hardly changed at all, held in place by the glue of intertribal hatred and distrust. The changes in the liturgy are just one more example of emptiness – like restaurant owners who redecorate after

losing business — as well as a kind of pandering to a tabloid
mentality.

After being out of the country for a long time I attended
Mass for a social reason and found myself next to a very pretty
girl. At a certain point in the ceremony she suddenly turned to
me and shook my hand. I was amazed by the gesture until I saw
that everybody else was doing the same. I could not resist
whispering to her that perhaps it was a good idea, that one
good thing could lead to another: whatever had been encouraged by the small act, it was not spiritual.

And that spiritual need will not go away. If it is no longer
able to express itself through the Church, it will take some
other form. A letter that Jung wrote to a colleague in 1933 I
find wisely applicable to all the violence that now surrounds the
religious in a rapidly changing society:

As you see, I am wholly incorrigible and utterly incapable
of coming up with a mixture of theology and science.
This was, as you well know, the prerogative of the early
Middle Ages and is still the prerogative of the Catholic
Church today, which has set the *Summa* of Thomas
Aquinas above the whole of science. It has been one
of the greatest achievements of Protestantism to have
separated the things of God from the things of the
world. With our human knowledge we always move
in the human sphere, but in the things of God we should
keep quiet and not make any arrogant assertions about
what is greater than ourselves. Belief as a religious
phenomenon cannot be discussed. It seems to me,
however, that when belief enters into practical life we
are entitled to the opinion that it should be coupled with
the Christian virtue of modesty, which does not brag
about absoluteness but brings itself to admit the un-
fathomable ways of God which have nothing to do with
the Christian revelation . . .

26 In the original letter he wrote to George de Lauris in 1903, Proust concluded:

> Ideas and beliefs die out but only when whatever they held of truth and usefulness to society have been corrupted or diminished, and they will do so even in a theocracy.

Seamus Heaney

SKIMS AND GLANCES

1

Finding the right stone, just weighted so
As not to lose momentum against air,
Just big enough to get the finger hooked
And triggered round it, just plump enough
To skip before it skimmed: the excitement of it
Got me like fiddle music every time.
And not just me. We were all the same,
Casual at first, then warming to the search,
Picking, testing, stockpiling, face to face
With the whole extent of water, refusing
To give up.
           But, in the end, just having
To give up, reluctant and far out,
At arm's length from the throw we never made,
The one that would skim on and on and keep
Momentum, lambency, direction, drag.

2

Another airy nothing? But in your bones
You felt the good of fluency and give,
The lovely danger of it — as years ago
The skid and waltz of a Volkswagen began
Across black ice and the road swam out from under
The whole carload of us, ballasted and braced
And helpless as we'd been an hour before
Careering off the dance-floor at full tilt.

So loosen up, cast off, and go with it.

If thou be'st too hard, thou wilt be broken.
But what of the little reed that was not shaken,
The one who let fly and would not be gone
As he smashed the byre windows at Mossbawn?
That pure refuser, stander of his ground,
Out in the yard, a picked stone in each hand
And a pile of them beside him – but it's me
Pitching in like mad, methodically
Taking out the quarter-panes of two
Fresh-puttied frames the yardsman dared me to.
What of it? Here's my father at the door,
Too late, uncomprehending and unsure,
Looking hurt-eyed, the wind out of his sails.
How answer to the name he calls and calls?
How but own up to it, walk up to him
And start the trek to the land of skip and skim
By way of the old scenes and escapades –
The whirled slingstone, the dangerous crossroads –
Then farther out, compelled and distance-faced,
Until the throwing arm is exorcised?
Until each one comes round, changed through and through,
Yet sheer and steadfast as a broken window,
All-heeding, strange, wide open, equal to.

EXTRACT FROM FAMILY

Roddy Doyle

Family *is a story for television, in four hour-long episodes. Each episode is followed from the point of view of a different member of the family. The family name is* SPENCER:
CHARLO, *the father;* PAULA, *the mother;* NICOLA, *sixteen;* JOHN PAUL, *thirteen;* LEANNE, *eight;* JACK, *three. The extract below is from the second episode,* JOHN PAUL'S *story.*

1. INT. SCHOOL/ATTIC. DAY.

JOHN PAUL SPENCER *and two friends,* FATS *and* TERENCE, *have climbed through a gap left by a broken tile in the school-toilet ceiling. They are in the dark – the attic – walking carefully along the wall dividing two classrooms.* JOHN PAUL *is leading. The three boys are in uniform but, in the gloom, this isn't clear.*

FATS *is very skinny; he's a bit of an eejit, a nice one.* TERENCE *fancies himself as a rapper. He says 'Yoh' a lot but when he's excited he forgets that he's not a black American.*

They say nothing as they edge dramatically forward; JOHN PAUL, *then* TERENCE, *then* FATS. *Then* TERENCE, *for fun, pushes* JOHN PAUL.

JOHN PAUL *falls through more ceiling tiles into a class room and lands on a desk.*

TERENCE (*hissing to* FATS):   Get back –!

FATS: Wha'? I can't turn.

30   2. INT. CLASSROOM. DAY.

JOHN PAUL *has landed in a first-year religion class; lots of screaming and laughter. The* TWO GIRLS *at the desk have nearly wet themselves.*

JOHN PAUL (*up to the hole in the ceiling*): You're dead!

GIRL ONE (*recovering*): Get off me drawing of Jesus, you, John Paul Spencer.

The TEACHER, *at the front, is dazed.*

GIRL TWO: It's all right, miss, it's not the devil; it's only John Paul Spencer.

BOY: There's more o' them up there.

JOHN PAUL: Shut up, you.

We see TERENCE'S *head disappearing. The* TEACHER *is recovering and is approaching the desk.*

TEACHER: You'll pay for this, John Paul.

JOHN PAUL (*affronted*): Wha'? It wasn't my fault . . .!

3. INT. SCHOOL TOILET. DAY.

We see FATS'S *feet hanging from a hole in the ceiling, searching for the cubicle wall.*

FATS'S VOICE: He'd better not rat on us.

TERENCE'S VOICE: Hurry up!

FATS'S VOICE: Will he?

FATS'S *feet are on the wall. The rest of him begins to follow. There's a* SENIOR PUPIL *sitting in the neighbouring cubicle, smoking, looking up at him.*

TERENCE'S VOICE: Hurry up!

4. INT. SCHOOL CORRIDOR. DAY.

A later day: JOHN PAUL, PAULA *and* CHARLO *are standing outside the school boardroom, waiting to be summoned in to a disciplinary committee meeting.* PAULA *looks worried,* CHARLO *hostile;* JOHN PAUL *has his head down. All are dressed in good clothes.* CHARLO *takes out his cigarettes, and wonders if he can light up.*

The PRINCIPAL *opens the boardroom door.* CHARLO *puts the fags back.*

PRINCIPAL (*suitably stern*): Mrs Spencer, Mr Spencer . . .

They, and JOHN PAUL, *walk past him into the boardroom. He closes the door.*

5. INT. BOARDROOM. DAY.

CHARLO, PAULA *and* JOHN PAUL *are seated at one end of a long table. The* PRINCIPAL *and other* TEACHERS *occupy the other three sides.*

Heavy silence: the DEAN *is flicking through* JOHN PAUL's *Progress Journal.* CHARLO *is staring at the table, then a photograph to the left of the* PRINCIPAL's *head; he notices a good-looking* TEACHER. PAULA *still looks worried;* JOHN PAUL *still has his head down.*

DEAN (*reading*): . . . late a.m . . . talking . . . disruptive . . . late p.m . . .

PAULA: (*almost apologetic*): He's always out of the house on time.

CHARLO: That's righ'.

CHARLO *gently thumps* JOHN PAUL's *shoulder.*

CHARLO: Sit up straight there.

JOHN PAUL *does what he's told; then his head goes back down.*

32 DEAN: . . . cheeky . . . homework not done . . . (*looking up*) That's just one day. (*looking down; reading*) late a.m . . . no gear . . .

PRINCIPAL (*interrupting*): It's intolerable, Mrs Spencer, you'll agree. Not just the attic incident . . .

CHARLO: He wasn't the only one that done it.

PRINCIPAL (*ignoring* CHARLO): We can't have it, and we won't have it. This is a school.

CHARLO (*to* JOHN PAUL): Sit up straight.

PRINCIPAL: Now, John Paul; do you wish to remain in this school?

CHARLO: Look at him; go on.

JOHN PAUL (*glancing at the* PRINCIPAL): Yessir.

CHARLO: He won't do it again; I'll make sure o' tha'.

PRINCIPAL (*ignoring* CHARLO): Are you prepared to abide by the rules?

CHARLO: Go on.

JOHN PAUL: Yessir.

CHARLO: Louder; sit up.

PAULA *cringes; she wants to hug* JOHN PAUL.

6. EXT. STREET/OUTSIDE SCHOOL. DAY.

CHARLO *is theatrically raging, ready to go back in and have it out with the* PRINCIPAL.

PAULA: Stop it . . .

CHARLO: Shower o' dry-arsed bastards. They can stuff their poxy school.

(*to* JOHN PAUL) Isn't that right?

JOHN PAUL *is nervously delighted.* PAULA *is furious.*

PAULA: For Jesus' sake, Charlo . . .!

CHARLO (*turning on* JOHN PAUL): If you ever make me waste my time like that again, I'll maim yeh, d'yeh hear me.

He hits JOHN PAUL. JOHN PAUL *is shocked and confused.*

CHARLO: And do your homework.

CHARLO *stops walking: he doesn't intend going home.*

CHARLO: It's their job. It's nothing got to do with us what goes on in there. That's their job, they're gettin' paid for.

PAULA *and* JOHN PAUL *have walked ahead a few paces before they realise that* CHARLO *is going no further. They stop.*

PAULA: He has to behave himself.

CHARLO: They should make him; it's what they're paid for. And their bleedin' holidays as well.

PAULA: You're ruinin' it.

CHARLO: Ruinin' wha'? Wha'?

PAULA *moves off.* JOHN PAUL *hesitates,* then follows.

PAULA: You're useless.

CHARLO: So are you.

PAULA: I'm not listenin' to yeh.

CHARLO: Good; don't then.

He heads over the Green towards the pub.

PAULA (*to* JOHN PAUL): Don't mind him. You'll be good for them, won't yeh?

JOHN PAUL (*meaning it*): Yeah.

34   PAULA: Good boy; do your best.

JOHN PAUL: I don't mess all the time, Ma.

PAULA: I know that.

JOHN PAUL: He hates me, Connelly does.

PAULA: No, he doesn't.

JOHN PAUL: He does, I swear.

PAULA: He's a teacher.

They walk together. The street is empty.

7. EXT. SUPERMARKET REAR. DAY.

A soft-drinks truck is being unloaded, watched by a gang of very young KIDS, *ready to pounce. The* DRIVER/UNLOADER *is keeping a very close eye on the* KIDS, *trying to estimate the distance from the truck to the door, and back.*

There is a waste field beside the loading/unloading bay.

8. EXT. WASTE FIELD. DAY.

JOHN PAUL, TERENCE *and* FATS *are sitting on an abandoned fridge in front of an old, cold bonfire. They're out of uniform. They're talking about the disciplinary committee;* JOHN PAUL *and* TERENCE, *in particular, doing a lot of spoofing and boasting.*

JOHN PAUL: My da stood up to him, he did.

TERENCE: Disc-ip-lin-ary committee, she-it.

FATS: My ma started cryin'.

JOHN PAUL: He said I was entitled to go to school.

FATS: She said I was adopted. And I'm not.

TERENCE (*reliving the event*): Yoh, fool! You're not going to suspend me; shit!

FATS: She always says that when I'm in trouble.

JOHN PAUL: Miss Shweppe said I'm very intelligent but I'm wasting my time.

TERENCE: She–it.

FATS: She said I was usually very nice . . . Did they make you sign a letter?

TERENCE: Yeah.

JOHN PAUL (*at the same time*): No . . . Yeah. But I wouldn't sign it. Me da said I didn't have to.

TERENCE: Say what? Yeh spoofer.

JOHN PAUL: Who's a spoofer?

TERENCE: You are, fool.

JOHN PAUL: I am not; what about you?

TERENCE: Spoofer.

JOHN PAUL: Spoofer.

TERENCE: Spoofer.

They try to push each other off the fridge, messing.

9. INT. SPENCER HALL. NIGHT.

The hall is dark; there is light coming from the kitchen.

CHARLO'S VOICE: Quiet now; loads o' hush.

LEANNE'S VOICE: What's goin' to happen?

CHARLO'S VOICE: Shush now; no talk, righ'.

36   10. INT. SPENCER KITCHEN, NIGHT.

There is a new microwave on the worktop. CHARLO, JOHN PAUL, LEANNE *and* NICOLA *are standing and sitting in front of it, waiting, staring.*

A tomato explodes inside the microwave. They all roar laughing.

JOHN PAUL: Deadly.

CHARLO: Brilliant, wha'.

LEANNE: Janey; it's after blowin' up. Did it?

JOHN PAUL: Yeah.

NICOLA (*enjoying it*): It's stupid.

JOHN PAUL *looks at* CHARLO *for permission, then loads another tomato into the microwave, and sets the timer.*

CHARLO: Good man.

They wait.

NICOLA: How does it do it?

CHARLO: Don't know. (*to* JOHN PAUL) Do you?

JOHN PAUL: Kind of . . . It just does.

LEANNE: Here it comes.

PAULA *enters during the next explosion. She hasn't seen the microwave before.* JOHN PAUL *tries to lassoo her into laughing. She attempts a smile for his sake, then –*

PAULA (*to* CHARLO): Where did you get it?

CHARLO: Found it.

JOHN PAUL *looks worried and aggressive, afraid that another fight is about to start.*

CHARLO (*to* JOHN PAUL): Show her.

JOHN PAUL (*eager; desperate*): Look it.

He loads the microwave and sets the timer.

PAULA (*quiet but insistent*): Where?

CHARLO: Don't worry about it . . . Look it now; watch.

The tomato explodes. PAULA *can't help laughing.* JOHN PAUL'S *relief is almost hysterical. He dashes to load another one.*

LEANNE'S VOICE: It's a terrible waste of good food, really.

Eiléan Ní Chuilleanáin

THE ARCHITECTURAL METAPHOR

The guide in the flashing cap explains
The lie of the land:
The buildings of the convent, founded

Here, a good mile on the safe side of the border
Before the border was changed,
Are still partly a cloister.

This was the laundry. A mountain shadow steals
Through the room, shifts by piles of folded linen.
A radio whispers behind the wall:

Since there is nothing that speaks as clearly
As music, no other voice that says
Hold me I'm going . . . so faintly,

Now light scatters, a door opens, laughter breaks in,
A young girl barefoot, a man pushing her
Backwards against the hatch –

It flies up suddenly –
There lies the foundress, pale
In her funeral sheets, her face turned west

Searching for the rose-window. It shows her
What she never saw from any angle but this:
Weeds nesting in the churchyard, catching late sun,

Herself at fourteen stumbling downhill
And landing, crouching to watch
The sly limbering of the bantam hen

Foraging between gravestones – Help is at hand
Though out of reach:
The world not dead after all.

STEPHEN

Anne Enright

By that time I needed anything I could get, apart from money, sex and power which were easy but hurt a lot. The angel rang at my door with an ordinary face on him and asked for a cup of tea, as was his right. He revealed himself on the threshold with broad comments about my fertility. Who needs it? I felt like taking the cup right out of his hand.

We wrestled for a while, which was just part of the job as far as he was concerned. I thought that he'd been wafting about since aye began, in that place where grief and joy are one, where knowledge is an old joke and Time is just another window. I thought he might do a lot of singing. I was wrong. The angels he knew were ordinary men who killed themselves once when times were bad. Now they had to walk everywhere, setting despair to rights, growing their wings.

I said I was glad that this was the way it turned out, that I thought everyone was too hard on suicides. It's not as if, I said, you did it just for fun. He said being an angel wasn't a free ride either. There was a lot of wrestling involved, a lot of regret. He wished, for example, that I would stop looking where his crotch kind of glittered while the rest of him glowed. He asked me how the despair was coming along. I smiled. I told him he was wasting his time on me.

Stephen had been gaffer for a construction company in Canada with some accounting duties and responsibility for a lot of materials and transport. He built a bridge in Regina and went on from there. Getting married was one of those surprises, he said, when you're just a kid yourself, but his daughters were the saving of him (they taught him how to read) and the bridges were great. Then there was all that clear sky and the crisp winters when your hand might freeze to the girders and you couldn't feel a spanner except as a burn. He was in Ontario in 1934, with a job nearly done, each side of the span cantilevered out over the water and gaping. One night he walked up to where the road stopped and stepped over to the other side. Actually, the noose froze. It was the cold that did for him in the end.

That was it, he said, and nothing left, apart from a lingering pain for humanity and a susceptibility to the cold. He gave me a smile of celestial beauty, which spread over most of him, but missed the marks on his neck.

'So what's it like since God died?' I asked, with a laugh. He looked at me.

'And how's your mother?' he answered. Which I thought was a little low since she is fairly happy now, considering. Besides, there are things between every mother and child best forgotten, when we all settle down and just get on with it.

Apparently it was just a stock question and second on the list. His own mother had doubled up with grief one day while clearing the dishes. She looked like she was trying to push her head into the teapot, because she had to press her face against something and she could not cry.

I was disappointed with all this mother-and-teapot lark. She was not the last thing he had thought of, before he died. I told him to get on with it and he went through the list.

The List

Did my mother weep, did my father die, did the two happen around the same time and which one caused the other.

Did I leave light bulbs burning alone, did I draw the curtains at night, did I ever put a plug in a socket just to make it feel happy.

Had I ever pissed myself in public, did I take pleasure in it.

42   Did I suffer from the feeling that I had left something behind on a train. Is that why I smoked, so I could check my pockets for cigarettes.

Had I ever been overheard in a private conversation. Had I ever put blood on a mirror. During the sexual act, did I suffer from regret.

Did beauty disgust me.

Did Jesus Christ die for me.

Did I ever hoard parts of another person's body, for example, a lock of hair.

Had I ever seen a pregnant woman swimming on her back.

I found my sexual feelings for Stephen quite disturbing. He had taken the precaution of sleeping with me at night. We were both looking for the question that was missing off the list and we needed all the time that we could get.

Besides, there were problems at work. I thought about him as he lay beside me, not making a dent. Just my luck, I said, cold hands and a rope burn, but he whispered in his sleep, until even the sheets looked happy.

And then there was always his ineffable smile of incredible beauty. There was also the fact that he was blessed, that all blessings ever given or withheld seemed to sit. in him, for example the blessing my mother never gave me, and the one I never gave her, despite the fact that we are both superstitious that way.

There was also awe, and awfulness, always a good one between the sheets. Not to mention the unutterable, the unspeakable and the inexpressible, lying by my side in hand's reach.

You're forgetting about purity, wisdom and grace, he said. Even a human can have them. 'No, I'm not,' I said, and made a pass at him saying, 'This is pure is, isn't it, this is wise?' and a lot of other very embarrassing things, as one does in these situations.

He said he thought that nymphomania was out of fashion now, but where he came from it caused a lot of parental concern. Various procedures might be followed, with or without the aid of anaesthetic, he said, and the mildest cure of all was a bag of powdered camphor attached to the back of the woman's neck. So he got out of bed to look for mothballs.

We were no nearer the missing question as he hovered four feet over the bed and cried all night.

By breakfast time I knew what I wanted to say. I wanted to say, 'It's not as if you don't think about it too, you bastard, about warming your cold hands in my hot crotch, not to mention the last thing you did before you died.'

'I cast my bread upon the waters,' he said.

My mother rang to tell me that I wasn't at work.

'You're not at work,' she said. 'Are you all right?'

'It's Saturday,' I said. 'How are you?'

'I'm fine,' she said, because we both lie the same way. 'Any news?'

'Nothing much,' I said. (There is an angel in the kitchen, breaking the toaster.) 'And yourself?'

'Oh nothing new here.' (Your father is dying, but so are we all.) So we hung up.

Stephen liked watching the television. He sat on the sofa and laughed. When the weather forecast came on he looked at the satellite picture, said, 'Wrong again! Ha ha ha.' He told me about an angel of his acquaintance, who had killed himself three different ways at once. His death, when it came, was so violent, that he was still scattering, and now, instead of walking, he fell like the rain.

And then there was the guy, he said, who died to the sound of kisses in the next room, which was, he thought, quite a nice way to go. 'He specialises in the sound of kisses, and their colour.'

'Really,' I said, thinking about blue.

We sat there all day, fighting over the remote control, waiting to see which one of us would snap. He cried at *The*

44   *News*, or laughed inappropriately. I did the same at *Little House on the Prairie*. He annoyed me by pointing out an actor in the crowd: 'I know him. *Cyanide*, 1964. Lovely guy. Specialises in the mothers of homosexual men, and shoes.' I said nothing.

I had to watch the show that I was working on. We called it *The Love Quiz*. I said, 'Have you ever seen anything so awful in all your life?'

And Stephen said, 'It is about Love, isn't it?'

So I went into work and made people love each other for a while.

The next weekend I took him into town. I was hoping that he might bump into someone more needy and snag on to their grief in the crowd.

I had to hold his arm walking down the street to get him through all the pain between the GPO and O'Connell Bridge. He knelt down outside Clery's and took some dirt up off the street like a child. I took him inside, down to the hardware department, and explained toasters to him, just to make the effort. I could tell by his enthusiasm that he missed the passage of time, he missed his body, more than he missed the body of his wife.

By the time we got to the river I loved him. He sang 'The Canadian Boat Song' for me. The rain didn't wet him and the wind blew right through.

We looked down into the water and I said that maybe we could make a go of it after all. I would give up money if he liked, and lust, if he had to be old-fashioned. I said that there was something between us that was real and strange, and just because he denied it, didn't mean that it wasn't there. The end of his nose went white, he said to me, 'If dying wasn't enough, how do you think that sex would help?'

'You're just like the last man I went out with,' I said. 'At least he put out.'

He began to sing.

He was still singing when my mother called to the house, with some food in a Tupperware. They seemed to get on fine.

'No one sang like that for me,' she said.

'If you want him, you can have him,' I said.

'Thanks for the chicken,' she said. 'It's nice to see you still care.'

'Don't be so bloody sarcastic,' I said and left them both in the kitchen, talking about God.

I went into the sitting-room and turned on the television to cover the sound of their voices. For a shy woman, my mother is remarkably loud. She said, 'I feel sorry for young women these days, so much is denied them.' She said, 'It is a pity that she can't sing. I always thought that a singing voice was the best gift of all. Never mind all the rest.' I turned up the television and started banging my head off the wall.

'You know what I think,' she said as I showed her out, 'about you and men.'

'Yes,' I said, 'now fuck off, Ma, and leave me alone.'

Stephen came into the hall. She turned to him. 'Where did I go wrong?' she said. 'The summer I was pregnant with this young woman, I swam in the sea every day. In the sun and in the rain. And I said to God that this would be my prayer for the child – whoever it was, whoever it grew up to be. And now,' she said, 'now look at her.'

That night I kicked Stephen out of the bed. When I got up to go to the toilet I found him naked, hanged by the neck in the shower. He said that it helped him to think. His small wings were a bit forlorn. By morning he was cheerful again. He announced that he had half an answer at least. It was not his place, he said, to care.

I rang my mother and told her that we were not to blame.

RIVER RHYMES
(FOR WILLIAM COLE)

Derek Mahon

1

Crossing the stormy Irish Sea
The Rev. King got drowned, I see –
But, lo! Young 'Lycid' skips in view
Twitching his merry mantle blue.

2

Beside the Tiber's icky mud
John Keats spat up a spot of blood:
Sighed he, 'I'd hoped to go to Greece
But now have fears that I may cease.'

3

Drifting drunkly up the Yellow
Went Li Po, the Chinese fellow;
Reaching down to grasp the moon,
He climbed too far and toppled in.

4

Beside the Black Sea's icy mud
The poet Ovid proudly stood:
'*Miserae mihi plura supersunt,*' quoth he,
'Old sport, *quam tibi felici.*'

5

Above the waves in Galway Bay
John Synge would smoke his pipe all day;
And later, when the day was o'er,
Listen to the people through the floor.

6

Beside the soiled and sunken Thames
Tom Eliot would play his games,
Impersonating a London cop –
Until his wife told him to stop.

7

Way out upon Dun Laoghaire pier
A light went on in Beckett's brain –
'I'll get this down when I'm in the clear
And nicely settled by the Seine.'

8

The Quaker Graveyard in Nantucket
Was where young Lowell said his piece:
'Will you stop killing sperm-whales, f— it,
And give us all a bit of peace!'

9

By Bantry Bay, his fame secure,
Jim Farrell lies who, taking ship,
Wrote *Troubles*, *The Siege of Krishnapur*
And, best of all, *The Singapore Grip*.

10

Beside the Lagan's oily murk
Seamus Heaney oft would lurk;
Though the clear waters of Lough Neagh
Were more his tea-cup any day.

DEAR MR JOYCE

Edna O'Brien

Was he garrulous? Did he wear a topcoat? Did he hanker after an estate? Did he play chess or cribbage? Once at evening time was he observed to step out, get into a carriage and immediately and for some mystifying reason get out again and disappear into the house? In short, was he a neurotic? Such questions we always ask about the deceased great, trying in our forlorn way to identify with them, to find some point of contact, some malady, some caprice that brings us and them nearer. Such questions are not satisfactorily answered in works of fiction (writers being by necessity conjurors), nor in the testimonies of friends because friends are prone to lie in the interests of love, hate, stupidity or venom. Ex-lovers are equally unreliable being for ever besotted or irredeemably wounded. But letters tell. Letters are like the lines on a face, testimonial. In this case they are the access to the man that encased the mind that was the genius of James Joyce, Aquarian, Dubliner.

He started to study medicine three times. No two occupations are closer than that of doctor and novelist. Both are trying to arrive at a diagnosis of some kind and hence a metamorphosis. Had he qualified he was bound to have gone on and been a gynaecologist, he with his obsession with wombfruit and the bloodflow 'chiding the childless'. In his youth he was suspicious, contemptuous, unaccommodating. He saw his countrymen as being made up of yahoos, adulterous priests, and sly deceitful women. He classed it as 'the venereal condition of the Irish'. Like the wild geese he had a mind to go elsewhere, it was not to follow an alien king but to

50   commence a revolution in words. He wanted to be conti-
nentalised. He liked the vineyards. He had a dream of Paris. He
likened it to a lantern in the wood of the world for lovers. He
had a craze for languages. In literature his heroes were Cardinal
Newman and Henrik Ibsen. To Ibsen he wrote, 'Your work
on earth draws to a close and you are near the silence. It is
growing dark for you.' He was nineteen at that time. Young
men do not usually know such things unless there is already on
them the shadow of their future. There was on him. He
descended into blindness. The eyes are the nearest to the
brain. He was beset by glaucoma, cataract, iris complaint,
dissolution of the retina. His nerves were like the twitterings
of wrens. His brain pandemoniacal. The sirens were always on.
He was having to take aspirin, iodine, scopolamine. It had its
funny side, this daily harassment of his. His eye doctor had a bet
with him that if the front wall of the lens of his eye was
removed would a cataract decide to form itself on the back
wall. He admitted that with such cryptic wit a man like that
could have written *Ulysses*. He was prone to betting. He
wagered a pound of dried apricots with his friend Ezra Pound
that his play *Exiles* would not be produced although at the time
there was a management in an agreeable tiz about it. A pound
of apricots, a pound of chops, plum pudding, Mass and
canticles. Religious motifs may have dogged him and Latin
words and Hades and Potsdam and melancolores and Atrahora
and the Portuguese for Devil but he remained a plain-spoken
man. In a tart and almost vulnerable rejoinder he was driven to
point out to his aunt that receiving a copy of *Ulysses* was not
like receiving a pound of chops and he urged her to give
cognisance to that fact and get it back from whatever hooligan
had swizzled her out of it, under the name of borrowing. His
mind was forever computing. In the next letter, or the letter
following, he plied her with questions. Had such and such a
house ivy on its seafront wall, how many steps were there
down to the sea, could a man climb over a certain railing into
Eccles Street. To him words were not literature but numerals,

digits, things that when he strung them together in his wild, prodigious way, took on another light, another lustre, and were the litany of his lapsed Catholic soul. He liked hymnbooks and tittle-tattle and all tongues to be welded in together. The English he strove for was pidgin, Cockney, Irish, Bowery and Biblical. To avoid being cloying, to run no risk of being literary, he always prefaced or postscripted his incandescent phrases with a joke. When asking Italo Svevo to collect a briefcase, he first described it with fiendish accuracy, its oilskin cloth, the approximate weight, the approximate measurement and the protrusion which struck him as having a likeness to a nun's belly. Then he said, 'In this briefcase I placed the written symbols of the languid lights which occasionally flashed across my soul.' Only by giving a pedestrian complexion to the whole thing could he communicate his real feeling, rather like having to make a declaration of love on a banana skin.

Love. Love as we practise it makes dotards of us all. Blackmailers. Infants. It is a solace to know that he sublimely fell into those traps. No detachment, no grand phrases but raging boiling lust and suspiciousness and doubt. His love object, and a lasting one, was from Galway, the city of his tribal name. Are such things total chance? She had reddish-brown hair and he wanted that she had fuller breasts and fat thighs. To achieve that he urged that she drink cocoa. Back in Dublin without her, where he was on the ludicrous mission of helping to have cinemas opened, he was racked with thoughts of their youth, their courtship, her absence. Was his son really his son? Was not the bloodstain the first time rather slight? Could he be smacked by her? Or better still flogged? Could he be her child? Could she be his mother? The brown stains on her girlish drawers sent him off on another rhapsody. Desire and shame, shame and desire. His own words for his own feelings were that they were mad and dirty.

The madness was there all right, the madness that through the long hours of day and night, when he attained divinity through language, murdered his eyes, his nerves and later his

52   stomach. He went far into far latitudes but he always came back. He came back with such weird reliability. He had to. He had to cope with poverty, piracy, lawsuits. Money was always on their agenda, or rather the absence of it. Borrowing and Lending. Checking the prices of food, of furniture, hotel rooms and much much later, the cost of mental institutions. He had dreams of grandeur. There were some very fine furs he wanted to buy for Nora. There was a necklace that he had made for her in Dublin, while at the same time he was sending his brother a telegram to say that he was arriving on the morrow, penniless. He suggested a linoleum they get for the kitchen, the shade of curtains and the armchair where he could loll. He asked his brother for Jesus' sake not to attack him with bills.

He attended to his own talent, not in the interest of bombast or self-aggrandisement, but rather like a faithful watchman. He had the fixity of the great and therefore no need of vanity. He estimated that three shillings would be a reasonable price for *Ulysses*. A tiresome book, he admitted. At the same time he was dogged by fear that the printing house would be burnt down or that some untoward catastrophe would happen to it. He assisted Miss Beach in wrapping the copies, he autographed the de luxe editions, he wrote to influential people, he hawked packages to the post office. He knew that the illustrious would change their minds many a time before settling down to a final opinion and he knew that many another would know as much about it as the parliamentary side of his arse. If there was a good review he rejoiced, simply because it might lead to another sale. If there was a bad review he asked sagely what method of suicide he ought to embark on. He was a distant man. Ambiguous. He wrote reams and reams of letters. and yet there was no knowing for certain what he truly felt about the people he wrote to. A slitherer, Jesuitically trained, and with a scorching wit. Getting shamrock so that it was a cloudscreen, a sham screen and from that to something else, derived from Syrian or Burmese or Heaven or Hell. Metamorphosis it is called. Then back to his bath buns. If he had a sign on his person it would be 'Beware of the Miserere'. He liked regional dishes. He liked a white wine that was named St Patrice. He knew that Oxford was where the best shirts were made. He asked an affluent friend for a spare tie and upon getting it was filled with a deferential effusion. Blind as only the visioned can be. His mind a conglomeration of colour, trinities, rainbows, double rainbows, Joyce knows what. Iridescent and onomatopoeic and sensifacient, all together. He must have often longed to have his brain dry-cleaned or exposed to the gales of the Atlantic Ocean. When he learned that the wild flowers of Carthage survived the devastation of centuries he likened that indomitableness to the lilts of children. He had two children, Lucia and Giorgio.

It was where his family pinged and impinged that his profound heart was bared. He believed that a mysterious malady had caught hold of them when they were small, in Switzerland. Lucia wanted to be a dancer and then an artist. Giorgio wanted to be a singer. Neither of them achieved their ambitions. At first he feared that their existence might sever him and Nora. As they grew older their needs became paramount. When they were absent from home he wrote daily and maundered into many languages because he liked to think that they were multilingual. For his son he copied out songs, sent sheet music, wished maybe that he be another John McCormack whom he both admired and ridiculed in that sparring way of his. Never the genius but always the father, livening them up with some story, some little memory that danced through his mind. Always in the cause of the 'mafacule', always.

Fathers and daughters. That terrible clench. He named her Lucia after the patron saint of eyes. She had to have an operation to have one of hers straightened. First she wanted to be a dancer, then an artist, a graphic artist. She was given to premonitions. She had the wisdom of the serpent and the gentleness of the dove, as he said. Again as he said, she was gay, sweet and ironic, but given to bursts of anger and eventually she had to be put in a straitjacket. He strove to right her. He must have minded terribly

54 not being God, he who had nearly attained a divinity through language. He praised her rubrics, her lettering, her designs. Long before he had loved the graphic fantasies of the old Irish monks. She was not Cézanne, as he noted, but he wanted her life to have point. It was more than fatherly concern, he saw into her. He tried to save her from institutions but she passed the line of demarcation, made too far a walk, out into the mental Azores, and had to be committed. One asylum was called St Nazaire. So like Nazareth. So like Joyce.

Towards the end of his life there came a thaw, a burstingness. He was famous then. There were picnics arranged in his honour. When he went to his favourite Paris restaurant the orchestra played 'It's a Long Way to Tipperary'. He was bowed to, at the opera. But it was not fame that caused him to mellow so, surely it was growth. He called on people, sent greetings, blessings, telegrams, entertained those he met with his clear tenor tones. He sent Mr Yeats an autographed copy of 'Work in Progress' and said that if Mrs Yeats cared to unsew the first pages of *Ulysses* he would happily sign it for them. He sent *Pomes Penyeach* to the Library at Galway University. They had a special reading desk made and he was delighted that his book, with Lucia's letterings, was on display for all the ex-hooligans to see. The spleen was growing out of his mind. He was the father of his family, a scattered family. He remembered Christmas, birthdays, old friends, he lifted a glass to old times. He had come to a height. He had achieved monumence both in his work and in his being. In neutral Switzerland where he and Nora went to be near Lucia he got pains that could only be relieved by morphine. The doctors and surgeons had a consilium and took him to the Red Cross hospital where they operated. There was a hole in his stomach resulting from an ulcer that had been his constant and undiagnosed companion for years. Two days later he died. It was January. He was bordering on sixty. It is hard not to believe in immortality, considering the death of dear Mr Joyce.

REMOTE CONTROL

Neil Jordan

I have a dream. I'm at a party, or reception, I'm not sure which. It has something to do with advertising. A group of salesmen enter who have developed new techniques in selling coffins. They are expert palmists. One look at your hand tells them when you will need it and how long you have to make your advance payments. They read my palm. Three weeks, they mutter. Pay us in cash.

I'm staying in the only bungalow available in the motel where John Belushi killed himself. The suspicion that it might be *the* one occurs to me every morning at roughly the same time – 4.30, when I sit bolt upright, wide awake with the uneasy impression that a stoned spirit has passed from the bedroom to the fridge. My imagination, which can work wonders, generally lies, so I attempt to get back to sleep. If it was a spirit it was definitely stoned, I tell myself, in a woozy opiate haze with no bad intentions. But sleep doesn't come and the pale orange light is beginning its march beyond the blinds. I know this light and its habits very well. It begins orange and lightens to a sliver on to the wall opposite me. This sliver grows imperceptibly into an elegant rectangle, long, stretching from ceiling to floor. Now although it grows, I can never see it move. A minor miracle in itself, I tell myself.

And as it grows, the colour of the light changes. From that orange, to amber, to the hue of dusty chalk. And as it changes, the rectangle widens, creates two minor, angled extensions on the ceiling and floor. And all these processes happen at once. And never, never can I observe the act of changing, I can only monitor the result.

56   Such are the delights of insomnia. And when recalled in retrospect, in the peace of one's home where the habit of drinking is not so despised and thus sleep is more readily available, they do seem like delights. But at the time, ten minutes' oblivion would more than compensate for all such observation. And sleep won't come, so observe it I must. And only when the light turns truly banal – when it's flooded the whole wall and assumed the colour of pale vomit, do I get up, put on my clothes and drive.

I drive because I need company, any kind of company instead of the isolation that seems the norm here. My car, parked in the wrong place, has a ticket glued to the windscreen. I can never get the hang of those things. I drive because the company of these strange, intent beings on their way to work is preferable to the company of nothing. I turn left down to Sunset and then make a right.

The street hoardings advertise the coming movies. Once I longed to get my name on one of those hoardings, I felt that people whose names were on those hoardings didn't end up doing things like watching the light come up when they couldn't sleep; they felt warmer than that, they belonged – they had their names on hoardings after all. Then when my name did come to be on a hoarding, a little one, tucked away to the side so that only very inattentive drivers would get to see it, I thought: this is not the feeling I'd expected, not the feeling I'd waited all those years for, with bated breath, the way the shyest daughter waits for her wedding-night. No, this is not the thing at all. I didn't feel more warm, more secure, I didn't belong to anything, I only felt stupid, standing with Steve Woolley in the middle of both lanes, cars hooting, saying get the fuck out, and somehow I knew then that having your name on hoardings was no guarantee whatsoever of untroubled sleep. In fact it made you sleep worse because you thought, why didn't they get a better hoarding, why do they have to be such cheapskates, maybe if the name was bigger or had a little line underneath it the way some names do, maybe that's the thing. And so you're awake once more, and you know that's not the thing, that's not the thing at all. I who wept for Dido's slave.

So anyway, I'm driving, a pathetic substitute for company. I'm looking for a restaurant serving breakfast at this hour. I know if I stop at one that is not quite yet open, that opens in ten minutes, a muddle will occur, one of those muddles that gives you the equivalent waking feeling of sitting bolt upright from your sleep. Something has made you uneasy and you don't know what it is. You suspect it is you of course, everyone suspects it is you, deep down in your heart you know it is you, and this mild confusion has only served to confirm your worthlessness. No, restaurants that are not yet open, or only half-open, are to be avoided.

I find one though – one that is open – and with the ease, the sense of belonging of a true man of the world, I slide beneath the sign that says Restaurant Parking. Now, approaching my view, is the gentleman whose job it is to open your car door, hand you a ticket, smile politely and park it. Now, someone who had driven in search of company, it would be assumed, would exchange some words, no matter how inconsequential with such a person. But for some reason I don't. I merely smile politely, thank him and walk towards the door. Now there's a strange thing. And walking in I ask myself why. Because it is not the done thing. I tell myself.

Now the restaurant is there, I enter the low door, it goes dark for a while and then the inside makes itself known to me. There is a smiling girl behind a cash-desk and behind her a kind of conservatory with seats for diners. Waiters, with a somehow European sense of boredom, are lounging on the seats.

Now, I know I need a paper to have breakfast with. A newspaper helps, in an indefinable way, somehow someone sitting with a newspaper knows what he's about; he has things to do, he's not just sitting having breakfast because he can't sleep. No, he eats as he peruses, he belongs. So I ask the girl for change for a dollar bill. In her slightly puzzled face I can see the

58 first hint of a major muddle; the first cloud forms, a slight shiver
of terror like the one caused by the stoned ghost who walked to
the fridge. The first thing you do when you walk into a
restaurant is ask for change. Explain yourself, something
whispers, so I do. It's for a newspaper. I say, and grin,
awkwardly, pointing to the row of newspaper receptacles
on the pavement outside. She smiles as if she understands
and the muddle passes. Thank you, I tell her, with inordinate
gratitude. I make my way out again, through the other door, to
the white sunlight out there and the pavement.

A word about these newspaper receptacles. First, about the
nomenclature. The name I've chosen is the wrong one: they
don't receive newspapers they dispense them, after you've
deposited a quarter in the tiny slot. They are simple, squat,
metallic things with a glass panel to display the particular
brand of newspaper imprisoned beneath. And I know brand
is the wrong word too, it seems to turn newspapers into soap
powder, but I am in a foreign country, trying to understand.
Now the newspaper receptacles, which they don't have in
London or Dublin, seem simple, ingenious solutions to the
problem of dispensing newspapers without involving people.
But there are hidden dangers. And the chief of them is these.
Once having got your quarter from the waitress, who
thankfully understands, the idea is that you drop the quarter
in the slot, lift up the glass panel and take out the newspaper
of your choice, which you are now free to read. But if in
your haste, or your misunderstanding of the process, or
through a pathetic attempt to be different about things,
you attempt to pull the glass panel while your quarter is
still rattling down the chute towards whatever home it finds
in there, the glass panel will get stuck, the quarter will be
lost, you will find yourself paperless, on the hot street, with –
God forbid – no more quarters. A muddle, if ever there was
one. You then have two options – if you have another
quarter that is. You can retreat gracefully, and have your
breakfast without the benefit of that form of discourse we call

journalism, or you can try again. And if you try again, the following steps are recommended. First, shake the panel firmly to make sure it is unstuck. Then, taking another quarter out, slide it down the hole, and after what any instruction manual would define as a decent pause, attempt to raise the glass panel.

So the paper comes out, bound by a piece of white plastic, a bundle of sections about one-inch thick, to be placed under one's free arm as one resumes an attempt at breakfast. So I make my way back from the hot pavement to the brown interior where I catch the eye of the girl behind the cash machine, who gestures me towards an immaculate waiter, again with a decidedly European air, who leads me to a place by the window.

By now the streets are buzzing outside, the hum of the traffic is a pleasing drone, the morning sun cuts the room in half and a girl in a pink tracksuit enters through it. The waiter sits her at a table near the door and comes to take my order. I refuse his offer of coffee and ask for tea. Coffee here is a generic concept, but tea is a rarity: there are varieties of the stuff one doesn't find at home. English Breakfast, I explain, and he nods benignly and leaves. The thought of insomnia has abated now, it seems OK to be awake with someone else in the room. Her pink tracksuit is quite immaculate, the colour Irish mothers favour for new-born babies, she has been given a plate of cereal and is reading a book. She is remarkable in that she has perfectly even teeth. A couple enter, also remarkable for their perfect teeth. The waiter brings my tea, and smiles, exposing his perfect teeth. I am in a culture, I realise, that has brought the science of dentistry to heights undreamed of in my philosophy. In early adolescence the teeth are ringed by metal braces, creating a mouthful of gleaming silver so that in early adulthood one can smile with comfort. If the chin is receding, or its opposite, creating what is known as an overbite, the jaw can be surgically broken. For those of us with unbroken jaws, without the benefit of a

60 steel-ringed adolescence, there is the option of keeping one's mouth shut.

Sipping tea without exposing one's rotting molars is not too difficult. Reading the pages of the *Los Angeles Times* is. A society where every fact is of equal interest, is reported with equal space and sonority, is one to be approached with circumspection. And such a society is Los Angeles, to judge from the pages of the *Los Angeles Times*. The acres of newsprint are endless, divided in alphabetical sections, devoted to world affairs, entertainment, civic affairs, fashion, cookery, property. And the dangers of muddle presented by the format are legion. I sit in my appointed place, balance the thing on my knee, try to break the piece of white plastic that binds it, and end up using the table knife.

It is the murders that interest me most, these triumphant expressions of contact in an isolated world. Currently running are the Millionaire Club Murders, the Cotton Club Murder, various serial treatments on serial killers and the ongoing saga of the gang killings. These are by far the most dramatic, with their portraits of young neighbourhood warriors with assault rifles, hand-grenades, Uzis and rocket-launchers. I read of how casualty wings have turned into battlefield hospitals. How medical techniques perfected in Beirut and Belfast are at a premium here. I remember a relative of a friend of mine who perfected a device known as the Sheehan knee, an artificial kneecap in great demand around Ballymurphy, and wonder whether I should give him a call. I wonder whether murder here has the same intimacy as it has at home and conclude that it must. The final, desperate expression of the need to have a chat.

But the day is in its element now and those peculiar traumas have passed. The restaurant is full, the place is buzzing and that peculiar self-loathing that happens in the twilight hours has gone. There are meetings to attend, calls to be made, the possibility of speech. I pay the waiter, smile without fear, grab the acres of newsprint into an awkward bundle and make my way outside, a citizen of something, of what I can't be sure, but then most others can't either.

Night comes and the muddle descends. I have to go to a preview of a movie I've made. The studio is nervous, the producers are nervous, the stream of traffic down Sunset seems to shake, I drive a convertible car with the hood down. The hood is down because I don't know how to get it up. The car, it seems, has some cachet since people wave at traffic lights, drivers of similar vehicles raise their heads in gestures of fellowship. I take the San Diego Freeway towards Long Beach and wonder at all the cars in the world. The signs flash by me with their unpronounceable, poetic names signalling the prosaic suburbs beneath. Taking the name of my destination at face value I anticipate a mass of white strand, a boardwalk, a long beach. But that is always a mistake. The presumption that place names hold a clue to what they signify is a peasant's one. The punishment for such presumption is murder.

I take the exit that seems the right one and find myself in that concrete, indeterminate purgatory that goes on for ever. Having forsaken all hope of beach I drive through the low-lit streets, past the gangs of kids at every corner, think to stop at a gas-station to ask the way. A phalanx of body-builders tries to shake me down, and I think twice about it. I drive on. I can picture the worst form of insomnia now, the one where you drive and you can't sleep because you can't stop. Now that the broader picture of Long Beach has failed, I concentrate on the specific, Lakelands, Long Beach. Getting wise to these things, I suspect there'll be neither land nor lakes. A Mexican kid on a street corner tells me in his broken Spanish to go to Willow and turn right. I go to Willow and turn right and drive for an age and find Lakelands. It is a mall, a small village devoted to commerce. People gather there, work there, sell things there, but don't live there. And in the centre of this mall is a movie complex which is previewing my film. It is here, I suspect, that

62 this isolation might end. I can see the cars and limos pulling up near the entrance and the queue of the chosen gathering at the desk.

A preview is a method of assessment. Movies are assessed in two ways: their playability and their want-to-see. The die for their want-to-see is cast at the outset, with the script chosen, the director, but most importantly, the stars. But their playability lies in the balance until they are shown. As with most aspects of film-making, the legends surrounding previews are numerous. About the movie previewed without its score, where the music got the highest ratings. About the movie previewed without its last reel. About the ones that scored high and bombed. But the reverse, I have been told, is never true.

And the thing about previews is that while the executives, agents and producers will tell you they mean nothing, you must never believe them. You must enter that theatre secure in the knowledge that they mean everything.

So you must enter the theatre in a calm manner, never fumbling with the glass doors or pulling them the wrong way. Resist all urges to smoke a cigarette. Dress neither up nor down. Shake hands politely with those who have given you the equivalent of the gross national product of Uruguay to make this tender little piece. They will tell you they *love* it – and it will be true. Their affection for your film is as genuine as their support for you was during the making of it. But you can see the nervousness, the terror that it might not work, the awful suspicion that what was so lovingly nurtured and constructed might turn out to be art and nothing else. And that thing that is so longed for, that necessary frisson between class and commerce, will have retreated once more until the next time, if there is a next time.

So the house lights go down and the picture comes up. A comedy of sorts, made by you who can never tell a joke, who always blows the punchline. Shot in sombre colours, with an opening reel so dark as to be terrifying. And you begin to question every instinct you ever had, every choice you ever

made, the very fact of your being born. Until the front titles 63
end and the first shots come up. And a small ripple of laughter
runs through the theatre. You are amazed; you never thought
this was funny, maybe they're laughing at the picture, not with
it. But then it happens again, and again and the thing takes off
with a life of its own like a horse let loose and all you can do is
follow it.

And you sit in the dark and think that life isn't so bad. Life
isn't so bad, after all.

THE BIRTH
Paul Muldoon

1

Seven o'clock. The seventh day of the seventh month of the year.
No sooner have I got myself up in lime-green scrubs,
a sterile cap and mask,
and taken my place by the head of the table

than the windlass-women ply their shears
and gralloch-grub
for a footling foot, then, warming to their task,
haul into the inestimable

realm of apple-blossom and chanterelles and damsons and
    eel-spears
and foxes and the general hubbub
of inkies and jennets and Kickapoos with their lemniscs
or peekaboo-quiffs of Russian sable

and tallow-unctuous vernix, into the realm of the widgeon –
the 'whew' or 'yellow-poll', not the 'zuizin' –

2

Dorothy Aoife Korelitz Muldoon: I watch through floods of tears
as they give her a quick rub-a-dub
and whisk
her off to the nursery, then check their staple-guns for staples.

MUSIC AT ANNAHULLION

Eugene McCabe

She put her bike in the shed and filled a basket of turf. Curtains still pulled across Teddy's window. Some morning the gable'd fall, and he'd wake sudden. Course you had to pretend to Liam Annahullion was very special. 'See the depth of them walls' . . . 'Look at that door; they don't use timber like that now' . . . and 'Feel that staircase, solid, made to last.' Bit of a dose the way he went on; sure what was it only a mud and stone lofted cottage, half thatched, half slated, with a leaning chimney and a cracked gable.

'The finest view in Ireland,' Liam said a hundred times a year. High to the north by Carn rock it was fine in spring and summer, very fine, but all you ever saw from this door in winter was the hammered-out barrels on the hayshed, the rutted lane, and a bottom of rushes so high you'd be hard put at times to find the five cows. Liam went on about 'the orchard' at the front put down by their grandfather, Matt Grue: a few scabby trees in the ground hoked useless by sows, a half-acre of a midden, but you couldn't say that to his face.

One night Teddy said, 'Carried away auld cod: it's because he owns it.'

'Shush,' Annie said, pointing upstairs.

'A rotten stable, it'll fall before we're much older.'

'We grew up here, Teddy.'

'Signs on it we'll all die here. They'll plant it with trees when we're gone.'

'It's home.'

'Aye.'

66   Teddy talked like that when he came in late. He drank too
much. His fingers were tarry black from fags, the eyes burned
out of his head. Even so you could look into his eyes, you
could have a laugh with Teddy.

She called up the stairs as she closed the kitchen door.
'Teddy, it's half-eleven.'

'Right.'

He gave a brattle of a cough and then five minutes later
shouted down, 'Is there a shirt?'

'Where it's always.'

'It's not.'

'Look again.'

She listened. 'Get it? In the low drawer?'

'It was under a sheet.'

'But you've got it?'

'I got it.'

'Thanks very much,' Annie said to herself. She hooked a
griddle over the glow of sods to warm a few wheaten scones.
She could maybe mention it quiet like, give it time to sink. He
might rise to it after a while maybe, or again he might know
what she was up to and say nothing. He was always low over
winter, got it tight to pay Liam the three quid a week for board
and keep. In the summer he had cash to spare, on hire through
the country with a 1946 Petrol Ferguson, cutting meadows,
moulding spuds, buckraking, drawing corn shigs to the
thrasher. Sometimes he was gone a week.

'Knows all the bad weemen in the country,' Liam once said.
'Got a lot to answer for, that bucko.'

Teddy came down and sat at the north window under an
empty birdcage, his elbows on the oilcloth. A tall stooped
frame. He ate very little very slowly, put her in mind often of
some great grey bird; a bite, a look out the window, another
bite. 'You were up at Reilly's?'

'We'd no butter.'

'Who was there?'

'George McAloon.'

'Wee blind George?'

'He's not that blind.'

Teddy lit a cigarette and looked out. He could see Liam stepping from ridge to ridge in the sloping haggard. The field had earthy welts running angle-ways, like the ribs in a man's chest, hadn't felt the plough since the Famine or before.

'Anyone else?'

'Only Petey Mulligan the shopboy. He kep' sayin' "Jasus" every minute to see poor George nod and bless himself, and then he winked at me, much as to say "mad frigger, but we're wise" . . . too old-fashioned by half.'

Teddy was quiet for a minute and then said, 'Religion puts people mad.'

'No religion puts them madder.'

He thought about this. He hadn't confessed for near forty years, lay in bed of a Sunday with rubbishy papers Liam wouldn't use to light fires. Sometimes they had bitter arguments about religion and the clergy. Liam and Annie never missed Mass.

'It's a big question,' Teddy said.

Annie filled a tin basin from the kettle. 'I saw a piana at Foster's.'

'Aye?'

'In the long shed at the back of the garden.'

'What's it doin' there?'

'They've put a lot of stuff out.'

'What kind?'

'Horsetedder, cart wheels, pig troughs, beehives, auld churns, a grass harrow, stuff like that.'

'Useless?'

'Less or more.'

'Over from the auction.'

'Must be.'

'Odd place to leave a piana.'

'The very thing, I thought.'

After a moment she said, 'It looks very good, shiny with two brass candlesticks, like the one in the photo.'

68   'Auld I'd say?'

'Must be.'

'The guts of fifty years.'

'And maybe fifty along with that.'

Teddy went to the door and looked out. Annie said to his back, 'Pity to see a thing like that going to rack and loss.'

'If it's worth money,' Teddy said, 'some fly boy goin' the road'll cob it . . . maybe it's got no insides or it's rusted or seized-up some way, must be something wrong with it or it would have gone in the auction.'

'If it come out of Foster's it's good, and it could come at handy money.'

Teddy looked round at her. 'Who'd want it?'

Annie shrugged.

'You want it, Annie?'

'A nice thing, a piana.'

'Everyone wants things.'

Teddy looked through stark apple trees towards the wet rushy bottom and the swollen river; rain again today.

'Who'd play it?'

'A body can pick out tunes with one finger, the odd visitor maybe, and you could put flowers on top of it, light candles at special times.'

Teddy was picking at his teeth with a tarry thumb. 'When one of us dies, Annie?'

'Christmas, Easter, times like that.'

He went on picking his teeth with the tarry thumb. 'It's a bit daft, Annie.'

'Is it?'

There was a silence and Teddy looked round; when he saw her face he said, 'Don't go by me, but it's a dud, I'd swear.'

'I'd say you're right.'

He took his cap from the top of the wireless. 'I'll see if there's letters.'

'Tell Liam there's tay.'

Annie saw him cross the yard, a scarecrow of a man, arms hung below his knees. Teddy wouldn't bother anyway. A Scotch collie bitch circled round him, yapping and belly-crawling. Guinea hens flapped to the roof of a piggery. She could see Liam blinding potholes in the rutted lane. Even in winter scutch grass clung to the middle ridge. Teddy stopped for a word; hadn't much to say to each other that pair, more like cold neighbours than brothers. Teddy went on down the road. Two years back Liam had put the post box on an ash tree near the gate . . . 'To keep Elliot the Postman away from about the place.'

'What's wrong with him?' Teddy had asked.

'Bad auld article,' Liam said.

'What way?'

'Handles weemen, or tries to, in near every house he goes to, anyway he's black Protestant.'

Teddy let on he didn't understand. 'Handles weemen? What weemen?'

Liam got redder. 'He'll not put a foot about this place.'

Annie thought about Joe Elliot, a rumpledy wee fellow, with a bate-in face, doggy eyes, and a squeaky voice. No woman in her right mind could let him next or near her without a fit of the giggles, but there was no arguing with Liam. He was proud and very private. Four or five signs about the farm forbade this and that. A 'Land Poisoned' sign had been kept up though there hadn't been sheep about Annahullion for twenty years. When stray hounds crossed the farm Liam fired at them. Every year in the *Anglo-Celt* he put a notice prohibiting anyone from shooting or hunting.

'Jasus,' Teddy said, 'thirty wet sour acres and maybe a dozen starved snipe, who's he stopping? Who'd want to hunt or shoot about here? There's nothin', only us.'

Near the bridge there was a notice 'Fishing Strictly For-bidden'. The river was ten feet wide, the notice nailed to an alder in a scrub of stunted blackthorn that grew three yards out from the river bank. When the water was low barbed-wire

70 under the bridge trapped the odd carcass of dog and badger; sometimes you could see pram wheels, bicycle frames, tins and bottles. Liam once hooked a pike on a nightline. She had cooked it in milk. It tasted strong, oily, Teddy wouldn't touch it: 'I'd as lief ate sick scaldcrows, them auld river pike ates rats and all kinds of rubbish.'

Annie found it hard to stomach her portion. She fed the left-overs to the cat. Teddy swore later he saw the cat puke. Liam was dour for days. She heard him crossing the yard now and began pouring his tea; he blessed himself as he came across the floor, pulling off the cap.

'Half-eleven, I'd say?'

'Nearer twelve,' Annie said.

Liam nodded and sucked at his tea. 'You could say midday.'

'Next or near, you could say that.'

Liam shook his head. Every day or so they had this exchange about Teddy.

'I'm never done tryin' to tell him,' Annie said. 'I get sick hearin' myself.'

'It's a pity of any man, he couldn't be tould often enough or strong enough.'

'True for you,' Annie said, and thought how neither of them ever dared a word, let alone hint. Teddy was his own man, paid steady for his room, helped about the yard or farm when he felt like it. Liam sucked his teeth. They were big and a bad fit, put you in mind of a horse scobing into a sour apple. He was squatter than Teddy, sturdier, slate-coloured eyes and tight reddish skin. He smiled seldom and no one had ever heard him laugh. Sometimes Annie heard him laugh alone about the yard and fields.

'Same as the Uncle Eddie,' Liam said, 'lazy and pagan and you know how he ended. In a bog-hole . . . drunk . . . drownded.'

Crabbed this morning, better leave it till evening. 'Teddy said you remarked a piana at Foster's.'

Oh God, Annie thought and said, 'I saw it from the road.'

Liam ate another scone before he said, 'Scrap.'

'I'd say.'

'Whole place was red out at the sale. Piana must have been lyin' about in a pig house or some of them auld rotten lofts.'

'That's what Teddy said, a dud.'

'He's right about that anyway.'

And that's that, Annie thought. Soon they'd all be pensioned, maybe then she could buy the odd thing. It was put up to her to run the house on the milk cheque. It could be a very small one in winter. She made up by crocheting, anything but approach Liam. All afternoon she thought of the piano. In the end she found herself crying as she kneaded bread. Yerra God, she thought, I'm goin' astray in the head . . . an auld scrap piana, an' not a body in the house fit to play, and here I am all snivels over the head of it. She blew her nose and put it out of her mind.

It was dark when Teddy got back. He smelled of whisky and fags and his eyes looked bright. Liam didn't look up from the *Anglo-Celt*.

'Your dinner's all dried up,' Annie said.

'No odds,' Teddy said.

Liam switched on the wireless for the news. They all listened. When it was over Teddy said, 'I saw your piana, I made a dale for it.'

'Ah you're coddin', Teddy!'

'It's out of tune.'

'That's aisy fixed.'

'Woodworm in the back.'

'You can cure that too.'

'There's a pedal off.'

'What odds.'

From the way Liam held the paper she could tell he was cut. God's sake couldn't he let on for once in his life, his way of showing he kept the deeds. Teddy winked.

'Who sould it?' Liam asked.

'Wright, the Auctioneer. It was forgot at the sale, hid under a heap of bags in the coach house.'

72   'Cute boy, Wright.'

'He's all that.'

'How much?'

'Two notes, he give it away.'

'You paid him?'

'He's paid.'

'That's all right,' Liam said and went out.

They heard him rattling buckets in the boiler house.

'Pass no remarks,' Teddy said. 'If you want a thing, get it. What's he bought here all his years but two ton weight of the *Anglo-Celt*, one second-hand birdcage that no bird ever sang in, and a dose of holy pictures.'

'Horrid good of you, Teddy,' Annie said.

'Ah!'

'No, it was,' Annie said. 'If you'd waited to chaw it over with Liam you'd be that sick hearin' about it you'd as lief burn it as have it.'

'Liam's a cautious man.'

Next day Teddy took the tractor out and went off about three o'clock. Annie lit a fire in the parlour. It led off the kitchen at the end of the staircase. It was a long, narrow room smelling of turpentine, damp, and coats of polish on the parquetry lino. The white-painted boards, ceiling and wain-scoting were yellow and spotty. Like the kitchen it had two windows at either end, a black horse-hair *chaise-longue* in one, a small table with a red chenille cover and potplant in the other. Two stiff armchairs faced the painted slate fireplace. On the mantelshelf there was a clock stopped since 1929, a china dog, and a cracked infant of Prague. Annie looked at the photograph over the shelf: Teddy with a hoop, Liam wearing a cap and buttoned britches. Her mother had on a rucked blouse, a long skirt with pintucks at the bottom, high boots and gloves, and that was her with a blind doll on her mother's knee. Their father stood behind looking sideways. At the bottom of the photograph 'McEniff, Photographer, Dublin Road, Monaghan 1914' . . . some fairday long ago, no memory of it now. The rough-faced man and the soft young woman buried. She was now twenty years older than her mother was then, and she thought now how her mother in her last sickness had kept raving, 'The childer, the childer, where are my childer?' She remembered saying, 'This is me, Annie, one of your childer.' Her mother had looked at her steady for a minute, then shook her head. Course she was old, dying of old age.

It was dark when they sat down to tea and Liam said, 'Long as he's not drunk . . . and lyin' in some ditch under the piana. That would be a square snippet for the *Celt*.'

'He'll be all right,' Annie said.

No noise for an hour but wind in the chimney, the hiss of thornlogs through turf, and the crackle of Liam's paper. She began to worry. Supposing he did cross a ditch, get buried or worse over the head of it. Then she heard the tractor, and went to the door. A single light was pulsing on the bonnet of the old Ferguson as it came into the yard. Teddy reversed to the front door and let the buck-rake gently to the ground. He untied the ropes and put the tractor away. Annie tested the keyboard in the dark windy yard. There was an odd note dumb. Guinea hens cackled and the collie bitch barked. Liam was watching from the door.

'What's wrong with them?'

'Damp,' Annie said. 'Nothing a good fire won't mend.' It was heavy, the castors seized or rusted.

'Like a coffin full of rocks,' Liam said.

'Time enough,' Teddy said. 'No hurry.'

They had a lot of bother getting it into the kitchen, Liam wouldn't let Annie help.

'Stand back, woman, we're well fit.'

It seemed very big in the kitchen. Teddy sat down and lit a cigarette. Annie took down the Tilley lamp and went round the piano. Made from that thin shaved timber; damp had unstuck some of it. That could be fixed. The keys had gone yellow but the candlesticks were very nice and the music stand was carved. God, it was lovely. She lifted the top lid and looked

74 down into the frame. She could see something . . . a newspaper?
She pulled it out, faded and flittered by mice. Liam came over.

'That's an auld one,' Teddy said from the hearth.

'The 7th November, 1936,' Liam read.

'The weight of forty years,' Annie said.

From where he was sitting Teddy could read an ad:

WHAT

LIES

AHEAD

FOR

YOU

Why not make the future certain?

'What's in it?'

Liam had put on his glasses . . . 'A Cavan man hung himself
in an outhouse.'

'Aye?'

'Last thing he said to his wife was, "Will I go to Matt Smith's
or get the spade shafted?" . . . and the wife said, "Damn the
hair I care but the childer have wet feet . . . don't come back
without boots."'

Liam looked up. 'Then he hung himself.'

'God help her,' Annie said. 'Women have a hard life.'

'God help *him*,' Liam said.

'Safer lave God out of it,' Teddy said.

'I must have bought that paper and read that maybe ten times
. . . and it's all gone . . . forgot . . . Do *you* mind it, Annie?'

'No.'

'You, Ted?'

'It's like a lot of things you read, you couldn't mind them all.'

Liam put the paper aside. 'Better get this thing out of the
way.'

He went to the parlour door, looked at it and looked at the
piano. The two last steps of the staircase jutted across the
parlour door. It was made from two heavy planks, each step

dowelled into place. The whole frame was clamped to the wall with four iron arms. 'None of your fibby boxed-in jobs,' Liam often said. 'That's solid, made to last.' He went to the dresser, got a ruler, measured, folded the ruler and said, 'Won't fit.'

'It'll be got in some way,' Annie said.

'How?'

'Let's try and we'll know.'

'If it doesn't fit, it doesn't fit. Damn thing's too big.'

Teddy took the rule and measured.

'We might jiggle it in,' he said, 'it's worth a try.'

'Won't fit,' Liam said.

Annie made tea and watched for an hour, measuring, lifting, forcing, levering, straining, Liam getting angrier and redder.

'For Christ's sake, don't pull agin me.'

'Where are you goin' now, up the friggin' stairs?'

'What in the name of Jasus are you at now?'

Finally he shouted, 'Have you no wit at all, the bloody thing's too big, the door's too small, the staircase is in the way, it won't fit or less you rip down them stairs.'

Annie tried not to listen. Teddy kept his voice low, but he was vexed and lit one fag off the other. 'Maybe we could strip her down,' he said, 'and lift in the insides, build her up again in the room.'

'Maybe we could toss the sidewall of the house,' Liam said, 'and drag her through, that's the only way.'

They said nothing for a while and then Annie said, 'I suppose it'll have to go out again?'

'Where else,' Liam said.

They got it out the door again and half-lifted, half-dragged it to the turf shed. Two castors broke off. The thrumming and jumble of notes set the guinea hens clucking and flapping in the apple trees.

Liam went to bed early. Teddy sat at the hearth with Annie and drank more tea.

'It's only a couple of quid, Annie.'

'No odds,' she said.

He looked at her. He felt a bit of an eejit; maybe she did too.

'What odds what people say.'

'I don't give tuppence what people say . . . never wanted a thing so bad, dunno why, and to have it in the house.'

'If you're that strong for a piana, we'll get one, the same brass candlesticks, one that fits.'

'No.'

Teddy looked at her again. If she'd come out straight and say what was in her head; women never did. They never knew rightly what was in their heads.

'Two quid is nothing, Annie.'

'I told you, it's not the money.'

Teddy sat a while at the fire.

'I'll go up.'

He paused half-way up the stairs. 'It's only scrap, Annie, means nothin'.'

'I know.'

Annie dreamed that night that Liam had hung himself in the turf shed. Teddy cut him down and they laid him out in the parlour. She looked at the awful face on the piano, and then the face of the little boy in the photograph, and knelt. She felt her heart was breaking, she wanted to pray but all she could do was cry. 'What are you cryin' for, Annie?' Teddy was standing in the parlour door. 'Everything . . . all of us . . . I wish to God we were never born.'

When she woke up it was dark. She lit a candle, and prayed for a while. It was almost light again when she fell asleep. That morning she covered the piano with plastic fertiliser bags. The guinea hens roosted on it all winter. Near dark one evening in February she saw a sick rat squeeze in where the pedal had broken off. By April varnish was peeling off the side. One wet day in July Teddy unscrewed the brass candlesticks. On and off she dreamed about it, strange dreams that made her unhappy.

It was winter again and one evening she said, 'I'm sick to death lookin' at that thing in the turf shed. For God's sake get shut of it.'

She watched Teddy smash it with an axe. In ten minutes the rusted steel frame lay in the hen mess of the yard like the carcass of a skinned animal. Teddy slipped the buck-rake under it and drew it out of the yard.

From under the empty birdcage Liam watched through the kitchen window. 'No wit, that man,' he said. 'Always bought foolish. His uncle Eddie was identical.'

Dermot Bolger

HOLOTROPIC
BOTANICAS

I close my eyes to find before me
  A wooden door with a silver handle
    Which I feel unable to open
      Which opens by itself inwardly

Beyond it a blackscape of stars
  Weakens down to the glimmer
    Of a sweating pane of glass
      Curved within corroding girders

The Waterlily house of the Botanic Gardens
  My son's face moisted in the sultry light
    We are seated by the plopping waterwheel
      And we are smiling across at each other

I only realise as the scene is dissipating
  That I am him and the tall figure my mother
    Goldfish flit through the green water
      And we are smiling across at each other

TELL THEM I CAME
AND NO ONE ANSWERED

(For Malcolm Bennett)

The back gate was tangled with Russian vine,
A square of light glimmered in the bathroom:
Our hedge had caved in to block the path
And buckle the rusted Corporation railing.

I heard your black bicycle clang behind me,
Our children hauling paraffin from the shop.
A cat stared from the cracked slates on the shed.

Tell them I came and no one answered

The cement path was rinsed blue by moonlight
As I stood outside our window to watch
Strangers play with a child they had bathed.

The nuns claimed that children in the wards
Would disturb patients preparing to meet God;
You brought me their photograph in the garden
Scrubbed and solemn in new black clothes.

Tell them I will come home down the back lane
To surprise them some evening at the Rosary,
The scrape of boots when they hear my voice again.

WHEREVER
YOU WOKE

There only ever was one street,
   One back garden, one bedroom:
Wherever you woke you woke beneath
   The ceiling where you were born,
For the briefest unconscious second
   An eyelid's flutter from home.

The envelope rests like a coffin
   in the glove compartment;
I have parked at this turning
   by the old schoolhouse
Where artists cheerfully work
   In batik and poverty.

Beyond an acre of stacked rafters
   Salvaged from an asylum.
Past a honeycomb of webbed tracks
   I glimpse the mobile home
Where you live at eighty-nine
   Among the building young.

I am taking my letters back
   In case they are burnt
In the fire after your death.
   I reread them last night
And it did not seem like you
   Who was facing oblivion,

Encompassed by this activity,
   But that excited youth
Who typed poems on to carbon
   over an extinct ribbon,
And hitched lifts to read them
   In your candlelit caravan.

When I hear that you are gone
   I shall recall driving at dawn
In that steadfast silence
   With which you carried home,
To a wild woodland lawn,
   The ashes of your son.

HOME

Paula Meehan

I am the blind woman finding her way home by a map of tune.
When the song that is in me is the song I hear from the world
I'll be home. It's not written down and I don't remember the
    words.
I know when I hear it I'll have made it myself. I'll be home.
A version I heard once in Leitrim was close, a wet Tuesday
    night
in the Sean Relig bar. I had come for the session, I stayed
for the vision and lore. The landlord called time,
the music dried up, the grace notes were pitched to the dark.
When the jukebox blared out *I'd only four senses and he left
    me senseless*,
I'd no choice but to take to the road. On Grafton Street in
    November
I heard a mighty sound: a travelling man with a didgeridoo
blew me clear to Botany Bay. The tune too far back to live in
but scribed on my bones. In a past life I may have been
    Kangaroo,
rocked in my dreaming, convict ships coming o'er the foam.

In the Puzzle Factory one winter I was sure I was home.
The talking in tongues, the riddles, the rhymes, struck a chord
that cut through the pharmaceutical haze. My rhythm
    catatonic
I lulled myself back to the womb, my mother's heart
beating the drum of herself and her world. I was tricked
by her undersong, just close enough to my own. I took then
to dancing; I spun like a Dervish. I swear I heard the subtle

music of the spheres. It's no place to live – but,
out there in space, on your own hung aloft the night.
The tune was in truth a mechanical drone;
I was a pitiful monkey jigging on cue. I came back to earth
with a land, to rain on my face, to sun in my hair. And
    grateful too.

The wisewomen say you must live in your skin, call *it* home,
no matter how battered or broken, misused by the world, you
    can heal.
This morning a letter arrived on the nine o'clock post.
The Department of Historical Reparation and who did I blame?
The Nuns? Your Mother? The State? *Tick box provided,*
we'll consider your case. I'm building a soapbox, I'm taking
the very next train. A citizen of nowhere, nothing to my name.

I'm on my last journey. Though my lines are all wonky
they spell me a map that makes sense. Where the song that
    is in me
is the song I hear from the world, I'll set down my burdens
and sleep. The spot that I lie on at last the place I'll call home.

BRINGING THE HOUSE DOWN: SHERIDAN'S MACHINERY

Fintan O'Toole

Frederic Reynolds, twelve years old, thought he was going to die. He was walking down the narrow passage between Vinegar Yard and Bridges Street late on a May evening, when he heard a terrible noise above his head. The sudden, tremendous rumble made him sure that the Drury Lane theatre which formed one side of the passage was collapsing, and that he was going to be killed. He covered his head with his hands and ran for his life, but 'found, the next morning, that the noise did not arise from the *falling* of the house, but from the *falling* of the screen in the fourth act; so violent and so tumultuous were the applause and laughter'. He had passed by the opening night of Richard Brinsley Sheridan's play, *The School for Scandal*, on 8 May 1777.

What had caused that noise, so full at once of delight and terror? On stage, a screen had been dashed down, and there, cowering behind it, was the scandal-monger Lady Teazle, her duplicitous relationship with the hypocrite Joseph Surface discovered, revealed, laid bare. What Joseph Surface calls 'my Politics' – scheming, double-dealing, injustice – had been stripped naked and brought to light. And the analogy with politics in the broader context was made unmistakably plain to the opening-night audience by barbed references to Benjamin Hopkins, political opponent of the radical hero John Wilkes, then engaged with Wilkes in a struggle for the office of Chamberlain of the City of London. If Joseph Surface's feckless brother Charles, and not the apparently moral Joseph, could be the hero of the play, then so too Wilkes the good-hearted rake could be a fit hero for the people.

That explosion of violent delight that made Frederic Reynolds think that death was at hand was also an outburst of political possibility. By the power of an illusion, truth could be revealed. Art could reveal the reality of Politics, both personal and public, and, once the truth was revealed, all would be converted to its cause. Lady Teazle emerges from behind the screen, and refuses the web of justifications and excuses that Joseph begins to spin. She confesses and capitulates. Once revealed by the falling of the screen, she must make amends, go forth and sin no more.

The School for Scandal, with the screen scene at its apex, was the dominant contemporary image in the London theatre from that night until the end of the century. No other contemporary play – leaving aside musical comedies like Sheridan's own *The Duenna* – was as frequently performed in those years. But, more than that, Sheridan took his own theatricality directly into the political world, and, at the height of his achievement, shook it by the power of performance.

Two years later, Sheridan was elected to parliament. By 1787, he and another Irishman, Edmund Burke, both outsiders born without rank or property, had persuaded the House of Commons to impeach one of the most powerful men in the world, the Governor of India, Warren Hastings. The power of artifice to force political revelation had been felt at the heart of the Empire. The noise that Frederic Reynolds had heard had assaulted the ears of the great, making it seem, for a moment, that the house might really be about to fall down.

Burke was the moral and intellectual force behind the impeachment of Hastings on charges of corruption and oppression, but Sheridan was the aesthetic and dramatic force. Sheridan, son of an actor and a playwright, himself a dramatist and theatre manager, wrote, staged and acted two extraordinary performances, understood at the time as essentially theatrical, in which he persuaded the House of Commons and the London audience that Hastings was a villain. The effect of his two speeches against Hastings, urging the impeachment

86   in 1787, and then at the trial in 1788, was not one of intellectual persuasion, but of emotional effect.

Sir Gilbert Elliot, afterwards Governor of Bengal, wrote to his wife the day after Sheridan's five-hour House of Commons speech, which he had witnessed. The relationship he describes is not that between politician and politicians, but that between actor and audience:

It was, by many degrees, the most excellent and astonishing performance I ever heard . . . It is impossible to describe the feelings he excited. The bone rose repeatedly in my throat, and tears in my eyes – not of grief, but merely of strongly excited sensibility . . . The conclusion, in which the whole force of the case was collected and where his whole powers were employed to their utmost stretch, and indeed his own feelings wound to the utmost pitch, worked the House into such a paroxysm of passionate enthusiasm on the subject, and of admiration for him, that the moment he sat down there was a universal shout, nay even clapping, for half a second; every man was on the floor, and all his friends throwing themselves on his neck in raptures of joy and exultation . . . All the Ministry and all the friends of Hastings were struck absolutely dumb, and sat confounded, not knowing how, nor daring to meet the impression made on the audience.

The 'tumult of applause' which greeted the performance, more appropriate to a theatre, was reportedly the first time this noise had ever been heard in parliament.

What had occurred was understood as irrational, inexplicable in terms of mere argument or political skill. A hostile observer, Sir Horace Walpole, evoked black magic as a possible explanation. 'How should such a fellow as Sheridan, who has no diamonds to bestow, fascinate all the world? Yet witchcraft, no doubt, there has been, for when did simple eloquence ever convince a majority? Mr Pitt and a hundred and seventy-four other persons found Mr Hastings guilty last night . . . Well, at least there is a new crime, sorcery, to charge on the opposition!'

All the force of Romantic sensibility – tears, rapture, passion – had been unleashed theatrically into the House of Commons itself, and the assembly and Government had no defences against it. Sheridan had managed to recreate in parliament the explosive exhalation of an overwhelmed audience that had terrified Frederic Reynolds ten years earlier. Having brought the house down with the screen scene, he now brought the House down with his performance on Hastings.

As with any great theatrical hit, there had to be a repeat performance. The trial of Hastings opened the following year, and Sheridan had again to present the same charges. This time, the theatricality was yet more explicit. The setting was Westminster Hall, a self-consciously ceremonial space. Tickets for Sheridan's performance were sold to the public, and prices of up to fifty guineas were offered. Queues for admission formed from half-past six in the morning, and many people slept overnight in the adjoining coffee houses in order to secure places near the front of the queue. The pressure of the crowd was such that many women lost shoes and had to go in barefoot, while others sat there with one red shoe and one yellow one, having picked up stray shoes to replace their own.

Sir Gilbert Elliot wrote to his wife on the first morning of Sheridan's performance that he had been down to the Hall early and had seen the crowds gathered, and predicted that 'when the doors open . . . there will be a rush as there is at the pit of the playhouse when Garrick plays King Lear.'

The theatres themselves understood the form of what was happening, and throughout the first fortnight in June, while Sheridan's speech was anticipated and performed, both the licensed houses played his work, *The Duenna* at Covent Garden, and *The School for Scandal* at his own Drury Lane. Audiences could thus make for themselves the connection between Sheridan's theatre and his own political performance at Westminster Hall. They could understand that Sheridan's desire was to make them feel and see and inhabit the oppression of India, as much as to understand and consider it.

88   Sheridan performed for four days. He again worked his audience into paroxysms of emotion, so that even Sir Gilbert Elliot, who had witnessed his House of Commons speech, and knew what to expect, confessed that 'as for myself, I never remember to have cried so heartily and so copiously on any public occasion'. This time, Sheridan's theatrical conclusion was physical as well as oratorical. As he finished, he swooned into the arms of Burke, who caught him, an image that imprinted itself more than any words on the minds of the audience. But Elliot and other observers such as the historian Edward Gibbon, though deeply moved and impressed by the performance, were no longer astounded by it, because they now understood it as a piece of theatre. Elliot noted that Sheridan's style drew 'the attention entirely away from the purpose to the *performance*'. He also saw the 'fine parts' of the speech as being too close to 'the higher kind of theatrical composition to be perfectly becoming or satisfactory in real affairs'. Gibbon, too, understood the performance as a performance. 'Sheridan, on the close of his speech, sank into Burke's arms, but I called this morning, he is perfectly well. A good actor.'

A year later, the Bastille fell, and the French Revolution divided Sheridan, who supported it, from Burke who became the mainstay of the intellectual counter-revolution. Sheridan's supporting player in the drama of his Westminster Hall performance became his bitter enemy. Gilbert Elliot, after agonised hesitation, took Burke's side. 'Real affairs' had turned Sheridan's aesthetic politics, his invention of a politics of performance which could subvert the politics of wealth and place, from a wonder to a horror. In France, performers and theatre people like Marie-Jean Hérault de Séchelles, Collot d'Herbois, Camille Desmoulins, the Chénier brothers, and Fabre d'Eglantine had demolished altogether the dividing lines between theatre, rhetoric and politics, and in the process done much, not merely to threaten to bring the house down as Sheridan had done, but to shower Europe with falling bricks and masonry.

The theatricality of Sheridan's politics, which Elliot had discerned, and Burke had, literally, supported, now stood out not as wondrous witchcraft, but as black art, dangerous and devilish. Sheridan's extraordinary moment of power, achieved by a fusion of the aesthetic and the political that disarmed his opponents and left them dumbstruck by its novelty and brilliance, had passed.

In his last speech at the trial of Warren Hastings, after the Revolution and after it had become plain that Hastings must, in this changed world, be acquitted, Burke could not resist a theatrical metaphor, could not get out of his mind the triumphant moment of revelation that had shaken Drury Lane on that May night in 1777, the screen falling, duplicity and conspiracy revealed, the guilty vanquished. In a last appeal to the Lords on the bench, he resorted to the language of theatre:

Now, my Lords, was there ever such a discovery made of the arcana of any public theatre? You see here, behind the ostensible scenery, all the crooked working of the machinery developed and laid open to the world . . . You have it all laid open before you. The ostensible scene is drawn aside; it has vanished from your sight. All the strutting signors, and all the soft signoras are gone; and instead of a brilliant spectacle of descending chariots, gods, goddesses, sun, moon, and stars, you have nothing to gaze on but sticks, wires, ropes and machinery. You find the appearance all false and fraudulent; and you see the whole trick at once.

The confidence of the appeal is belied by the loss of faith in the metaphor. The astounded delight of the screen scene is gone, and now, in Burke's language, it is theatre itself that is the illusion which must be swept away. By now, Burke has broken with Sheridan over the French Revolution. The screen of pomp and power has really fallen and Burke is frightened by the noise. The trial of Hastings, begun in such hope of revelation, is

90   about to end in bitter defeat. Whereas Sheridan had held out the promise of theatricality as a way to political reform, Burke now sees it as itself a trick of sticks and wires, ropes and machinery. He wants to hark back to that period of hope when the screen fell and Hastings was impeached on a wave of rhetorical emotion, but he cannot convince himself, let alone the Lords. In his head is an extraordinary hatred of the theatre, which he now associates with his worst enemies, the French revolutionary Directory, the evil politicians whom he will compare in the bitterest terms to actors: 'candle-snuffers, revolutionary scene-shifters, second and third mob, prompter, clerks, executioners, who stand with their axe on their shoulders by the wheel, grinners in the pantomime, murderers in tragedies, who make ugly faces under black wigs – in short the very scum and refuse of the theatre'.

The link between French revolutionaries and the theatre in Burke's mind is Sheridan, Burke's confederate in the impeachment of Hastings, now, to him, a dangerous and disgraceful ally of the sansculottes. Sheridan's metaphor of revelation in the screen scene cannot be ignored, since the energy it released was essential to Burke's impeachment of Hastings, but now it fills Burke with disgust and hatred. He reverses it, turning theatrical trickery from the means of revelation to itself the fraud which must be revealed.

And Burke, not Sheridan, is the victor. It is Burke's detestation of the Revolution, not Sheridan's support for it, that commands the high ground of English politics from then on. It is the moment between that May night in 1777 when the theatre exploded with delight and astonishment and the acquittal of Hastings in 1794 that will come to seem astonishing in retrospect. How did this Irish actor's son manage this trick of sticks and wires that almost brought the house down?

Simon Schama has written, in the context of France, of the period of Sheridan's plays, and of his most successful fusion of theatre and politics, as one in which 'public diction was public power', in which 'it was oratory that created "the People", not vice versa. Conversely, failure to be heard could be a death sentence.' Sheridan was uniquely fitted by his background to understand both sides of this equation. His father was not merely an actor, but the compiler of a dictionary that rivalled Johnson's and, above all, a theorist and teacher of rhetoric and oratory. Yet his antecedents were not in any useful sense Anglo-Irish, but merely Irish. He grew up in a Protestant family, but one which was Gaelic, Catholic and Jacobite in origin. The extraordinary, virtually hereditary caste of writers of which he is a part, stretching from the sixteen-forties to the death of Joseph Sheridan Le Fanu in 1873, was founded by his great-grandfather, Denis Sheridan, who took part in one of the most deeply symbolic literary acts in Irish history, the translation of the Protestant Bible into Gaelic, carried out under the Anglican Bishop Bedell. That Gaelic was at least understood in Sheridan's family is clear from the Gaelic phrases and puns in his father's play, *The Brave Irishman*.

This Gaelic culture was, in the world in which Sheridan operated, a silence. It was unheard, and this silence, could be, in Schama's phrase, a death sentence. Sheridan thus emerged from a country, and more specifically a family, which was both full of an extraordinary linguistic self-consciousness on the one hand (his mother, too, was a distinguished playwright and novelist) and yet aware of a great silence in its own recent history. Speech – conceived of by his father as polished performance, with little difference between acting and political rhetoric – is not a social adornment, but a battleground. It was a path to social advancement, a mediation between two worlds, a way of constituting an acceptable reality for a strangely dislocated family. In other words, a politics. Sheridan's father is a bizarre and comic figure, obsessively devoted to the ideals of correct pronunciation and the reformation of public morals through rhetoric. His career as an actor, theatre manager, playwright and educationalist is subordinate to this overriding dedication on the part of a penniless Irish interloper to the task of instructing

92 the English how to speak English. Yet this absurdly comic enterprise is also a route to power.

Thomas Sheridan's arrival in England with Richard in tow comes at a moment when two related things are happening. One is that the English language is at a vulnerable moment of transition from loose and diverse orthography and usage to standardised and centralised speech. A standard form of discourse is being established. The second, and related, matter is that, because of incipient democracy, a mass language for mass politics is being invented. Because it is shifting in these ways, the power structure is vulnerable, accessible to outsiders. Because that vulnerability is constituted by language, it offered access precisely through language. Thomas Sheridan, for all his pretension and absurdity, was able to exploit this vulnerability to such an extent that he became, for instance, the instructor in elocution to the Duke of Buckingham. His son Richard was able to exploit the vulnerability at a yet higher level, to insert himself, and not merely his linguistic theories, into the power structure itself.

For one extraordinary historical moment, defined by the two-stage assault on power by the Sheridans father and son, an Irish obsession with language born of the trauma and shame of the oppressed and an English obsession with language born of the need of the powerful to redefine the rhetoric of rule came together. The result of that accidental conjunction was Richard Brinsley Sheridan's accession through language to a position where he could both make the voice of the silent oppressed heard at the heart of imperial power and be himself so intimately involved with that power as to be the ghost writer of private letters between the Prince of Wales and his father the King.

Yet the grand nature of this moment is founded on comedy. It is the laughable nature of his father's personality – the earnest innocence of the Irishman abroad – that makes it possible. And it is the manipulation of that comedy through the theatre – sometimes, as with Mrs Malaprop, directly inspired by Thomas

Sheridan's obsessions – that gives Richard the fame on which to found a political career. Sheridan's life and work is a comedy of terrors and thus a profound metaphor for the long inter-relationship of Ireland and England.

The bitter and complex relationship between Richard and his father can be traced in terms of this paradigm. That Richard felt abandoned by his father both physically and economically, that he saw his childhood torn apart by his father's pursuit of the reform of the world through speech, that he grew up with the prospect of being a prisoner of his father's language (his father's plan for Richard was that he would be a 'rhetorical usher' at a projected academy of speech, a Kafkaesque fate of linguistic entrapment) – these are good grounds for the unhappiness of the relationship. Yet his father's exposure of language as a route to power for those without property or social standing, his notion of rhetoric as a way of reforming the world and of theatre as a way of reforming rhetoric, the links through Rousseau between his father's educational theories and the French Revolution – these were inheritances so important to his own achievements that he could not ever break from his father or from his father's convoluted Irishness.

Sheridan's power of affect, in which language replaces property and position as the ultimate source of personal and political influence, is the link between his theatre and his politics. The Enlightenment's search for a new morality on which to ground a new politics of freedom, Rousseau's cult of sensibility which had such a crucial cultural bearing on the French Revolution is at play in Sheridan. His father's educational ideals – in which Nature, not discipline, leads the pupil onwards – are Rousseau's and the political turn given to these ideas by his father in explaining the importance of studying classical oratory is quintessentially that of Enlightenment republicanism: 'Liberty could not subsist without virtue, nor be maintained without wisdom and knowledge; and wisdom and knowledge unless communicated with force and perspi-cuity, were useless to the state.' Persuasive speech, therefore, is

94   not just an adornment to the aristocrat, but the essence of the virtuous state, in which society is held together, not by the power of monarchy, but by the eloquence by which the wise induce the beneficent sentiments of those who hear them. Speech replaces power and wealth as the glue by which virtuous society is held together.

These are the crucial questions of Sheridan's time, questions to which the French answer is a revolution against authority powered by rhetoric. Sheridan's two major plays are comic testings of his father's propositions. The tyrannical nature of love which is merely a function of wealth and position is set against a comic view of the excesses of Romantic sensibility. Equally, Sheridan's private life is a testing of the extent to which Romantic rhetoric on its own really can confound the hierarchies of established power. And his political rhetoric is the ultimate testing of sensibility, of the extent to which an appeal to the emotions can actually override the realities of his own, and his people's powerlessness.

There was not, in Sheridan, a shift from theatre to politics in any absolute sense. A key text for understanding the continuity is the political tract on which Sheridan was working immediately after the first production of *The School for Scandal* in 1778. An 'Essay on Absentees' was drafted (though never finished) at the height of Sheridan's theatrical success, and two years before his election to parliament. It is of immense importance to understanding his political motivations, both because it is entirely about Ireland, and because the rhetoric of sensibility that it employs is a direct case for a politics and an economics which is touched by the virtues of theatre and politics.

In the essay, Sheridan ventilates one of the great grievances of the silent dispossessed, and largely Catholic, mass of tenant farmers, forced to pay rent to Protestant landlords who do not even live in Ireland. The danger and boldness of the subject in an English context can be judged by the fact that even the leader of the most radical group in parliament, to which

Sheridan will align himself, the Marquis of Rockingham, is an absentee landlord with vast Irish estates. The core of Sheridan's arguments is that those who detach themselves from their tenants can never be made to feel their pain and suffering:

But granting an undiminished benevolence to exist on the part both of the landlord and of the agent, yet can we expect any great exertion of pathetic eloquence to proceed from the latter to palliate any deficiency of the tenants? – or if there were, do we not know how much lighter an impression is made by distresses related to us than by those which are *occulis subjecta fidelibus*? The heart, the seat of charity and compassion, is more accessible to the senses than the understanding. Many, who would be unmoved by any address to the latter, would melt into charity at the eloquent persuasion of silent sorrow. When he sees the widow's tear, and hears the orphan's sigh, every one will act with a sudden uniform rectitude because he acts from the divine impulse of 'free love dealt equally to all'.

This is a theatrical version of radical politics in which justice and equality proceed from seeing and feeling rather than from abstract understanding. From the beginning, Sheridan's political adventure is animated by the eloquence of a silence – the silence of the buried Catholic Irish majority from which he springs – which, once it can be made audible and visible in the heart of the Empire, will produce, he believes, a sudden, uniform rectitude. The astonishing thing is not that this, in the proper sense, naive project fails, but that it succeeds to the limited but nonetheless breathtaking extent that it does.

Far from being separate compartments of his life, Sheridan's political power is at its height when he is most a playwright. In the Regency crisis, because of his intimacy with the Prince of Wales, he literally writes the script. Much of the Prince's correspondence, including his letters to his father, is written by Sheridan. So convincing is his performance that he even gets to act the part of the future George IV.

96   It could not last, and Sheridan could not win. Such a fellow as Sheridan with, as Walpole put it, no diamonds to bestow, could fascinate all the world, but could not change it. The Irish dazzlers who followed after him – Oscar Wilde, George Bernard Shaw – would fascinate too, and make a politics of their theatre, but they would never get so close to bringing the house down as Sheridan did. By then, the world of power was more fixed, more invulnerable. By then, the trick had been discovered. All the workings of the performance had been laid bare. The sticks and wire, the ropes and machinery, could be gazed upon with a knowing eye. There were no more tears in the House of Commons.

Leland Bardwell

DANCING WITH
BEEZIE IN
JORDAN'S PUB

With Country and Western suit
gangster tie, bell-bottoms
he sings to us:
Dancing with Beezie in Jordan's
As gangster guest
in this company
the soft-shoe rhythm
tidies the throb:
Will you waltz, my love
Will you waltz with me
again.
We women talk of rain
and chemotherapy.

TWO SEASONAL POEMS

WINTER

Weeds through the curragh's ribs
grass on the jinnet's hames
rust on the tall ship's anchor

God's acre splits
cows tumble, moan
kestrel rides the wind

arranged in this landscape
I await the wound of winter
the coming of the geese.

SPRING

When the moon aligns the sun
the ocean gathers

when the weeds find light
the ring of the eye expands

when the scar of the torrent knits
the boulders flatten

when the hares rut
the rhizomes shiver

when the loam breathes
the earthworms sing.

That winter they fell in love
over the cross cut
that bitter winter of '47
when the country slept
under a stretched white canvas.

No bird called that winter
only the saw's song
was the persistent nudging
of the earth.

ICKLE CHUBBIES IN THE CLAY
Patrick McCabe

What started it all was Mrs Mc Adoo's baby waking up in the middle of the night and the yowling out of it was enough to put anyone astray in the head so that was why she brought it up to the doctor who gave her some medicine and said don't you worry your head Mrs Mc Adoo babies are a divil if they're not getting one thing it's another you just make sure you give him this medicine and come tomorrow night he'll be right as rain you'll see. When she heard this she was as happy as Larry and whoever she met on her way down the street she said to them I'm an awful eejit to be worrying my head sure there's not a bother on him the doctor gave me a tonic and he says by tomorrow night he'll be right as rain. By the time she got home she was so delighted with herself about it all she had to hold herself back from having a party to celebrate her son Thomas's visit to the doctor. Which would certainly have been pre-mature because by the time tomorrow night came around far from being right as rain or anything else he was yowling worse than ever and on top of that again white as a ghost and when she saw that a hot dart of fear shot right through her and she thought to herself my baby is going to die. Then she caught herself on and said what am I talking about I'm making an eejit of myself sure didn't the doctor tell me he was in the best of fettle. Run down – that's what he is. I know what I'll do. I'll take another walk up to the surgery just to be on the safe side. And that is exactly what she did and the doctor gave her more medicine and no sooner than she had said goodbye to him and gone off down the street than she was laughing and smiling away with the neighbours and the shopkeepers who were standing in the doorways chatting and laughing as usual and it would certainly be very good to be able to say that that evening saw little Thomas back to himself but it didn't unfortunately and the yowling bad as it had been before was now unmerciful so it was no wonder when the neighbours said to Mrs Mc Adoo would you not think of bringing him up to the Canon don't you know that he can work miracles that she replied right then I will because by that time she would have done anything. If the neighbour women had said don't you know that wood shavings are very good for stopping babies yowling she would have fed him a spoonful.

She put him in the pram and wheeled him up to the parochial house and told the Canon that her child had the disease and he said to her I see. Right so – bring it out the back. Of all the women in the town there was no one who could argue that Mrs Mc Adoo wasn't a holy woman and she most definitely wasn't one who would speak back to the priests especially not the Canon but when he asked her to bring him around the back and then put him down into the barrel of holy water she wasn't so sure any more if she wanted a miracle performed in fact she was almost one hundred per cent sure that she didn't want one and although she was a little bit afraid she did manage to utter the words but Canon what if any of it gets into his mouth? There's all green stuff on the top of it there. It's just that I'm afraid it might make him sick Canon if you know what I mean. When the Canon heard this he didn't know what to do, whether to fall about the place laughing or just draw out there and then and hit her a skelp of his walking stick because he just could not understand what had gotten into the woman or what was wrong with her. Fortunately for her in the end he just sighed and said ah daughter will you come on now and stop your cod-acting like a good girl and put him into the holy water I've to be in Castleblayney before seven. When Mrs Mc Adoo started to sniffle a bit he said more forcefully this time Mrs Mc Adoo will you please put the baby in or what is wrong with you. So then at last she put him in and when she took him out she hesitated for a minute or two because she wasn't so sure about putting him in the second time because he was as she had said all covered in the green stuff but the Canon was insistent that it had to be the three times or nothing. Immersed three times in the water or the whole thing was a waste of time – that was what he said. So in he went the third time and the Canon said there now – that wasn't so hard was it good girl yourself. Mrs Mc Adoo reddened although not all that much. Just a little because she was confused. Then she replied no Canon it wasn't hard Canon thank you very much Canon I want to thank you very much. And the Canon said that there was no call to be thanking him. He said never mind thanking me Mrs I'm doing no more than my job that's all I'm doing no more no less so the thanking is out the window.

After that he said it was near time he was off because he had to hit the high road for Castleblayney he never said what for not that Mrs Mc Adoo had in the slightest bit worried about that aspect of it because she was in a state of near-elation and as she carried Thomas all the way down the hill towards the town she felt she was cruising at least three feet above the ground she was so happy. And if she was sure of one thing it was that that day which was an ordinary misty-wet day in September was the happiest day ever in her whole life so far and it seemed to her that nothing would bother her ever again as she said to Thomas tweaking his cheek in the pram isn't that right Thomas isn't that right it certainly is my little man and it definitely did seem at that moment to be the rightest thing in the whole world and went on being like that until around half-past eight or nine when she went into the bedroom to see if he was awake or did he maybe need another cot feed and she was still so happy she was singing a little song which was by Burl Ives and went with his legs all dangling down-o! and the words of it seemed so silly she was going to say to Thomas did you ever hear such silly-billy big words in your whole life ickle chubbies that was what she wanted to say to her little man and if she had she would have expected Thomas to give her one of his big wide baby grins that said back to her no mammy I didn't but he didn't unfortunately and there was only one reason for that and one reason alone the fact that he was dead and when she saw that what could Mrs Mc Adoo do only let out one of these yowls that would make your skin crawl.

After that no matter where you went you'd hear one set of people saying this and another saying that and others who not if they were paid would they know what to say. At least Benny Doyle seemed to be clear in his head about it. He said everybody makes a mistake. Are you going to sit there and tell me there's nobody in this town makes a mistake? I guarantee you this. For every ten tables made above in Johnny Mc Gee's joinery there's one with a bockedy leg. Am I right? And don't tell me the doctors don't drop the odd stitch either. There's men buried up there on that hill would still be walking the streets of this town if the doctors and surgeons had been minding their 'p's an 'q's. Mistakes? We all make them. And the boys above in the parochial house are no different. Of course it's very sad that the little baby got drownded it'd be a hard-hearted class of a man that'd say different. Glory be to God sure there's no sweeter sight on this earth than the smile of a bonny baby inside in a pram. Of course it's sad – there's no heavier cross to be asked to bear and poor Mrs Mc Adoo Lord bless us and save us God knows what it'll do to her for what with her poor father passing away not two years back she wouldn't now be the strongest class of a creature if you know what I mean but lookit for the love and honour of God when all's said and done what can you do about it? Eh? We're hardly going to go up to the parochial house and march the Canon down to Mc Adoo's to make the child come alive again. Jesus Mary and Joseph sure we're not going to do that. And if we're not going to do it then what are we going to do? I'll tell you what we're going to do we're going to do damn all damn bucking all that's what we're going to do because there's nothing we can do and why because the Canon is a very nice man the best of a fellow. A gentleman that's what he is no two ways about it it's just unfortunate that whatever happened this time things didn't work out and I'm afraid that's all there is to it when all's said and done. After he had said all that the men who were sitting beside him on the seat couldn't really think of much to offer by way of reply, they just sat there staring into the greasy bowls of their caps and dragging long and hard on pipes as they said aye and true for you Benny.

The funeral took place a couple of days later and Benny was proved right again. He had estimated that there would be an attendance of two thousand and his prediction turned out to be very accurate indeed. He said the child y'see you can always be sure of a big draw when it's a child. Do you mind the Mahon infant? Close on the same. They put the small white coffin on trestles in the chapel for all to see and anybody who saw it could not stop the tears coming into their eyes. They said this is a sad sad day. The chapel was like the Botanical Gardens with all the flowers. Taped to the lid of the coffin was a small card edged in black with a photograph of Thomas on it. It read Thomas aged six months. All the shops in town closed as a mark of respect. Usually they only closed for a little while but now they remained shut all day. As the funeral cortège arrived at the cemetery everybody waited for the Canon to speak. He was standing by the grave in his surplice holding his missal. He said that it was a sad occasion and when he said that everybody bowed their heads and stared at the grass. But he said that although it was a sad occasion it was also a beautiful one. And that was because there was always something special about a pure white unblemished soul returning to the welcoming arms of Jesus and then as he looked all around the graveyard what he wanted to know was who could deny or ignore the feeling of peacefulness that now pervaded the entire cemetery the peacefulness of a community united as one in grief. He raised his arms heavenward and proclaimed it wonderful that at times like this everyone gathered together as members of a community could put aside small differences which it had to be admitted occasionally came between us such as the unreturned

106 spade the hasty word the broken promise and so on. He said today Christ walks amongst us on this happy occasion. Then he closed his eyes and said no on this happy happy occasion. It was a great speech. It was a speech that had a marked effect on everyone present and there wasn't one person who was not close to a state of blissful contentment thanks to his beautiful well-chosen words. It was a magnificent transformation and there would have been very many happy almost ecstatic people leaving the graveyard that day if the Canon had been allowed to continue in that vein and Mrs Mc Adoo had not thrown herself into the grave and started to rant and rave like a madwoman. And not only that but began to tear away at the lid of the coffin with her nails like a werewolf or something shouting Thomas Thomas come back to me. I don't want you to die. I don't want you to go to limbo either. I want you to come back to me so we can play building blocks. At first no one knew what to do but the problem was that the longer it went on the less they seemed to know what to do about it. All they could hear was the scraping on the coffin and they weren't sure what to do. One thing they were sure about was that the peaceful harmonious and undeniably wondrous atmosphere of togetherness and unity which the Canon had been talking about had all but disintegrated and they found themselves standing there with big red faces trying their best not to hear which was impossible because by this stage she wasn't shouting she was roaring. John Joe Gavigan wasn't sure who exactly it was standing behind him he thought it might have been Reilly of the shop but no matter who it was he articulated almost everyone's inner feelings when he said this is great carry-on. This is a grand how-do-you-do I must say. Or what in the hell is wrong with her? Jesus Mary and Joseph such a thing to happen on the day of a funeral.

  Eventually it went too far far too far as Johnson the plumber muttered under his hand, and two men climbed in after her and said come on now Mrs you can't be shouting like this you'll have to come up now out of that and when they saw this everyone heaved a sigh of relief and said to themselves at last it's all over thank God but then what did she do, drew out and hit one of them whether it was by accident or not no one could tell but she was screaming leave me alone leave me alone. The screaming was bad enough to begin with but then it became so unbearable that in the end there was no point in anyone pretending or even hoping that they could ever go away from that cemetery saying it had been a magical day of community solidarity or anything like it. It was beginning to look increasingly likely that the only authentic description of it would turn out to be a complete and utter unmitigated disaster. John Joe looked around and saw Benny Doyle lighting his pipe and tossing the match away into the flapping wind as he said out of the side of his mouth I seen a mad buck cat one time that had the rabies. That's what she reminds me of. I wouldn't get into that grave for love or money.

And it looked like he was right because not long after he said that the two men came climbing back up out of the grave with nothing to show for their trouble only one bruised eye and a jacket covered in spittle all over the shoulders. There was a sort of last lingering hope that Mrs Mc Adoo would appear up out of her own accord and when she didn't a black gloominess descended and all anyone could think of doing was looking down at the toes of their shoes and producing something to examine in great detail such as wallets rosary beads etc. The Canon did his best under the circumstances but he was only wasting his time trying to reason with her and after he had spoken a few soft sentences to her she swore at him too and told him yes there was something he could do for her die in his bed that night. That particular comment more or less put paid to any hope of sympathy there might have been and after that everyone became very agitated indeed. Benny was the first to break the silence flicking another match away ah this has gone to hell it's about time someone did something I'm supposed to meet Herbie Molloy in the hotel at seven-thirty we're going to Longford dogtrack. Someone asked him did he think the

108 Guards would have to be sent for and he said all I know is I'm supposed to be meeting Herbie and look at the time it is now. An argument started beside John Joe as to whether the Guards should be called or not. Some were for and some against but in the end it didn't matter anyway because Mrs Mc Adoo's head appeared out of the grave and she came climbing back up and out and walked off in the direction of the cemetery gate without a sound. When they saw her a few of the women cried out and ran after her calling Mrs Mc Adoo! Mrs Mc Adoo! I say! Mrs Mc Adoo! But they were only wasting their time because no matter what they called after her she just ignored them and carried on walking towards the town with bow legs like she was after wetting herself.

After that the crowd began to disperse and they all went off home in dribs and drabs and there was such a feeling of bitter disappointment hanging about the place it was like a drab grey sheet. You could almost reach out and touch it. Any time for years afterwards that the funeral was mentioned Benny would clench his pipe between his teeth and go into his speech don't mention it don't mention it it'd be a queer sort of a world if we were all to go jumping into graves every time a bit of trouble comes your way. Jesus Mary and Joseph does she think she's the only one in the town. Sometimes he would leave it at that but other times it would get too much for him and he'd shake spits out of the pipe and hiss a sorry-looking sight now a sorry-looking bloody sight a sad pathetic sketch and no mistake. Then he'd say: he went off and left me standing outside the hotel Herbie.

So there was nothing much more about Mrs Mc Adoo after that, the only ones it was important to now were Thomas and Mrs Mc Adoo themselves, as everyone else said it turned their stomachs to even think about it the way she went on that day. It was best forgotten about for it would aggravate a saint. Probably the only one left in the town who didn't forget about it was John Joe Gavigan and he didn't think about anything else. He used to see Mrs Mc Adoo in there in the cemetery sitting beside her son's grave. The first time he saw her he barely knew it was her at all because she was less like Mrs Mc Adoo now more like a skeleton with big deep eyes and the skin hanging off her. Sometimes he went in and sat beside her but she didn't talk not very much anyway. One day he asked her why are you waiting here Mrs Mc Adoo and she said I'll be joining Thomas shortly. Other times she answered questions in ways that made no sense at all. Once she said I won a book at school for never missing a day and another time she said Tide has gone up a penny. When she said about waiting to join Thomas John Joe thought she was joking but not long afterwards he looked in on the way home and there was no sign of her and when he was going past her house he saw there was a black-bordered card in under the knocker above the letter box that said she was dead and when a bit further on he met Benny and he told him that Mrs Mc Adoo was dead he said is that right and went off up the street opening the lid of his tobacco tin.

GHOSTS IN PROGRESS: WRITING ABOUT YEATS, 1992–3

Roy Foster

'Swift is round every corner.' Yeats in old age became haunted by the Dean of St Patrick's, writing plays about him, identifying with his rage, his savagery, his repudiations, his Dublin. As I begin to write the fourth chapter of a biography, I think of Yeats walking Dublin and physically sensing Swift around its corners.

Should biographers identify with their subjects? I once opened a magazine on an aeroplane and found an article by Denis Donoghue on why he gave up writing Yeats's biography. The perceived difficulty was not so much restricting access to the family papers, but the horrors of living so long with your subject that you might become like them: the biographer possessed (an image from Poe or Le Fanu). Denis has a way of being right about things. Was this a case in point? (But he occasionally has a way of being wrong about things, too.)

Yeats was the impresario of his own life (and of his death). I sit in a Dublin pub and suffer, yet again, being told a 'Yeats story' – the one about his demanding to be taken to a pub by R.M. Smyllie, the editor of the *Irish Times*, because he had never been inside one. 'I have seen a pub, Smyllie: now take me home.' But, I want to shout, that is nonsense; as a young man Yeats went to a pub every *week* with the Rhymers' Club. I keep quiet, of course; I collude with the story. Which Yeats probably invented himself, to fit his late hieratic person-ality. So I collude with Yeats.

When did the mask slip? 'I was not entirely serious,' he once said wearily to an acolyte who reverently repeated one of his more dotty pronouncements.

I walk down O'Connell Street and think of Yeats leaving the Gresham Hotel, noticing the red-headed girl selling *An Phoblacht* on the corner of Cathal Brugha Street, and going on to write 'Politics': which revisionism now places at the climax of the canon, the last poem in the rearranged *Last Poems*. 'But O that I were young again/And held her in my arms.' She probably wouldn't have thanked him. Crossing O'Connell Bridge in the evening I stop to look down the river, and uncomfortably remember that he paused there too. 'When I stand upon O'Connell Bridge in the half-light and notice that discordant architecture, all those electric signs, where modern heterogeneity has taken physical form, a vague hatred comes up out of my own dark . . .' But I don't feel like that, yet.

Back in Oxford, I pass by No. 4 Broad Street and think of him living here: his great speech to the Oxford Union denouncing the Black and Tans, Maurice Bowra squirrelling away stories about him to sustain a lifetime's dining-out, George Yeats's dislike of the dons' wives' hats. I step out into the street and am nearly killed by a donnish woman on her bicycle (hatless).

Another ghost in Oxford: Richard Ellmann, still the best biographer. I remember him, subtle, courteous, secret. Recently I worked on his papers in an American university library. Through his correspondence from the late-forties, when he was researching Yeats, I sensed the young Ellmann: a different man. Did he become his later self through writing about Joyce? Denis would think so.

Sligo in the summer is a non-stop Yeatsfest. On my way back from the Summer School I drive through Galway, and take a French hitch-hiker to the Tower at Ballylee. Ezra Pound, always sharply attuned to a symbol, called it 'Bally-phallus'. Now it is all gift-shop and *son et lumière*. But I am tempted to hide behind a homespun curtain and wait until the tour guides have gone home. Even the hitch-hiker (a geology student from Lille) says he senses an 'atmosphere'.

112   The ghosts in Swedenborg or Le Fanu walk among the real world, describing repeated patterns. Yeats believed that the dead take part in the lives of the living. Andrew Motion has tapes made by the man who supplied Philip Larkin's hearing-aids. After Larkin died, he still sent messages down the air-waves, thoughtfully recorded by the mediumistic engineer. Words like 'satisfactory'. Motion thinks the voice sounds authentic. The biographer listens in.

Years ago at a conference a woman told me, 'Better be careful writing about Yeats. A friend of mine wrote something about him he didn't like, and he tried to drown him when he was out swimming.' I thought desperately: where did Yeats swim? Rapallo in the late-twenties? Roquebrune in the thirties? Was this something else the Steinach operation did for him? But when I ask her she says, 'Oh it was at the Forty-foot, last year. Something got him by the ankle. He knew it was Yeats.' Now, as I begin to write, every near-accident, every twinge and itch, suggests a supernatural fatality on its way. The woman on the bicycle: the Curse of Yeats?

Everyone thinks they own him (except, paradoxically, his family – who have been exemplary in their generosity and evenhandedness towards the Yeats industry). In the Haughey era, a Fianna Fail politician told me reverently, 'Yeats is the Taoiseach's favourite poet.' Fame at last. His voice booms from the radio, the famous recording of 'Innisfree', which he grew to hate. An innocuous Sunday magazine article on fly-fishing suddenly mugs me by quoting 'The Song of Wandering Aengus'. Yet another biographical study is on its way: its author says to me, possessively, 'I had to come to terms with him.'

I think about ownership of Yeats, of Irishness, of Irish history itself: competing claims, debatable lands. I think of the Kulturkampf in Ireland, past and present. Who qualifies as Irish? Does nationalism exclude or include? What do you have to give up in order to possess it? The voice of D.P. Moran is heard in the land. Some Irish papers announced after Yeats's

death that he was an 'English' poet (of the 'sewage school'). He 113
built up defences and they out-lasted him. The affectations and
ambiguities that lie behind even his most ringing endorse-
ments; the audacity of his pronouncements and conjunctions.
That extraordinary voice: will it ever be picked up posthu-
mously by a manufacturer of hearing-aids? Or bellow its rage
through a medium, as Yeats makes Swift do in *The Words Upon
The Window-pane*? Will I be there to hear it?

Need I? He is round every corner.

JACK B. YEATS: THE MOIST-BRIGHT PIZZAZZ OF IRISH LIGHT

Tom Paulin

In a brief and scarcely known prose work, 'Homage to Jack B. Yeats', his friend Samuel Beckett celebrates this magnificent painter's 'desperately immediate images'. But the celebration is terse and curtailed, for Beckett refuses to expatiate on 'this great internal reality which incorporates into a single witness dead and living spirits, nature and void, everything that will cease and everything that will never be'. Calling Jack Yeats 'this supreme master', Beckett concludes that we simply have to bow before his work 'wonder-struck'.

Beckett's magisterial reverence is just, impressive, heartfelt, but we need to do more than bow helplessly before Jack Yeats's canvases — here is a major painter who has not been accorded the recognition he deserves.

Jack Yeats (1871–1957) had a long and fulfilled artistic life, but unlike his elder brother, W.B., he has yet to achieve international recognition. Revered in Ireland, his work has only been fitfully praised in Britain (notably by Herbert Read, Kenneth Clark and John Berger), though the exhibition of Yeats's late paintings at the Whitechapel Gallery last year did stimulate some interest. Like one of the travelling figures in his wildly dazzling canvases, this visionary painter is still moving down the road towards the promised land:

> Left, Left
> We Left Our Name
>   On the Road
>   On the Road
> On the Famous Road

On the Famous Road
On the Famous Road
   Of Fame.

Yeats devised this chanting ballad-refrain as the title for one of his finest paintings, and his tramping – tramping *not* marching – use of 'we' embraces all the tinkers, strolling players, ballad singers, boxers, sailors and fairground crowds this republican democrat identified with. So pervasive is the sense of outdoor openness and travelling exposure in the paintings that they seem to be tragi-comic answers to the question his brother puts at the end of 'The Cold Heaven':

   Ah! when the ghost begins to quicken,
Confusion of the death-bed over, is it sent
Out naked on the roads, as the books say,
                              and stricken
By the injustice of the skies for punishment?

The homeless on-the-road quality in the paintings embodies Jack Yeats's intense love of popular culture and his gloriously deracinated communalism. It expresses many centuries of historical suffering, but it wears that experience lightly – like bright rags figured in raw oilpaint under a sky like 'a tinker's twisted withy tent'.

Yeats is the painter as ballad-singer. He often used snatches of ballads as titles for his paintings and he loved to collect sudden epiphanies like this:

I married a tinker's daughter
in the town of Skibbereen
but at last one day she galloped away
with me only shirt in a paper bag
to the shores of Amerikay

Yeats is a deeply oral painter who is fascinated by singers and actors – he seems to be sketching in oils in order to catch the

116   intensity of the vocal moment. This means that he is an insouciantly rootless, unplaceable painter whose work embodies the pervasively empty, the abandoned quality, of the Irish landscape. Implicit in his spontaneously cascading brushstrokes and the deliberately makeshift look of his paintings are the ruined cottages, the barren fields and aching emigrant atmosphere of what he termed in one of his prose works 'an only-just island'. They carry, too, the absence of a significant indigenous tradition in the visual arts. His figures come out of nowhere, carrying minimal baggage.

In another prose work 'The Amaranthers', Yeats describes a ballad-singer walking home with a bundle of ballads 'flittering in his hands'. This flittering or 'whiffling' quality is essential to the profound surface excitement of the paintings. It is vividly expressed by Sickert in a letter to Yeats where he praised the movement of his figures within landscapes which have 'water, sky, houses ruffling like flags in support of them'. Yeats sought what he termed 'continuosity, impetuosity and exuberance'. He aimed at what in a lovely phrase he called 'the living ginger of Life' and this means that his paintings are always in process, always seeking a human absolute in 'the power of the moment'. He is therefore a highly theatrical painter who never falls into the trap of offering a premeditated staginess. Like the characters invoked in his friend Synge's *The Playboy of the Western World* – the 'pirates, preachers, poteen-makers . . . the jobbing jockies; parching peelers' – his figures are carefree, impoverished, exuberant travellers.

In one of his finest paintings, *In Memory of Boucicault and Bianconi*, he identifies a group of travelling players with a high tumbling waterfall and this expresses his love of theatrical, especially melodramatic, excitement. The moist-bright pizzazz of Irish light, the experience of popular theatre and cinema, movement, emigration, singing, talking, thinking, all become identified. Even his interiors – the tragic *Nothing Has Changed*, for example – have a sense of being open and exposed before an audience that is all buzz and hum or raptly present attention.

No painter more favoured the present participle when devising titles for his works: *Rushing Waters, Man in a Room Thinking, Looking Forward, Looking Back, Tinker Whistling 'Donal Abu', Going to Wolfe Tone's Grave, Something Happening in the Street.* There are many similarly active titles which point to what has been termed the 'quiveringly intensive vitality' of his brushstrokes or flicks of the palette knife.

If we seem to view many of his paintings through a proscenium arch, Yeats must also be seen as a highly literary painter. As Hilary Pyle has shown in her *A Catalogue Raisonné of the Oil Paintings, On Through the Silent Lands* is based on the opening lines of Christina Rossetti's sonnet 'Remember':

> Remember me when I am gone away,
>   Gone far away into the silent land;
>   When you can no more hold me by the
>
>   hand,
> Nor I half turn to go yet turning stay.

This late masterpiece shows an elderly bent man with what looks like a bowler hat pressed under his arm as he walks painfully down a hill towards a flimsy bridge over a swollen river. Beyond it are a lough and a strange cascading icy mountain. Yeats was nearly eighty when he painted this extraordinary picture. Like all his best work it powerfully communicates a sense of life bleak, joyous, eternal. It may be because this painting hangs in the Ulster Museum that I've come over the years to think of Yeats's figure as an Orangeman, perhaps one of the bowler-hatted Sligo Orangemen he knew as a child. His figure anticipates the tramps who also wear hats in *Waiting for Godot* and who may in some future production of the play be portrayed as wittily derelict Loyalists. By placing the hat under the old man's arm – he looks like an out-of-work actor or an impoverished auctioneer – Yeats signifies something of the enormous imaginative humility he brings to all his subjects. Rejecting any impulse towards the

118   monumental and permanent, Yeats is able to make his paintings live in the moment, to exist, as he titled one painting, *Now*.

It's this volatile, momentous sense of the present moment that makes Yeats such a paradoxical master – more, to adapt his brother's phrase, the master of the 'flaming door' than of the fixed, the 'still stars'. He approximates the painter to the strolling player or the faith healer – Friel is another dramatist with a kinned or cognate imagination – and though Yeats's paintings have that desperate immediacy Beckett discerns, they are also joyously immediate in a celebratory, rapt and ecstatic manner. The awe, the sense of loss and renewal with which we contemplate them is rooted, I feel certain, in the experience of emigration. This is the experience which also produces and informs the pathos in some of the paintings – for example, *The Exile from Erin*, which shows an Irish businessman reading a newspaper in an office overlooking what must be Kilburn. This painting is the illustration that accompanies George Birmingham's witty essay on expatriate nationalism in *Irishmen All*. The sense of ontological displacement at the core of emigrant experience is also the subject of *The Island Funeral* which deploys the Blaskets setting as a figure for the whole island – if that's the right adjective. The angular coffin, open boat, shawled women and the more distantly placed, anxious male figure pressed against the mast build an image of impoverished exposure that expresses the binary tension of island/mainland or island/other-island which is the essence of expatriation.

The sense of exile as process is often shown overcoming pathos and tragedy to vouchsafe the feeling of 'life endless, the great thought/ By which we live, infinity and God' as Wordsworth terms it in 'The Prelude'. This is not the pragmatist's or the realist's mental universe of ends, means, destinations and plain hard facts, but a spattery, complete vision of eternity. It's high time Jack Yeats's eternal travelling images were better known.

MAGGIE ANGRE

Billy Roche

Maggie Angre, a rolled-up towel under her arm, stood on the edge of Rainwater Pond and gazed out at the very spot where her brother Steven had perished. This old, abandoned quarry which had been filled up to the brim with a mixture of seawater and rain, black and bottomless, tanged with salt, home of the otter and the eel, where the drowning Steven had called her name, called out to her even though he must have known in his heart and soul that there was no way could she swim out that far. And even still his voice echoed here, echoed through the trees, was blown on out to sea only to return year in and year out to this desolate and magnetic place.

On the far side the marsh reeds bowed like pageboys and, in the distance beyond the railway tracks, the mountains lay heaped against the sky as Maggie began to undress, kicking off her muddy shoes, taking off her pants and jumper and flinging them up into the bushes. She had her bathing costume on underneath her clothes; it was straining now to bear the brunt of her bulging physique. She knelt down and dipped her hand in the water. She blessed herself and looked up at the cloud-rolling sky, remembering once again what it was like on the day he drowned. Their little gang huddled together on the bank – Steven and Albino Murphy and big fat Anthony Mahoney from Selskar, herself and one or two others – and how they all got a bit of a fright when two white swans materialised out of the reeds opposite and started to drown the little ducks, holding them under the water with their wings. Albino walking along the top of the old submerged quarry wall which made him look as if he was walking on the water and he waving to the wide-eyed passengers on a passing train. It was a fine afternoon. There was a blue sky. Or was it raining? No, it was . . . It was all kinds of weather on the day he drowned. And it was no particular time of day. It was all day and every day and all day long there were sun showers. They sheltered under the dripping bushes. They ate beans and crab apples and they sang a little calypso song that Albino had taught them:

> Rich man underneath the apple tree
> Rich man singing you can't catch me
> I own the apple
> I own the pear . . .

Steven was a good-looking boy. Handsome. Not like Maggie at all. You'd never think for a minute that they were brother and sister. He was brave too. He was the one who had swum all the way across to the other side of the pond while the rest of them were afraid of their lives to venture more than a couple of feet away from the shore. Steven was fearless. And he was very good with people. Ask anyone about him. He was well liked. Ah poor Steven was a right laugh.

Maggie stood on the jutting-out piece of bank where Steven had stood. Awkward and ugly she felt in the daylight as the folds of flesh fell down around her and the fatness of her chilblained legs reflected in the water. And then she dived, leaving behind her footprints on the mucky bank, dirty bits of clay clinging to the soles of her feet as the river rose like a shroud to hide the monstrosity that she called her body. And when she dived her arched body resembled a bird in flight and when she rose up it was with an amphibian grace that she ploughed through the water, eating up distance with every stride, cutting up space with every stroke, her head rising and falling, her arms shooting out little white spurts of water as she swam. Maggie Angre was a powerful swimmer. When she swam people stopped to look at her. She could swim out to the Ballast Bank and back again and then without a feather off of her she would turn around and swim the entire length of the Woodenworks. She loved the water. Maggie was in her alley when she swam.

She was reaching the far bank now, touching it, kicking away from it, travelling underwater for maybe ten or fifteen strides. And then she surfaced, her drenched hair behind her like a wet mane, plunging onwards gracefully until she came to the spot where Steven . . . well, where it happened . . . Here's where he splashed. Here's where he kicked. Here's where he called out her name. She could still hear those pitiful sounds now and that last inarticulate yelp before he was swallowed up by the dark, treacherous place known as Rainwater Pond.

What did you call out to me like that for, Steven? I mean, why me? You must have known that I wasn't able to swim out there and save you. You must have known! I mean, why not Albino Murphy or one of the other bigger boys? Why me? Or were you just calling out to your only kin in sight, Steven, was that it? That was it, wasn't it? You were saying goodbye to the little sister that you loved. You did love me, Steven, didn't you? Ah of course you did. Sure wasn't I your little sister and weren't you always minding me and holding my hand and all and didn't you take me with you everywhere you went nearly . . . Me da was dying alive about you, Steven, so he was. He wasn't the same at all after you were gone. He just couldn't get over it. He never put much pass on me one way or another but after you were gone I disappeared too. I was drowned too . . . I should never have let you go out there alone anyway, Steven. I should have learned to swim sooner and then I would have been out there with you. I could have saved you. I could! If only it was now, Steven. Why couldn't it be now?

Anthony Mahoney is back in town, Steven. You should see him. He's an awful size. Compared to him there's none of me in it at all and God knows, that's saying something. Oh by the way I never told you, did I? They're after putting me out of my little house. I'm only out of it a couple of months and already the place is gone to the dogs. The windows have all been

122 smashed and there's a rotten old smell out of it. I'm after moving into the old . . . I'm living somewhere else now. God help me, Steven, but I don't know what's going to become of me at all, to tell you the truth.

And so once again Maggie Angre wept for her dead brother Steven, wept once again for her lonely self and as the salt tears she shed dropped into the water she remembered the first time that she had been brave enough to swim out this far and how the taste of her own teardrops had led her to believe that it was Steven's last few tears that had turned this stretch of water to brine.

On the way back she swam with all her might, every inch of water purging its own portion of blame, every foot of ground washing away another sin from the face of the world. She was swimming for Steven now. She was swimming for herself. She was swimming for Albino Murphy who was killed at Krudersberg. She was swimming for each and every one of us who have stood on the shore and watched while our brothers drown.

When she got back to the other side her eyes were still red from crying and so she sat shivering on the bank with a towel around her until her grief had subsided.

She rolled her wringing wet costume up inside the towel and then she climbed to the top of the ferny bank to sit in the sun. She lit up a cigarette and examined her nicotine-stained fingers and then she gazed down into the tranquil waters where two white swans swam.

Aidan Murphy

WHISTLING

The man going home alone
stares intentionally at nothing
& whistles. In bed I hear
his song of concentrated terror,
the tension of controlled breath.
It is a million years ago;
axe in hand he wades in slime,
slugs bubble at his knees
Somewhere in the wet forest
another advances. A perfect
double, his own armed &
cautious image, whistling
as he whistles, notes of fear.

Is this what music is? This
gentle Schumann spinning here
snowing on the world? Is it
born of an old reluctance,
a turning from silence & self?
I feel relieved. The symphony
is over, & the man? The street
is empty, his tune gone.
Under the sheets I watch
lights fencing with the dark.
Pins are dropping on the quilt,
I purse my lips and blow.

SLIGHTLY LIKE A WHEEL

The guru is retarded.
Quick! the water! fetch and carry.
The lion is injured, come back with a pliers,
and don't forget the lunchbags –
fixing life is hungry work.
Elastoplasts for Jupiter – holy cow!
Hurry! the emergency cord,
the fallen bodies are blocking the front-line,
we'll have to fill the ugly holes with glue
or maybe burn the lot, pyromaniacs for ever,
and after that it's anybody's guess.

She's angry again. Calls for safety manoeuvres,
pronto! cut the eyes out,
change into something pretty,
dinner for two and a moonlight sonata.
Hide your heart in the cutlery.
Quick! paint the babies,
quick! the water,
the guru is unconscious . . .

THE PARKGATE
BOOK OF THE
DEAD

Away from the scourge of daylight we sit,
transfixed by manmade darkness and uncomplex calm,
in hieroglyphic poses.
I am the Jackal, confounded –
you are the Ibis greedy for beauty –
and we watch with the other beasts
our lives departing
into the tunnel of the original mystery tour.
And we drink to our final journeys,
to the tattered passports of our souls,
and pray that mercy has a sense of humour.

Immured in space,
planets of banter orbit between our elbows,
feeding on photons of strain and silence.
And all that was said before is said again –
the reason and the rubbish,
the smashing of promises –
in the cultivated language of destruction,
while we suck each other's bruises
and find each other always on a fallow footing.

126   *Once* was a perfect day in summer
Loaded with the restful heat of eternal deceit.
Once was an open book
its white pages waiting to burn.
Now, as we relate – browbeaten Jackal, ageing Ibis –
our singular falls,
our eyes become a single eye,
a telescope of pain and longing
scouring earth sea and sky for its lost cunning,
poor waxworks tinged with worthless pity!
And the screen hollers death in vivid kodakchrome,
and the corpulent general informs the room
that he, also, doesn't give a rat's butt,
and the kerb beyond the door is cracking
pushing gas. So be it.
We drink again and breathe it in,
and breathe it in,
and breathe it in . . .

EXTRACT FROM RESURRECTION MAN

Eoin McNamee

Statement of John Arthur McGrath:

I John McGrath would like to state that the events I describe in the following happened as if in a dream so that it was as if I did not participate although I know that I did and this is a source of regret to me. We drove up to the gate of O'Neill's depot at ten o'clock in the morning of 10 May 1975. I remember a sign 'Trade Only' at the gate which gave me a moment of panic at being recognised as not being trade. I felt foreign to my own nature from that moment. We stopped the car at the entrance to the warehouse. We got out and walked in. Big Sam's eyes were gleaming and he looked from side to side as if his head was afflicted by madness which I also started to feel although I had no notion of a bloodbath at this or any other point. I do not wish to give the full name of Big Sam.

There was another man with us who I also do not wish to name as he is notorious for being involved in killing and has not a spark of mercy in his nature. This man I shall call Mr M. He had wrote out this car parts order which was a fake on a piece of paper tore from a children's exercise book. He seemed to be in high good spirits at this point. Two assistants came up to us and Mr M handed one the note but before they could read it Big Sam had them covered with a gun he took from his pocket and he said lie down on the ground. They lay down at that point.

Then Mr M said where's the office? One of the assistants looked up at us and pointed. I would like to say that there was no look of fear on his face or on the other one's. They seemed to lie down in a kind of blind disbelief. I remember Big Sam

128 said we should've brought a van and took some of the car parts were sitting round the place but M said we were there for the money. M kept looking at me and saying things like are you all right and smiling at me to make me feel part of things. Apart from the incident with Stewartie Robinson which was a mistake with a gun going off by accident this was the first time I ever done anything like that and I hope I will never be involved again. This is a statement of my remorse.

M indicated that I should go with him to the office. I cannot remember how he said it or if he used words at all. We went up these old wooden steps which creaked with a noise to wake the dead. M seemed to change somehow as we went up as if it was a climb to murder. He had these blue eyes which seemed to get smaller and he did not speak.

The office had two glass windows looking over the depot and a glass door. There were two men inside. They looked up and seen me and M outside the glass. You could see them looking nervous and talking to each other but you couldn't hear them through the glass. Seeing them and all it was still like they weren't really there. It was like watching an event that happened some time ago recorded. M opened the door and we went in.

I had never been in a proper office before and it was just like you imagined a real one, or one on television. There were green filing cabinets and a desk with this big typewriter on it. I had this notion to type my name on it like a typist with big fingernails but M saw me and said not to do it.

The older man came forward and asked what we wanted. He had grey hair and was like your uncle or someone you know well who gives you that look like he was disappointed in you but not surprised to tell the truth. M said that we come for the money and that we were serious. He said it was early on Monday morning and that there was no money yet in a voice like everybody knows that. The younger one didn't say nothing but just looked at us. I am sorry for the younger one. M said for them both to kneel on the floor. The older man looked at him and he said it again to kneel.

I am of the belief now that robbery was not the motive for the actions of M on that day and that he had the whole thing planned from the start. There have been questions as to the mental state of M in that period and I would like to state that there was no sign of madness from when we reached the office but that he was calm and smiling during the incidents described.

When they were kneeling on the floor with their backs to us M put his gun to the older man's neck and I put my gun to the younger man's neck who started to say something I think it was a Roman Catholic prayer. This seemed to cause displeasure to M. He fired his gun and mine went off also. I remember nothing of the office after that except that there was more smoke from the guns than you would think and that it gave you a taste in your mouth like when you touch a battery with your tongue to see if there is still any power left in it.

We went out of the office. Downstairs we saw that the other two were shot as well. M went behind the counter and looked until he saw headlights for his car. There was much laughter and talk in the car on the way back and no mention of the money. M said that I done well but I knew what would happen if I opened my mouth. I wish to say that I have now embraced Christian values and express repugnance at my deeds and that having made this clean breast I am at ease now in Christ.

★　★　★

Jim Curran left the snooker hall at a quarter past twelve and walked towards the Cliftonville Road. He had been playing snooker. He played every night. It was something a man could lose himself in. The green baize under hooded lights, men standing in the shadows along the wall, a purposeful drawing together, attentive to the passage and reclusive click of the balls. Curran loved the studied movements from place to place around the table, sighting along the cue and selecting their

130   footing with precision as if they were working towards a theoretical end, an abstract perfection. Something a man could seek guidance in.

He appreciated the clarity of thought that he brought away with him when he walked home from the club. He had an exhaustive knowledge of the great sportsmen who had come from the city. People whose names you rarely saw in books. Men of icy control and self-knowledge whose greatest victories grew in his mind as feats of unendurable loneliness. Curran had a deep respect for the sporting figures of the past. Rinty Monaghan. Dixie Dean.

It seemed that he could see the city clearly on nights like this, and it was a place of age and memory. He thought about the *Lusitania* and the *Titanic* built in the shipyard, the closed linen mills, the derelict shirt factories, the streets of houses built for workers. Then there were the other edifices, constructed by speculators who seemed to have this modern city in mind, their designs weathered down to create a setting for injured lives; this city like gaunt others they had created on shallow, muddy deltas or desolate coasts guided by infallible principles of abandonment.

At first he didn't see the yellow Escort emerge from a side-street, its motor idling. He had travelled another hundred yards before he became aware of the car following him at walking pace, keeping its distance in a way that seemed obedient, as if it were awaiting a command that he might make. He did not alter his pace. It could be the police. It could be a taxi looking for an address. Nevertheless he looked along the street for shelter, a house light, some warm billet to offset against the sudden conviction of lasting solitude. There was a row of locked garages to his right and the wall of a motorworks to his left. He could hear the noise of traffic in the distance, a sound he had been unaware of for years coming to him now as if there was something gentle-natured and sorrowing in the distance. It made him think of a country song about mothers that brought a tear to his eye. Thinking about this he stumbled on the

pavement and immediately heard the car behind him rev
wildly. He began to run. He thought if he could only reach
the end of the street. An image of Roger Bannister breaking the
four-minute mile came into his head. A man in flapping white
shorts and singlet, running with his knees high and elbows
tucked, upright and fleet, determined to imbue his passage with
dignity, aware that history would demand no less of the
moment.

He imagined that he was passing people in the street. A pair
of lovers in a doorway fixed in a attitude of solace, a drunk
watching him mildly, as though inclined to leniency on the
basis that much of life propels men into headlong necessities.
He felt that that the dead from his past were in the shadows.
Parents, brothers, uncles. He had the impression that they wore
expressions of strange urging. He felt that the untiring dead
were somehow gaining on him now, the soft patter of their
ghostly sprints almost audible. When the car drew level with
him he knew that he had lost. A man spoke to him from the
passenger window.

'What's your hurry, big lad?'

Curran stopped and bent over double, gasping for breath.
The car door opened and three men got out. One of them was
holding a tyre iron.

'You're coming with us, son.'

'A big trip in the motor car.'

'Fuck's sake, mister, you're not fit at all. Wee run like that
and you can't get a breath.'

'He'll be fit by the time we get done with him.'

'Fit for fuck-all.'

Curran held up one hand. He wanted permission to catch his
breath before speaking, a respite so that he could begin to form
words again. Please.

EXTRACT FROM THE ONLY TRUE HISTORY OF LIZZIE FINN

Sebastian Barry

Above Inch Strand in Kerry. Right, a structure suggesting the old house tower, a sort of lumber room, where rest bits of lawn sports, trophies from wars and old items, old dolls, a basin to catch a quiet drip, the newest thing being three army uniforms on a rough rack, all in a dusty solitude, with a few wooden steps leading up to it. Left, the comfortable sitting area of a drawing-room, appropriate to a small gentleman's house, good chairs and a richly embroidered sofa, and a little elegant table for a lamp and a vase. There's a little pair of reading glasses on this table. Downstage, the garden leading off from the drawing-room, a roll of trim lawn, with a deal of rhododendron, fuchsia and peony, and roses. An open-enough feeling, but also the sense of shelter from the high wilderness beyond the house. The garden thick with birds, the fresh pounding of the sea in Dingle Bay below, running in on to Inch Strand. A fresh, hot high summer's day towards late afternoon. Now through the pulse of sun comes BARTHOLOMEW *Grady, the gardener, a stocky man of about seventy with a fire of white hair still. He carries a basket lined with wet dock leaves which he will put cut roses into for moistness. He waves his old cutting knife, a contraption tied about with ancient string, at the retinue of black flies above his head.*

BARTHOLOMEW: Can not a Christian gardener cross his lawn without assassins? All winter, wrapped by my fire, I think of you sleeping in the icy stones, waiting for these sprightly summer days.

He manages however to select a few blooms, expertly snipping them into his basket. LUCINDA GIBSON, *Robert's mother, tall, dark, with a plain silver cross on the breast of her brocaded black mourning dress, comes through the drawing-room with a rectangle of paper, looking for good light to read it by. She steps out into the garden, closely scanning the paper.*

Lady, now, don't come out here without your netted hat — these black men will divide in the air, like demons, and ambush you too.

LUCINDA GIBSON: A little rough boy has just come running along the sea road from Castlemaine with this telegraph message. I'm sure his father sent him, with all the haste that is due to a telegraph message. And, look, I can't read it at all, Bartholomew. It is smudged of course.

BARTHOLOMEW: I've the responsibility of these blooms, Lady. You know how the heat runs in under the dock-leaves. I can't be scanning over messages at the same time. You'd best be burning a thing like that, Lady — that's my counsel.

LUCINDA GIBSON: Of your charity, Bartholomew Grady.

She gives him the telegram.

BARTHOLOMEW: Fortunate for you I've still immaculate sight. Here, hold it for me again, please, Lady.

He hands her the telegram back and she holds it unfolded for him. He steps back a few paces.

By Napoleon's ghost, I can read anything, at four paces. There now. All nicely read now (*heading off*).

LUCINDA GIBSON: But what does it say, Bartholomew? Is it good or bad?

BARTHOLOMEW: I don't know if it's good or bad. It will be as well for me to say nothing, Lady.

He heads off, stooping at the bucket briefly to skite a handful of moisture on to his selections.

LUCINDA GIBSON: I'll fetch on my reading-glasses.

134 *She goes to the little table where her glasses are, examines the paper.*

LUCINDA GIBSON: That old man doesn't get any saner. (*reads*) What could this be? Bartholomew?

BARTHOLOMEW (*just about to escape*): Yes, Lady?

LUCINDA GIBSON (*coming back out*): Was there anything in your newspaper about Robert?

BARTHOLOMEW: No, Lady.

LUCINDA GIBSON: Nothing at all?

BARTHOLOMEW: The *Castlemaine Herald* confines itself mostly to the state of the country and the frequent occurrence of murder in Irish life.

LUCINDA GIBSON: You spotted nothing through-out the newspaper that would cast light on this telegraph message?

BARTHOLOMEW: Believe me, Lady, I combed it through as is my custom when I am ingesting my sausages at noon and, *mirabile dictu*, as Virgil often said, there wasn't a blessed thing about your son.

LUCINDA GIBSON (*ignoring his sarcasm*): Then it's a mistake. (*stuffing the message away*) It has been taken down wrongly at the post office. Honoria Fanning is half-deaf as we all know and her husband is half-blind. The perfect people to run a post office.

She goes back into the house.

BARTHOLOMEW: Half-blind, says she.

Goes off.

The ringing of a telephone somewhere deeper in the house. Light up on ROBERT *upstage at a wall telephone, his back turned. The telephone rings for a while. Then, offstage,* LUCINDA GIBSON'S *voice.*

LUCINDA GIBSON: Yes, yes, Red House.

ROBERT: Hello, Robert – this is mother.

LUCINDA: No, you are Robert, I am mother. Robert, dear, how lovely to hear your voice. How lovely. It's three years, isn't it, dear? Do you know they sent me the uniforms back, all the way from Africa. I was astonished.

ROBERT: Did you receive my telegraph?

LUCINDA GIBSON: Yes, I received it, dear.

A pause.

ROBERT: I'm here at the station in Castlemaine. Do you think Honoria Fanning is still on the line? We're married, abruptly, I'll grant, but married just the same. I know it seems strange and ill-mannered, but it seemed the best course to take.

LUCINDA GIBSON: Are you telling me that you and Honoria Fanning are married?

ROBERT: Mother, don't be satirical.

LUCINDA GIBSON: It's just the way you put it. I knew she already had a husband, of sorts. Robert, I really must attend to Teresa in the kitchens. She's been trying her hand at a strawberry fool and it may need rescuing. Goodbye, Robert.

ROBERT: Mother, mother, I'm coming out on the trap . . . Mother . . . Oh, dear (*light away from him*).

BARTHOLOMEW *wanders on again with his pipe, directing the smoke purposefully at the flies. The sky above is reddening into long streaks, with lines of gold. The birds are hushed. He stops at the well.*

BARTHOLOMEW: A well is a kind of unturned bell, that will ring neither matins nor evensong. (*smoking his pipe*) Ah, yes.

136   *The sky deepens to the slate and crimson of late sunset, the dark filling slowly. Upstage, on a high trap, with the strike of the pony's trotting hooves, ROBERT and LIZZIE, with a chequered rug across their legs against the night.*

ROBERT (*exhilarated*):   Glorious, oh glorious, my lovely Kerry. Three years, Lizzie.

LIZZIE: Those are woods, aren't they, on the headland? I don't ever recall woods in Kerry. Isn't that strange?

ROBERT: They're my woods, Lizzie. Your woods. Our woods. See the lovely swagger of Inch Strand, Lizzie. That's your strand now.

LIZZIE: It's white as a snow bear that I saw once in a menagerie.

ROBERT: It's famous all over for its beauty. I was happy there often with my brothers. That was our Africa once. And now we'll fill it again with brothers and sisters!

LIZZIE: It's handsome, Robert.

ROBERT: There's the house peeking through the trees – Bartholomew's windbreakers, they are, to protect his garden. I've missed his bitter tongue. Oh, I'm so proud to be bringing you here, Lizzie.

LIZZIE: I don't see the house you mean. That little place there by the strand?

ROBERT: Lizzie, that's the village, as we call it. There was an old body there that gathered the periwinkles.

LIZZIE: Not those big roofs and the dark tower?

ROBERT: That's your home.

LIZZIE: But, Robert, that's a landlord's house, isn't it?

ROBERT: Well, and if it is? What did you think you were coming to?

LIZZIE: Not a great place like that, dark against the incoming night.

ROBERT: It's not so great, believe me. Just a little place, Lizzie. Just a little place for the Gibsons to lay their heads. Are you so shy of it? Will we rest up another night in the hotel in Castlemaine?

LIZZIE: I might have been happier approaching in daylight. Twilight is so full of things past. But since we're this far, let's drive on. I can imagine the three of us, my father and mother and me, on this road.

ROBERT: Remember, Lizzie, you're my wife. You're strong and right and legal here.

LIZZIE: Oh, I'm not afraid.

ROBERT: There's nothing to fear.

LIZZIE: Go on away up so.

A deep light in the drawing-room, brown shadows shoaling between the chairs. TERESA, *the general servant, a little birdlike woman of twenty, comes in, with* BARTHOLOMEW'S *roses carefully in her arms. She sets them down gently and digs in her pocket for a Lucifer, strikes it, removes the glass of the lamp, lights it. The room shrugs in the blowing light till she replaces the glass. She arranges the roses in the vase intently, casting shadows everywhere. At the other side of the house, the iron clanging of the bell. She hurries excitedly from the room. Echoing phrases, bang of things, silence for a little, then* TERESA *reappears showing* LIZZIE *into the drawing-room.*

TERESA (*breathless*): You go in there, do, miss, there's a heap of nice places for sitting (*watching* LIZZIE *all the while*). Would you like your coat off, missy?

She takes LIZZIE'S *coat, lays it on her arm, stroking the material. She takes* LIZZIE'S *hat in further wonder.*

138   I have never seen an English lady before, missy. You do look lovely, if I may say. Are everyone in England so trim! I imagine so, missy.

LIZZIE: England has its style, that's true, girl. But that's a nice frock you're wearing yourself.

TERESA (*overcome*):   This old thing, missy? It's only a yard of dross material the mistress bought for me in Tralee.

LIZZIE: Well, it's not the dress but the girl in the dress, we used to say.

TERESA: Oh, missy. You've no notion of the excitement you've caused me. Barty has been sputtering by the stoves with all sorts of black words, poking at the ashes with his pruning knife and doing it no good, but I couldn't get my rest last night for thinking of you. Oh, don't mind my give-out, missy. I'm worse than a goose. (*going, then worriedly*) You know what a goose is?

LIZZIE: I do.

TERESA: Ah, geese are all over. I knew that!

Goes.

LIZZIE *left alone. She looks about for a mirror or something to see herself in, attends to her hair.*

LIZZIE: I didn't know he was a king, I didn't know.

She sits ill at ease on a chair, looks at the fireplace.

He'd be sat there on a hearth like that, singing. Lovely Neapolitan songs to break your heart. He'd be given a pair of hard shoes to stand in, so as not to cause offence. Then they'd take them off him at the door. And off into the night with us with our sixpence. Oh Lord.

A while later, ROBERT *sitting beside* LIZZIE, *and* LUCINDA GIBSON *facing them. There's a certain strain in the room.* TERESA *arrives with tea things on a tray.*

LUCINDA GIBSON: Well done, Teresa, well done. Set it down there. Good girl. (*smiling out to* ROBERT *and* LIZZIE) Yes. Will you do the salmon for the travellers' supper?

TERESA: Oh, it's well on now, Lady, well on.

LUCINDA GIBSON: Poached, I trust, Teresa? I can't abide salmon, really, unless someone poaches it.

LIZZIE: You mean stolen?

TERESA: No, no, missy – broiled. It is, Lady – just as you told me.

LUCINDA GIBSON: Thank God.

She pours the tea with TERESA'S *help.* TERESA *hands out the cups.*

That's the girl. She has trained up beautifully, hasn't she?

TERESA: Will I bring in candles, Lady? Now that there's more folk than one?

LUCINDA GIBSON: Do we need candles?

ROBERT: There's light enough.

LUCINDA GIBSON: The light of candles draws us in from outdoors, I always think. Draws our hearts within the house. The countryside lies about us, but the candles draw us away from it. Usher in our souls, as it were. A lamp doesn't have the same effect somehow.

LIZZIE: You like the garden and the countryside?

LUCINDA GIBSON: I could stand all evening in the garden listening to the bay running in on Inch, I could. Do you like the tea?

LIZZIE: Yes, I do, Mrs Gibson.

LUCINDA GIBSON: Oh, Lady Gibson, it is. My husband was knighted for his jurisprudence hereabout, but, Lord knows, they flattered him.

LIZZIE: Excuse me – I didn't know.

LUCINDA GIBSON: At any rate, you're Mrs Gibson now, so there won't be too much confusion between us. (*seeing that* TERESA *hasn't moved for a while*) What's amiss, Teresa, are you all right?

TERESA: I have a scream coming on, Lady, you must forgive me. I got a terrible cold feeling in my bones when you spoke of souls and suchlike.

LUCINDA GIBSON: Well, don't scream in here, please. You go and scream in peace in the kitchens. When you get a chance, you may unpack their suitcases and portmanteaus.

TERESA: Yes, Lady.

LUCINDA GIBSON: We'll manage here.

TERESA: Yes, Lady. Thank you, Lady.

She goes.

ROBERT: Still mad as a March hare.

LUCINDA GIBSON: But very malleable, very. I'm quite pleased with her. Of course, she'll be yours now to perfect.

LIZZIE: I don't understand you, Lady Gibson.

LUCINDA GIBSON: This is Robert's house, you know. You've married him, and you must be mistress. Of course, if you wish, I can go to my people in Yorkshire.

LIZZIE: Oh, Yorkshire.

ROBERT: Your people in Yorkshire are underground these many years. There's no question of you being ousted in any way.

LUCINDA GIBSON: Oh, dear me, ousted, no. Thank you, Robert. The plain fact is, dear, since the government transferred the bulk of our farms, it has proved quite difficult to keep things going. Since our whole economy was based on rents.

ROBERT: I mean to look into all that. I'm sure we can manage for the three of us.

LUCINDA GIBSON: So many in recent years have had to leave their efforts here and go. It's quite sad, really.

ROBERT: We have a touch of new capital now.

LUCINDA GIBSON: (*looking at* LIZZIE): Oh, have we? How nice. Where are your people from, Mrs Gibson?

LIZZIE: My mother was from Ventry and my father I believe from somewhere near Cahirconree, but they moved about Corkaguiney.

LUCINDA GIBSON: They moved about?

LIZZIE: He travelled from place to place with us.

LUCINDA GIBSON: And did he have property here?

LIZZIE: He had a wife and a child and a splendid singing voice.

LUCINDA GIBSON: You mean your father moved about, singing?

LIZZIE: Yes.

LUCINDA GIBSON: How unusual, Robert. And they are both deceased, sadly, your parents?

LIZZIE: Yes, Lady Gibson. They died of fever.

LUCINDA GIBSON: So much death. Robert, after giving me an account of his brothers, tells me you were married in the Presbyterian church in Rutland Square. Does he mean you are a Presbyterian rather than of the Established Church?

142   LIZZIE: Yes, of course.

LUCINDA GIBSON: I don't want you to think me bigoted, you see. I just wished to know. It's the kind of thing one likes to know about one's daughter-in-law. If you have a little fortune, dear, how did it come to be?

LIZZIE: I gathered it for myself over the years.

LUCINDA GIBSON: How very extraordinary. How did you do that remarkable thing?

LIZZIE: You don't follow the halls, I think.

LUCINDA GIBSON: The halls?

LIZZIE: The music halls.

LUCINDA GIBSON: Oh no, dear. Do you?

ROBERT: Lizzie is a very independent woman, Mamma, and has lived an independent life, for which she is to be admired. She suffered here in Corkaguiney as a young girl, and I think it is wrong of you to question her like this, if I may say so.

LUCINDA GIBSON: Well, Robert, you know I have the highest regard for you, and I understand how dreadful it has been for you out there in Africa, and indeed I feel the force of our tragedy just as horribly as I know you do, but this is the plain world out here in Kerry, and the people hereabouts will want to know about your wife before they bring her into their houses. That's just how things are. I know these are modern times, and we are surely heading into darker times yet, but people are very simple and they like to know who they are talking to. That's all.

ROBERT: I should think they must be proud to know Lizzie.

LUCINDA GIBSON: My dear, these are very ordinary people out here. They expect a marriage in Christ Church like all your family before you. They want to read about her trousseau in the *Irish Times* and they want to feel that their world is going on at least as it always has gone on. You can't expect any better of them, especially in these hard times. I hope you won't disregard that. Because I myself feel quite put out, even to a degree, put upon, by this, I'm sorry to say.

ROBERT: I don't know why you would be, Mamma.

LUCINDA GIBSON: Well, I've tried to explain to you as gently as I can. I can see you have fine qualities, Mrs Gibson, but you mustn't expect to thrive here immediately. Go about with some care for people's foolish expectations. If you wish to gain your ground eventually. You are very different to the run of girls we get around here.

LIZZIE: I expect so.

LUCINDA GIBSON: (*rising*): Now, if you wish me to, I'll see to dinner. I'm sure you're both famished. In a private sense, I bid you welcome to Red House. In other senses, I don't know how I will enjoy describing you to people, but be that as it may.

ROBERT: You needn't try, Mamma, believe me.

LUCINDA GIBSON: We shall see, my dear.

A few minutes later. ROBERT *kneels before* LIZZIE, *holding her because she's upset.*

ROBERT: It's only history chooses a person's circumstance.

LIZZIE: Partly I love you because you don't care about all that.

ROBERT: That's it. I admire you, Lizzie. You didn't lie down and die in Corkaguiney. We are all very much equal under

144 the clothes that history lends us. If you can sing or dance or go soldiering, so much the better for you. No one knows exactly the through-going of their days. You made yourself secure in England. You don't require telling whether it was well or ill done.

LIZZIE: It was better than many of the doings of Corkaguiney, let me tell you, Robert. How it comes back to me, sitting under these dark skies.

ROBERT: You are the finest person I've ever met, and I've met my share of fine people, in the army and generally.

LIZZIE: Shall I go up and help little Teresa to unpack our things? She's a nice little creature, I think.

ROBERT: We'll both go up. We'll put on our finery and have a lovely supper of Corkaguiney salmon and the devil take the lingerer.

LIZZIE: You haven't let me down, sweet.

ROBERT: Nor will I ever, Lizzie.

They go.

The house as if empty, the little ruckus of moonlight through it and the fresh falling of the sea below. A rising and falling music. After a little, TERESA *emerges, staggering under the weight of some empty cases. She climbs the steps to the house tower, and lets the cases drop.* LIZZIE'S *stage knickers fall out of one of them.*

TERESA: My, what dust! I'll ignore it. That new missis is full of style. She has dresses!

She spots the knickers, takes them up, examines them in some wonder.

Ho, there's style for you. Will you take a gander at them stars. Would you deck them?

Holds the knickers against herself. They seem enormous.

Ha, ha. Oh. They must be winter knickers. The heaviness of   145
them. Now I've seen the heaven of knickers. She must have
been a empress before Robert Gibson found her. Oh, the
Holy Christ, that'll keep me going till Christmas. I needs see
nothing else till then. (holding them aloft) Oh, what
knickers!

CURTAIN *for Act One.*

EXTRACT FROM A NOVEL-IN-PROGRESS

Deirdre Madden

Although Claire did not know it, less than a quarter of a mile away Anna was also passing a sleepless night. She went down to the white kitchen and made herself a mug of camomile tea. Herbal teas were one of the few things of which she brought supplies from Holland to Ireland every summer. She sat with her hands around the mug, waiting for it to draw and then cool sufficiently for her to drink it. Tonight for some reason the light, straw-like scent which she usually found so soothing made her feel slightly queasy. She was in a worse mood than she had pretended to herself. Acknowledging this, she poured the tea down the sink and made herself a hot whisky instead.

Anna hated insomnia, which she regarded as one of the most severe penalties of growing old. She had slept so well when she was younger; she remembered Peter saying to her, 'Sleep is your natural element.' He used to get up in the middle of the night to feed Lili when she cried, and she wouldn't hear him either leaving or returning to the bed. She'd wake in the morning still in a fug of drowsiness for a good hour or so after she got up, as if the night was something she couldn't shake off. It had been particularly hard in Holland where everything started at the crack of dawn, she'd always had to be up so early to get Lili out to school and herself ready for work. When she came to live in Ireland she regretted that she hadn't lived there earlier, for in Donegal nothing much ever happened before ten in the morning. But as was the case with many things in her life, it was too late by then. Now it took her so long to get to sleep and the slightest sound woke her. Tonight the wind had been blowing about the eaves, but that was nothing new. No, it was her own frame of mind that was keeping her from sleep, and that drove her down to the kitchen and to the whisky bottle.

To some extent she blamed Nuala, who had called to visit her that afternoon, and confided in her more deeply than ever before, mainly on the strength of some Jenever which Anna had rashly produced for her to try, and for which Nuala had instantly developed a great liking. After three glasses she began to tell Anna more about her circumstances than Anna perhaps wished to know, Nuala growing lachrymose and self-pitying in the process.

Anna was used to being Mother Confessor to some of the local women. Generally she didn't at all mind that they confided in her, for she understood the rationale behind it. They were women she knew well, they were her friends. First they would tell her their worries, later they would tell her their secrets. She knew well that it was her being an outsider that also attracted them, as much as any personal affinity. Her scale of values was different; her frank godlessness both shocked and consoled them. They expected her to be more tolerant, more shockproof than they would be with each other, and in this she never disappointed them. Such secrets as they blurted out to Anna in her kitchen were mild enough, the familiar litany of drunken husbands, wayward children, long-held resentments against parents now old and dependent. Rita once remarked to her, 'It's foolish that you're the only person around here who I can talk to like this. What do secrets like mine amount to anyway? There's not a house round here where you wouldn't hear the same, if they chose to tell you. If you got every woman in this parish together and made her write down the thing they were most ashamed of, and then read them aloud, I bet you'd have half a dozen women claiming the same story. Oh yes, we all have our skeletons. Sometimes I wish we had the courage to bring it all out into the open, to stop pretending. But we never will.'

By making friends with the local people, Anna felt she knew and understood more about the area, but in the mood she was in tonight, she could only see their confidences as isolating: they trusted her because she was an outsider. But what did it matter? She loved Donegal, and never regretted having bought her house there. She'd loved the place from the moment she arrived there, just after Peter's death. They'd been living apart for such a long time, and after all they'd been through (or rather, after all he'd put her through) she hadn't expected that she would be greatly troubled by his dying. In her worst moments, she'd even thought that she would feel relieved, that she would be free of him at last.

But she wasn't relieved. She was devastated. Never for a moment had she thought they would get back together again, but she had hoped, even if only in some vague, half-formed way, that something would be worked out between them, that some day there would be some kind of resolution. It didn't happen. If he'd died in the early years of their marriage, just after Lili was born, before all the trouble, then it would have been different. Certainly she would have grieved for him, but it would have been a clean grief. There wouldn't have been this feeling of bitterness, of failure, of unresolved rancour, all of which was compounded by a deep sense of loss. And she hadn't expected to feel like this at all.

She didn't go to the funeral. Lili asked her not to: no, that wasn't true, Lili told her not to go; asked her why she wanted to add hypocrisy to all her other faults and shortcomings. He died in the summer. Anna's best friend had been about to leave for two weeks' holiday in Ireland, and persuaded her to come too. She had rented a cottage and was going there by car, so there would be no problem in accommodating her.

And so Anna left for Donegal. She had no idea which part of the country that was, for until then, Ireland was a place to which she had given no thought. She was glad that it was, for her, a neutral place. She expected little or nothing from the trip, it was to be nothing more than an escape from a difficult moment in her life.

The only time Anna cried during her first visit to Donegal was on the last day, when she was putting her case on the roof rack of her friend's car. The thought that she might never see this place again was unbearable to her. They drove off, and at the first town they came to, she asked her friend to stop. 'I'm not going back,' she said. She spent another week in Donegal, and by the end of that time had entered into negotiations to buy the cottage from the German family.

Her idea at that time was that she would sell up everything in Holland, and move permanently to Ireland. This had presented practical problems, and by the time they were resolved, she had changed her mind. She was glad now that that plan hadn't worked out, for she knew that it would have been a mistake. She came for Christmas one year, but she didn't enjoy it. It was dark and cold, she felt isolated and lonely there for the first time ever. As she came to know the place better, she lost some of her illusions about it. There was malice and spite here too, if you cared to see them. It didn't bother her greatly, Anna was more realistic than many visitors, and even felt relieved when she began to catch glimpses of the darker side of life she knew must be there, for she knew then that she was really getting to know the place in which she had chosen to live. She now came to Ireland every spring, and returned to Holland at the end of the summer. It was a pattern that suited her perfectly.

Sitting tonight in her kitchen, she thought of her apartment back in The Hague. She loved both her houses. Anna was an interior designer, although she now only worked part of the year on a freelance basis. She'd been successful in her career, and she'd enjoyed it. At least that had worked out. It was some compensation for the unhappiness in her personal life. Her marriage, her relationship with Lili: sometimes she could be philosophic about this side of her life, shrug, reason that she knew more people whose marriages had failed than had made a success of it. The hidden miseries her Irish neighbours told her were further proof that she was not alone in her unhappiness.

150   But tonight those regrets had the upper hand, and she could do nothing to get them into perspective.

It was three years now since she'd even seen Lili, and years again since the meeting before that. She'd looked quite different to how Anna had remembered her, looked older than she'd expected, with her hair cropped short in a style that didn't suit her. It was a mild shock to see how much she'd changed, for it brought home to Anna how much of Lili's life had passed in which she had had no part. Not that she wanted to interfere, as Lili claimed, no, she didn't think she had a right to know everything that went on in her daughter's life, but it did hurt to be so completely excluded from it. It wasn't fair for Lili to blame Anna for every failure and lack in her life. It certainly wasn't fair either to hold Anna exclusively responsible for the break-up of her marriage to Peter. That was the heart of the quarrel between Lili and Anna. She wanted to avoid talking about it on this visit, but feared that they would degenerate into wrangling about that very subject.

'I'm so glad to see you again, it's been too long, Lili. You look well,' she lied. 'How do you find me? I must look much older to you.'

'Yes,' said Lili, 'you do.'

'I won't always be here,' Anna said evenly. Peter had died so suddenly. She wanted to mend fences with her daughter if only to spare her the bitter, unresolved emotions she had experienced then. She still loved Lili enough to want her not to have to go through that; no, she'd not have wished such pain upon anyone, least of all her only daughter. But Lili had fixed ideas about her parents' marriage.

'Are you happy?' Anna asked timidly.

'Of course not,' was the reply. 'How can I be? Haven't I told you time and again the upbringing you gave me left me so lacking in confidence and self-esteem that I don't expect to ever find what you call happiness.'

Anna knew she would have to reply carefully to this. What she wanted to say was that Lili was being ridiculous, she was a woman in her thirties, her destiny was in her own hands. No one was dealt the hand they thought they deserved in life, you just had to make the best of it. To blame your mother for your misery at Lili's age was just wallowing in self-pity, as far as Anna was concerned. She had been a good enough mother, of that Anna was convinced. She had always given Lili her freedom and respected her independence. What did Lili want? That her mother live her life for her? Only by completely abdicating responsibility for her own life could Lili hold Anna to account. She didn't say any of this aloud.

Instead, she took a deep breath and said quietly, 'One thing which you should always remember, and yet one which you always choose to overlook, is that I didn't leave your father. He left me.'

'But then he came back and you wouldn't take him in.'

'Why should I have done so?' Anna was dismayed to see how quickly she was losing her temper, when she had wanted so much to stay calm. 'Have you any idea what it's like to have a man walk out on you like that? The man to whom you promised and devoted your whole life? Do you know what it's like to have a child with a man, and then to have him humiliate you in front of all your family and friends?'

When Lili was ten, Peter had left Anna for his secretary. He was forty, Anna two years younger. The secretary was nineteen. Anna hadn't suspected a thing. She had thought they were happy together. One evening he didn't come home from work. He rang her later to say that he wouldn't be home that night, that he wouldn't be home again at all, except to collect his belongings. Anna felt she aged ten years that evening. She had never given a moment's thought to getting older, had noticed slight, gradual changes in her skin, her body, as just that, changes, not as a deterioration of which to be frightened. She'd had nothing but contempt for women who thought they should look at forty as they did at twenty. After Lili was born she was never as shapely as she'd been before, but she didn't care. She was proud of her body. The changes wrought by motherhood made her feel more womanly, not less. But then Peter walked out on her for a teenager, and Anna felt he might as well have said straight out she was old and ugly. She still knew she had been right in her earlier attitude, but the shock of his betrayal completely destroyed her self-confidence. She rebuilt her life, but she never really got over that particular shock.

'It was just a silly little fling, Mother, anybody could see that. I remember at the time, everybody told you it would just blow over. I've never understood why you took it all so seriously, it was just too banal.'

'Banal!' Anna shrieked, jumping up from her seat. 'Don't you realise what you're saying? That's what made it so humiliating for me. Why can't you see that? Are you a woman at all, Lili, that I can't make you see that?'

'But then he wanted to come back and you wouldn't take him.'

'No,' Anna said, 'that isn't true. It wasn't that I wouldn't take him back: I couldn't. He had stayed away too long.'

'Ten months! You call that long!'

'Yes. Yes I do. You don't measure that sort of time by the calendar. You can't quantify pain like that. I spent those months hardening my heart just so I'd be able to go on living, and look after you. It was the only way I had to protect myself. By the time they got bored with each other and she kicked him out, it was too late. I couldn't just forgive and forget and go back to being as we had been before. Maybe you can turn your heart on and off like a tap, but I can't.' She forced herself to be calm, and spoke quietly now. 'My marriage failed because your father left me, not because I refused to forgive him. It was not my fault. I did everything I could to try to protect you, to lessen the hurt, but I had my limits. I think I gave you a good upbringing under the circumstances, but all you do is blame me. It isn't fair. The troubles of your life are not my fault, Lili. Can't you understand that? They are not my fault.'

She was shouting again by that point. Lili walked over to the door and coldly requested that she leave.

That was the last time she saw Lili, although Anna had attempted to contact her several times since then. All letters remained unanswered. Once she went to the apartment block where Lili lived. She rang the bell repeatedly, but there was no response, even though there were lights at the window, and Anna knew that her daughter must be there. The block was protected by a complex set of security devices. When Anna rang the bell a light came on, and a closed-circuit television camera was activated. Standing on the doorstep, pleading through the intercom system, 'Let me in, Lili, please, just for a moment, I must talk to you,' she imagined her daughter standing in a warm hallway, looking at the image of her mother's face on the tiny grey screen, listening to her tearful, pleading voice, but not yielding, making no reply, showing her no mercy.

Once Rita had asked her what she liked most about Donegal, and Anna, remembering that evening, had replied, 'I like the way everyone leaves the key of their house sticking in the front door.'

These thoughts and memories had tormented her tonight as she tossed in bed, longing for sleep to come. She'd been reminded of Lili by Nuala that afternoon, even before the young woman started to pour out her woes under the influence of the clear spirit Anna offered her. Like Lili, Nuala had strikingly beautiful hands. Both wore tinkling bracelets and rings set with precious stones which showed off to advantage their white fingers and perfectly manicured nails. Lili was a bank teller, and Anna had often noticed that women whose job involved counting out money tended to be vain about their hands. The similarity between the two women was compounded when Nuala launched into her peevish litany against her mother's shortcomings, and her unhappiness in life which had been the result. Everyone, it appeared, had short-changed Nuala in life. When her baby was born, she hadn't felt the love

154 for it she'd been told she would feel – told she ought to feel. She'd wanted a little girl, anyway. She hadn't been at all happy over the past year, so much so that she'd taken to stealing things. Well, you could hardly call it stealing, the things she'd taken were so insignificant she wondered that anyone bothered about them. Kevin had made such a bloody fuss about it. Anna didn't make much response to this information, but she narrowed her eyes and mentally revised her opinion of Nuala.

She wanted to say to Nuala, 'You're responsible for your own life, you know. You must never blame anyone else.' But she didn't trust herself to say even this. She was afraid that she would go too far, and vent on Nuala all her pent-up resentments against Lili. With effort, she kept her counsel, and spent the night drinking whisky to insulate herself against the pain of her own memories.

ELBA

Mary Beckett

'Holy Mother.' Connie sighed as she stretched in the narrow
hotel bed. The words came out in her original Dublin accent
long overlaid like her religion during the thirty years she'd
worked in London. Annette Fisher who was already asleep in
the bed nearer the French door was nearly twenty years older
than Connie. She had been called Hannah as a child but she
changed to Annette in her teens. Connie did not yet know that.
Connie ached in every bone. They had been travelling all day –
Florence to Pisa in one minibus to meet other tourists coming
off the plane from Gatwick, then, after a delay, another minibus
from Pisa to the coast to catch the boat to Elba. Annette had to be
helped around, good seats found for her, cases carried. Alessan-
dro, the courier, took her big suitcase under protest until the
boat arrived after they had been hanging about the harbour in
hot afternoon sun. Faced with the steep steps up to the boat he
refused. 'I go to my home,' he said. 'My duty is finished.'

'I can't carry this!' Annette bleated. 'I'm in my seventieth
year.' So Connie carried Annette's suitcase up first, leaving it
just inside the door to the deck, and came down again for her
own. She had a malicious hope that somebody would steal
Annette's while it was unguarded, but she checked the
thought. She knew it would be her job to search for it.

Connie had made all the arrangements for the holiday. She
had picked the town and booked the hotels. She thrived on
organising and her work as a superintendent of typists did not
give her enough scope.

But the hotel did not please Annette. 'It's not a first-class
hotel,' she said several times in a confidential voice to other

guests. 'I always go to a first-class hotel. Connie chose this one because it was in a quiet place. After Florence, you know. We were in a really good hotel in Florence. The sheets were changed every day. Every day! And a palatial bathroom. Not like this at all. Connie should have known this was not what I'm used to.'

Connie heard it all but she kept talking brightly to different people. It was not a first-class hotel but it was in a lovely wooded end of the island with steps down to a beach. And it was cheap. Florence had been dear, even going without meals, and making do with coffees and packets of biscuits. Here, dinner was included in the very reasonable price.

Dinner had caused more complaints – the soup was tepid in a cold plate, the salad was rough lettuce and tomato, the meat was tasteless and the dessert was ice-cream. Coffee could be bought in the bar. 'Wonderful *cappuccino!*' Connie enthused to stop Annette finding fault. Mists had rolled up from the sea, the bar was in a kind of summerhouse, not very warm, not crowded. There was nowhere else to go on foot. The road ended just beyond the hotel. People had driven away in cars. Italians herded their children off to bed and did not return. Germans talked to one another in German. There were some English-speaking couples but Annette had complained to all of them before dinner so they avoided her now.

'We'll go to bed early,' Connie said. 'We'll be fresh tomorrow. We'll go into town on the bus.'

'That gentleman says there is no bus on Sunday,' Annette said and Connie was horrified at her own carelessness in not checking.

The bedrooms were separate block houses with a glass door leading to a terrace in front of each. Overhanging their terrace was a fig tree. Connie was eloquent about the marvel of their very own fig tree but Annette pointed to several so ripe they had split open on the tree. 'Disgusting!' she said. There was a smell of wood smoke in the bedroom. It reminded Connie, for a minute, of turf smoke until she sorted out the difference.

Annette had the bathroom first, as usual, pottered about muttering to herself, got into bed and fell asleep at once, giving the odd rattle of a snore. Connie, for a long time, was too tired to sleep. She heard what she took to be rain pouring, but the French door was shut and the curtain down so she could not see. How would she keep Annette happy if it rained. She remembered the rain in Dublin at her mother's funeral over a year ago – deluges of rain from the time she arrived, late, at the airport until they straggled out of the graveyard after the burial the following day.

She had been at work in London when her brother telephoned to say that their mother had died during the night. She had gone immediately to Heathrow but the plane was delayed. She waited in one lounge after another. She did not even buy anything duty-free because she thought it would look unfeeling. She was sorry her mother was dead, but she was old and had been miserable for years, shunted from one son and daughter-in-law to another after they decided she could no longer look after herself in her own house, and sold it for her.

She had taken a taxi from the airport to the church on the south side of Dublin but even so, she met her family coming out, after the reception of her mother's coffin, huddling under umbrellas, not waiting to receive condolences. Connie had no umbrella because the weather had been fine in London and her auburn hairstyle had gone a bit limp with the wet.

She heard her youngest brother say, 'There's Connie,' and his wife answer, 'Goodness, so it is, I thought she wasn't going to bother at all. She doesn't look great. The years are beginning to show.'

Another sister-in-law, Mildred, turned and came over to her. 'There you are at last, Connie. We're all going to our house because it's the biggest. Can you squeeze into the back there?'

Connie got into the car beside two teenage nieces in their usual black with hair hanging over their eyes and mouths. She felt herself too gay and summery in her beige skirt and suede jacket. They did not return her smile and for the moment she could not think of their names.

'You'll stay with us overnight,' Mildred said and Connie was grateful.

'I'll even have to borrow a nightdress,' Connie said laughing. 'I came straight from work as soon as Brian rang me.'

'Oh did you?' Mildred said.

'We thought you waited until after you'd had your lunch,' one of the schoolgirls said and her mother told her to hush.

At the house, people were standing awkwardly in the hall and Mildred rushed past them into the kitchen, calling back, 'We'll feel better after a cup of tea. Aideen, show Connie her room and the bathroom.'

When Connie came back down into the sitting-room the women turned and looked at her. The men seemed to be in the dining-room. 'Well, Connie, you'll never get the chance now of having your mother to stay. We did our share. We have nothing to reproach ourselves with, thank God,' Bríd said, settling her skirt over her rather stout knees.

'She was too old to bring to London', Connie said, although she thought she'd be better saying nothing.

'She wasn't always too old,' Bríd said.

'We'll say no more about it,' Mildred said, laying down the tea tray. 'Grandma's gone to her reward. She won't have to worry any more about being a burden.'

'Many mansions,' Bríd said, nodding emphatically.

Connie was not a sensitive young girl. She did not care about these women. She and her brothers had got on well enough when they were young together, but she had been away from them for so long that she could feel no great attachment. She drank her black tea and enjoyed the ham sandwiches that the two teenagers passed round. She knew that her long strong legs and slim body looked younger than her years, unlike her sisters-in-law who were sagged and waistless, as a result, they claimed, of having families. If it had not been pouring she would have gone out somewhere, but she had no way of keeping off the rain.

When she had left home for London her mother had been a capable woman needing no help from anyone to run her affairs. When Connie had a job in Dublin she was expected to hand up her unopened pay packet to her mother. She managed the money. Connie's father had gambled a bit on the dogs before he got married, so to preserve him from that, his spending money was pared to a minimum. He had provided the red hair for Connie and her brothers but their height and physique came from their mother. Why had they all married small women? Connie could never understand how they had persuaded her mother to sell her house. She supposed even the toughest people are scared just after pneumonia. But they had got the money into their hands and divided it up. It had helped some of them with their mortgages but Brian was too well-off for that. He had bought Mildred an expensive diamond ring and she had had her engagement ring reset with added big stones in the middle so that it would live up to the new one.

'It's well to have two,' Connie had said at the time. 'Your two daughters won't have any reason to quarrel over who will get them.'

Mildred had looked startled and Bríd said, 'You were not entitled to any share since you're not having your mother to live with you,' and Connie had answered, 'Fine by me. I'd hate to help to rob my own mother.'

They had kept on at her over the years about how her mother felt neglected because her only daughter would not invite her to London. She *had* asked her mother to come over but not very pressingly because she valued her independence and knew she'd lose it while her mother was around. Connie could take only brief visits to Dublin because it was awkward staying for more than a night or two in the strained atmosphere she brought into any of her brothers' houses. She gave as good as she got and she knew her mother did the same, until her health failed her.

On the night before the funeral she went to her bedroom early, saying she had no need of a meal since she'd eaten on the plane, and she went straight to the airport from Glasnevin cemetery as they all agreed there was no sense in her heading back to the other side of the city for just a few hours. Sitting in the lounge upstairs in the airport looking at the sodden grey sky over Dublin she felt bereft and almost let tears come to her eyes. She had now no mother between herself and old age and no Dublin ever again, to perpetuate her youth. But it was many years since she had cried, not since her last love affair. Red eyes and red hair do not go well together.

While Connie was in Dublin Annette Fisher had moved into the flat above hers in London. She was knocking on Connie's door an hour after Connie had kicked off her high-heels and changed into a turquoise track suit.

'I've come down to say hello,' Annette said in a little high voice. She was a little round woman. 'I've taken the apartment upstairs. It's so important to be sociable with one's neighbours, I always say. You can do without friends but you can't do without neighbours – isn't that true. Although indeed I have lots of friends, all absolutely devoted to me, absolutely devoted. But a friend in Bury St Edmund's isn't much good if I want help here. I must say your place looks wonderful – mine is at sixes and sevens for the moment.'

There was nothing Connie could do but invite her in for coffee and listen to the life story Annette told. She was a widow with a son and daughter. 'They live their own lives,' Annette said. 'I would never want them to put themselves out in the slightest for me. I am a very independent woman, just as I see you are. I run a very successful little business.' She compressed her lips and nodded.

When she shut the door after her, Connie sat down and laughed, remembering stories in magazines and ads on the television where the new neighbour is an eligible man. Here I am, she told herself. I've just buried my mother. I've been avoiding responsibility for her all my life, and a mother surrogate arrives at my door.

The next morning Annette asked her for a lift to the station. 'I'm not accustomed to the traffic round here,' was the excuse.

She will batten on me, Connie thought but she did not prevent it. She introduced Annette to her friends and listened to her boring them until they were loath to spend an evening in her flat. She did shopping for her and accepted criticism of what she had chosen. It emerged that she owned a string of crèches, staffed by young girls who were to look after large numbers of small children for low wages. There was a constant turnover of minders and, therefore, constant crying of children.

'I love children,' Annette told her many times. 'Those young women who go back to work can leave their tinies with me and know they are perfectly safe. I provide a very necessary service. They are so grateful.'

While Connie was arranging planes and hotels she frequently imagined Annette telling people how grateful Connie must be to her for her company on this holiday.

When she woke in the morning Annette's bed was empty, the curtain was pulled back. The sky was blue and Connie said out loud, 'There wasn't any rain. That rainy sound came from the wind in the dry leaves of the fig tree.' She was dressed when Annette arrived back.

'A beautiful morning, Connie. Really beautiful. But I can't get down to the beach. Such steep steps and so many of them. With my arthritis I'll never manage them. We'll have to do without the sea until we get the bus tomorrow. I had hoped we'd go to see Napoleon's villa tomorrow but I suppose that will do later. Do you know, Connie, about Napoleon's escape from Elba? One of those gentlemen I met last night told me all about that just now. A very cultured gentleman.'

Connie threw open the French door. Some figs had plopped down on the tiles with juice oozing round them. Swarms of ants worked at clearing them away. Connie laughed, but Annette, noticing them for the first time, put her hands up to her face in horror. 'Oh how disgusting. Connie, get rid of them. We'll send for the cleaning women.'

'What's wrong with them?' Connie said. 'Do they remind you of the children in your baby dumps, there are such crowds of them?' She caught Annette's shocked look. 'Sorry, Annette. A joke.' They walked to the dining-room along a little path through trees. The warmth was balmy.

'After breakfast,' Connie said, 'I am going down to the beach and I intend to stay there most of the day. I'll bring some fruit for lunch.'

'And what will I do?' Annette asked.

They were at the paved entrance to the dining-room. A stout cleaning woman stood aside, her dark head bent submissively over her mop.

'*Buon giorno*,' Connie greeted her and she looked up.

'*Buon giorno*,' she smiled at Connie.

'What am I to do?' Annette demanded.

'Oh I'm sure you have your own resources,' Connie answered, her high-heels clipping on the terracotta tiles.

Gerard Fanning

ST STEPHEN'S DAY

After the church service
We park beside the cemetery,
Waiting for the drenched mourners
To pass by.

Leading us in trenchcoats
They resemble the break-up continuity
Of that civil war film,
And we the peripheral characters

Smirking in the almost out of shot.
Though we may genuflect
And catch the squalls
Trailing their five-minute lulls of blue,

We take this chance
To stand and listen
To the bleached white epiphanies
And the little offices,

Where space conceives infinite space,
And breviary translates into missal.
So stand clear
On this St Stephen's day

164   At the edge of one version of events,
      Where our thinning shadows
      Define the hours
      Of the pale immaculate sun,

      But fails to retrieve
      The picnic sites,
      From Kinnegad to Kilcock,
      The truck stops on Route 66.

PREAMBLE

Like a limpet recording its fastidious journeys
I may never know the music of the world
But can fathom time. This trail begun
Through ten thousand neap tides, sees Amundsen,
A watcher of the pools, trace silver coils
Rounded like ear-lobes, listening for the footfalls.
Glimpsed as a prism on the radio telescope,
Hauled like a bow on the raised strings of the bridge,
Was that a change of pace or tone?
A wave or a particle? Or just the ice floes arguing.

ABOUT ABSTRACTION

No more unusual are the salmon smolts.
They flee Killary, sprouting wings,
In a droning helicopter out of their element
Into the weightlessness of things.

FREEDOM OF SPEECH
Hugo Hamilton

The first thing she wanted to do was to travel. Anywhere, everywhere, just to be moving, to see somewhere new. She had recently come out of a bad marriage. It also had to do with a new freedom of movement and the end of the travel restrictions since the wall came down; because I can, I should. Back in the GDR days, she had never been further away than a Romanian resort. She had once had a bath in a Prague hotel where the water was brown and hot like molten lava. At a nudist colony near Rostock, she got a sunburned bottom and couldn't sit for a week. Travel was not a Soviet concept.

Mostly, it was to the Hartz mountains that her husband brought her, year after year, forcing her into those heavy walking boots, trudging silently beside him in cement feet, neither of them saying a word. It was all right for him, he was a schoolteacher, but she was an archaeologist and wanted to get to Greece, Turkey, Byzantium, Babylon. In the end she became a desk archaeologist at the Alte Pinothek. The most interesting thing she ever found herself was a porcelain cup which somebody had left on a window sill for a few years.

OK, there had been an expedition to an excavation site on the Polish border which is proven by photographs of her red-freckled face smiling up from dry, dusty trenches, holding up a trowel or as in other shots one of those miniature pickaxes that make you think of Trotsky's head. You don't want to dig too deep on the Polish border, she commented about the fact that nothing was ever found on the site. The excavation had been purely an exercise. There were shots of her with her husband

Gert too, on those Hartz walks with his stick and hat, and a smile of deep-rooted contentment. But of course, he's in the past now, as much as Trotsky or Philoctetes. Or the Berlin Wall.

Mechtild Vogel. She was thirty-two when I met her. Originally from Magdeburg, East Germany, one of the most troubled midEuropean towns in history; sieges, fires, hunger and fifty years of dictatorship followed by the abject plunge into the free market. After the bad marriage came a period of feckless promiscuity, naturally. Random uninformed travel which, for an archaeologist at heart, must have appeared like scraping the top soil for Coke caps. Come on, let's fuck off out of here, she said when we first met.

I found myself standing beside her at one of those human chains against racism, somewhere between Munich and Augsburg. She relit her candle from mine and told me she was getting bored standing around, she had itchy feet. Straight away she announced that it was all over between her and her husband, as though it was the first thing I wanted to know. She was anti marriage, anti life partner, anti house-pet, anti anything that promulgated a settled life. 'Up to here,' she warned, raising her finger up level with her long Thuringian nose.

Her apartment was full of artefacts, shards and stones, bits of pottery, all of which came from museum vaults while she worked there. She seemed to have half of the Acropolis in her bedroom and when you went to the loo you found yourself pissing in the company of a stone goat and a Celtic cross. She had no time for Soviet artefacts. There was a champagne cooler which had come from a London hotel. There was a wooden horse with white teeth and glaring eyes and colourful strips of cloth which she had brought back from a *mardi gras*. Her journeys since German unification could only be called casual.

In bed she soon started talking about going places. 'On that fucking thing?' I demanded, pointing at the wide-eyed horse. But she remained serious as though sex had sparked off a latent

nomadic obsession. She understood my concerns and began to
explain how she had benefited from the estate of an uncle on
the West German side, if that's what I was getting at. Her uncle
was a medium-sized advertising magnate to whom she referred
as an arsehole, showing nothing but contempt for the money
he left her. It tainted her life with the kiss of commerce. But
what wasn't tainted these days? Basically we were living in a
shagging supermarket. So let's get out of here, she urged.
Somewhere Third World. She wanted to burn up some of the
blood money.

I suggested Morocco and some weeks later we found
ourselves in Fez, walking down through the ancient streets,
driven into a torpor by the heat. She wore John Lennon-style
sunglasses and beat off the flies like a raging pilgrim. She was
unable to pass by a fruit stall. In the unremitting Moroccan sun,
fruit very soon became the substitute for sex. Any time I looked
at her, or half-suggested a path towards the bed, she would
offer me a tangerine, or a passion fruit, or a banana from
Tetuan. In the hotel bedroom, she installed a massive basket,
towering with an exotic harvest, grapes hanging over the edges
like fat necklaces.

It was as though she had a diploma in fruit eating,
meticulously peeling back the skin of a pear with her Swiss
army knife. I watched her with lust in my eyes, juice dripping
down from her mouth on to her bare breasts and legs. When I
asked her if I could suck the stray liquid from her body she
stared back and tilted the fruit basket towards me. My thumb
sank into the fruit flesh of a pear, a reservoir of juice spilling
across my hands, and I wondered if it was a sign of how ripe the
fruit was or how desperate I was.

'I'm still not over my husband,' she explained. She said it
with a smile that made me wonder whether the act of smiling
had not originated in primal times as a show of aggression and
only later evolved into something more dubious. I put it down
to the heat. Her suspended sexual interest came as quite a
shock. Nothing during the first wild three weeks in her

170 apartment back in Munich could have precipitated this. It was like fucking with a fatwa hanging over you. We hardly stopped to eat. All right, she ate melon slices while we were screwing, but I never imagined fruit taking over.

I looked for an explanation. She had seen some fairly distasteful things along the journey around Morocco; faeces, backing up toilets, that kind of thing. We saw flies drinking from the corners of children's eyes. Once I gave a small girl a tin of sardines in Oarzazette and she ran home with it like a prize. In the night we heard a woman in an alley below our hotel window being beaten by her husband, or brother, or pimp. The sound of a fist meeting a face has an unmistakable smack of reality about it. A woman offered me her seven-year-old daughter for the afternoon. In a mountain village Mechtild watched, in a demented way, a boy crossing the road carrying a cow's stomach like a sack over his shoulder and leaving a trail of purple spots along the road. It was more 'Third World' than her wildest imagination.

Would this put you off sex? I argued with her. Threatened to go home if she wasn't interested. The human body had a duty towards pleasure and happiness. The heat made us talk in circles. Thirst made us belligerent. Above all else I wanted to sort out this discrepancy between fruit and sex. Her lack of lust seemed to have degenerated into a purely linguistic problem rather than a physical one. Could sex not be an exchange of fruit fluids? It was a problem of definition.

In the late hours at our Fez hotel, with the bedroom window open on to the din of the old city, the sickle moon stuck on a blue-black sky, we decided to clarify every word. Even if we had to invent a whole new vocabulary for our relationship, it was essential that we redefined the exact meaning of each word as it pertained to us.

Fruit: the closest thing to fucking. Fez: medieval Moroccan city visited by many Americans and Germans in shorts and sunglasses. Thirst: a physical (sometimes metaphysical) imbalance which increases at every attempted reduction.

Outside our hotel the following morning, we met Mustafa. He became our guide, simply because he announced that he was our guide. I first tried to shrug him off but Mechtild quite liked the idea of being shown a few things. So we spent the day following Mustafa through the hyperactive souks with its dealers and donkeys and symphonies of smells. Every street had a thousand eyes. The eyes of women in *haiks*. The eyes of traders. The eyes of bald, lethargic dogs, motionless in the shade. The eyes of chickens bound together at the feet, five in a bunch. And the eyes of Moroccan men, each of them skilled at telling exactly what is going on inside your head.

Travel: extended foreplay. Tourist: a person coming from the last orgasm and on the way to the next.

Mustafa knew what was on Mechtild's mind. He pulled her aside to sit under an awning where he brought her some orange juice. Her thirst was getting out of hand. Three times she had to stop for juice. Mustafa showed us everything; where to eat, where to find the best pastries, where to drink lemon tea and watch the swallows over the city walls while the evening shrank back into a blue, yellow, then black night. Somewhere close by there was always music, drums and whistles. Mechtild was happy. She became generous. She searched in her bag and gave Mustafa some money, more than he ever expected. Then she put her head on my shoulder and watched the moon over Bab Boujaloud.

Money: that which makes the bearer attractive beyond all order of merit.

Back in the hotel bedroom I asked her why she had given Mustafa so much money. Was it some new substitute for sex, this generosity to strangers? Still there was nothing doing between us. I had completely lost my powers of persuasion. My penis stood up in the room, massive and inappropriate, as out of place as a missile marked for nuclear disarmament. I told her Mustafa would expect the same money the next day. It was her money, she said. She had too much of it. She would never get rid of her past until she got rid of the money.

172   The following morning I went out early after breakfast while Mechtild stayed at the hotel. She was exhausted. When I came back before lunchtime, I met Mustafa on his way down the stairs. He was running. He told me he had been sent out to get something urgently for my lady. Cream crackers.

Mechtild, my lady, was just about to take a shower when I got to the room. I lay on the bed listening to her body under the water. Music from the radio somewhere drifted in around my ears like the high-pitched whine of a mosquito. I could hear the water cascading down, accelerating over the slope of her breasts, across her hips, leaping on to her raised knee. I imagined drinking the cool water as it rolled off her bottom. I must have fallen into a dream of paralysed lust. After a while the water stopped and by the time Mustafa came back, she was dressed again, wearing a long, loose white T-shirt with a pink elephant on the front.

Breast: that which fits perfectly into a cupped hand. Cream cracker: dry, square-shaped biscuit of unstable, flaky composition. Lust: modern-day slavery.

I got up and stepped into the bathroom to shave. In the mirror I could see Mustafa standing at the door with the packet of cream crackers in his hand. Mechtild asked him to come in and sit at a small table. She placed the cream crackers in front of him. From her money belt she took out a crisp new 100 DM note. Mustafa's eyes lit up.

'Do you know how much this is worth?' she asked.

'Yes,' Mustafa nodded.

'Well,' Mechtild went on. 'If you eat this whole packet of cream crackers, the money is yours.'

Jesus, I couldn't believe it. Mustafa took it up as a perfectly normal challenge and sat down. He looked at the cream crackers, checked Mechtild once more to make sure she wasn't joking, and then began to eat while Mechtild lay back on the bed fanning herself with the pristine blue bank note. The shape of her nipples showing through the T-shirt.

'What the fuck are you doing?' I whispered, the lather on
the left side of my face giving me a speech impediment.

'Don't interfere,' she said.

Encouraged by the sight of the 100 Mark note which
Mechtild was now rolling into a fine tube, Mustafa vora-
ciously threw himself into the meal of cream crackers. There
was nothing with the cream crackers, no cheese, no drink or
anything. He didn't get very far before his mouth began to clog
up. His chewing slowed down. He attempted to swallow. His
head moved forward and back with the effort. His mouth was
open, full of pulpy white dough. The heat didn't help.

'Give him a glass of water at least,' I urged.

'That's not part of the deal,' she insisted.

I told her she was carrying it too far and she conceded, giving
Mustafa a capful of mineral water. If anything, the water only
made matters worse. It was like masticating patching plaster, or
fireclay, and very soon, his chewing came to a complete
standstill. He looked pale. He made another brave effort to
swallow and then allowed his head to sink down in defeat. A
large, white ball of dough rolled out of his mouth across the
table and fell to the floor.

'I'm sorry,' Mechtild said. 'You did very well, though.'

Mustafa sat there dejected. To encourage him, she told him
he might have another chance the following day. Same time.
He was to bring a new packet of cream crackers.

'You can't do that kind of thing,' I said after Mustafa had
gone.

'Why not?' she laughed, putting away the unfurled bank-
note. 'Why the hell can't I? It's only a bloody game.'

'You can't fuck around like this down here. You can't
behave like a complete arsehole in the Third World.'

'Don't start,' she sneered.

I watched Mechtild reach for the blue plastic bottle of Sidi
Harazam mineral water. The water ran down her neck inside
and outside. The radio was still playing outside somewhere in
the distance. It was too hot to talk.

The following day, Mustafa came back to try the game again. A new packet of cream crackers was placed on the table. Once again he was eager to get on with the meal. This time Mechtild added a new incentive. Along with the 100 Mark note, Mustafa could also have her. For my benefit she loudly said, 'You eat the whole packet, you have the money and you can also fuck me.' She pulled up the T-shirt to let Mustafa see her jet-black triangle. Pointing towards him with her finger, she then patted her cunt lightly with the tips of her fingers. For a moment I thought she was going to place the 100 DM note in there.

The money was one thing, but the additional promise of sex made Mustafa dizzy with ambition. He ate like a savage, swallowing the first few cream crackers whole. Again around half-way, the feast slowed down. His mouth lugubriously churned the floury paste like a cement mixer until it got stuck altogether. With tears of failure in his eyes he extracted a long baton of grey dough from his mouth and dropped his head.

Game: the act of contriving superiority along abstract rules. Cunt: that for which, and in which, a man would suffocate of his own volition.

Later on that evening, we met Mustafa again in a bar. He was as friendly as ever. He seemed undisturbed by failure, accepted the fact that he had given it two good chances. I bought him a few beers in consolation. He was eager to try the cream crackers again the next day, but Mechtild said she wasn't offering another chance. He swore he could do it. He got drunk very quickly and proclaimed that we were his greatest friends. He loved Europeans deeply. He wanted us to meet his family, his brothers and sisters, his mother.

'You come to my house,' he said suddenly with glazed expression.

'No, not now,' I said. 'It's too late.'

'No, no. Tomorrow,' he begged. 'You come to my house. You and your wife. My mother will cook for you – very good. You must come and eat the couscous.'

The idea of Mechtild being my wife was a delicious piece of irony. She ignored it.

'Of course we'll go,' Mechtild said, jumping at the idea. I think she was doing it only to dislodge the grin on my face.

'At last,' she said to me later, back at the hotel. 'A chance to see what family life is like in these countries.'

Next day, Mustafa was waiting for us outside the hotel door. Everybody seemed to have forgotten all about the cream cracker game. I had forgotten what sex was like. We followed him through the narrow streets of the Medina, through a maze of alleys all leading downwards. I lost all sense of direction. I knew only that we were descending into the heart of another ancient civilization, Mustafa occasionally pointing out things with great excitement: his school, the tanneries, the mosques. We followed him through the narrow alleys, gazing around in awe. He showed us doors or houses which had two knockers, one for horsemen, the other for pedestrians. All the time he was saying, 'Not far, not far,' and finally brought us into a quiet alley, no wider than a metre, where we had to walk in single file.

'Here is our house,' he eventually announced.

Mechtild was beside herself with excitement. Her eyes were wide open. We stepped inside and were led into a small room at the back. As soon as I entered the room I got the feeling I wanted to reverse everything, go back to zero, like a board game. We were surrounded by four men. They couldn't all have been Mustafa's brothers.

Mustafa whipped the sunglasses off Mechtild and put them on himself before she could react. We were told to sit down on the floor. Mechtild smiled as though it was all a joke. She defied at first but then she realised that things had gone wrong. Mustafa's manner changed completely. He took her bag. Our possessions were piled on the stone floor in front of us: passports, money, traveller's cheques, American Express. Cameras, watches, guidebooks, and Mechtild's contraceptives. Why the fuck she had those with her I don't know.

176   The last things that came out of her bag were two beautifully ripe pears. One of Mustafa's brothers bit into one of them, smiling. I could hear the smack of the fruit chunk giving way, his mouth sucking up the exploding juice with it. It was as though he had just taken a bite out of Mechtild's breast, as though I was forced to watch him screwing her. I wanted to kill him. I might have only for the fact that Mustafa now held Mechtild's Swiss army knife in his hand.

'What the fuck are you doing,' Mechtild shouted indignantly. Maybe she was still pretending not to understand.

'You find out now,' Mustafa said, picking up some of the traveller's cheques to examine them. He had already pocketed the blue 100 Mark note which Mechtild had shown him the previous day. I had visions of Mechtild eating hundreds of cream crackers. Maybe it was heat, maybe it was fear. I imagined Mechtild and Mustafa coupling on a bed of cream crackers.

Fear: narrowing of the anal passage. Shitting cream crackers.

I felt the Swiss army knife at my throat. In the corner of my eye, I could see that Mechtild had a long rusty blade at her throat too. The hair at the back of her head was in the grip of a fist. There was a faint smell of urine in the room. There was no sound anywhere.

'All right,' Mustafa said out loud. 'This is a very simple game. We are not going to take all your money, just some of it. You will go to the bank and get cash. One first, then the other one.' I saw Mechtild giving me an incredulous look. Maybe it was fear. Or maybe she had begun to regret the missed opportunities, all those wonderful orgasms I could have arranged for her. Maybe she was thinking of my poor penis standing like a folly on the landscape.

'You get the money,' Mustafa said. 'Then there is no trouble. I will go with you. OK. Who wants to go first?'

So this is what sex leads to. If it wasn't for lust we wouldn't have been in this mess together. I told Mechtild to go first, hoping that she would have the sense to make a break for it as soon as she got to the bank. I encouraged her with a discreet wink. She got up and allowed herself to be escorted to the door from where she looked back giving me a silent, desperate glance, perhaps thinking of all the fruit we could still have eaten together in our lifetime. Mustafa dropped his knife on the floor and, as he bent down to pick it up, I saw him lick the calf of her bare leg. Mechtild jumped as though she had been licked by a rabid animal. Then they were gone.

I wasn't expecting her back. When she returned half an hour later, I was worried. She looked pale and exhausted. She was soaked in sweat. Her brown legs were shining in the heat.

'Allah will be pleased,' Mustafa said as he pocketed the money.

It was my turn to go to the bank. I tried not to look at Mechtild but Mustafa stopped me and made me look back. I couldn't make out if she was in tears or whether it was beads of sweat in her eyes. She said nothing. Nor did I. The point of a knife slightly altered the perfect roundness of one breast beneath her damp T-shirt.

Penis: instrument of war and pleasure. Allah: a man with a penis so big it strikes terror into the heart of all nations. God: a man who falsifies the size of his own penis. Believer in the afterlife: a man who can fuck himself.

On the way to the bank I must have thought of a hundred ways to get out of the trap. Mustafa would not talk to me. We passed a group of American tourists and for a moment I thought I could ask them to help. There was nothing I could do. I had to remain loyal to Mechtild. My last memory of her became unreliable in the heat.

At the bank, I stepped towards the counter to get the money as required. The money didn't matter. A small price for Mechtild's freedom. I had visions of us back at the hotel again, free, penniless, making love like savages, fucking again like people in a war zone. Maybe all this would teach her a lesson. Fucking is all that matters in this world. But then I had a stronger urge to fight my way out. I turned suddenly and threw

178   my arms around Mustafa, clutching on to him like a drowning man, trying to drag him down with me, shouting all the time, 'Thief, thief.' But nobody seemed to pay any attention. It was like a stupid embrace. I must have appeared like somebody who had lost his reason in the intense heat, a tourist with sunstroke, malaria, bilharzia. Mustafa punched me discreetly in the stomach as he struggled free. He made it look like he was helping me to lie on the floor, to rest myself. Within seconds, he had disappeared into the crowded street outside, leaving me in the doorway bent over, with the eyes of onlookers penetrating my skull.

Loyalty: a self-imposed virtue characterised by the eagerness to sink with others in preference to surviving alone. Sex: sinking together. Oral sex: singing without accompaniment. Erection: the power of illusion. Love: the science of self-deception. Corpse: a body no longer capable of giving or receiving pleasure.

I ran to the police, but there was little point. There was no way I could give descriptions or lead them to the house where Mechtild was being held. And all the hours running around the Medina looking for her proved just as futile. I got lost every time. All I had now was my money and my passport.

Three days later, Mechtild turned up at the gates of the old city: Bab Boujaloud. I found her sitting in a small café staring in front of her at a lukewarm glass of mint tea. I rushed over to her. I was so excited to see her alive. Was she unharmed? I couldn't see.

She would not let me embrace her or comfort her in any way.

'Mechtild, are you all right?' I said emptily under her passive stare. 'Those bastards. I tried everything to find you. I was so worried about you. The police were out everywhere. I did everything I could.'

I might as well have spoken to a corpse. She stared straight ahead, her eyes vitreous with hurt and indifference.

'What happened?' I asked.

'I'm going home,' she said without looking up.

Nothing I could say would change her mood. I asked her how she got the bruised lip. I wanted to know had they done anything to her? Had they raped her? Had they taken all her money? I took her away and got her something to eat. All she would accept was soup which she spooned slowly past her swollen lip. She was starving.

'What happened?' I asked again. 'What did they do?'

When she said nothing, I began to explain and invent reasons for why I had acted to save myself. Mechtild wasn't interested. She held up the spoon to stop me talking. The flies kept bothering her and I tried to chase them away. It was useless. She looked past me, staring at the traffic in the street outside, at the laden donkeys, at the people waiting for buses in the distance.

Spoon: instrument for conveying soup.

Fly: thoughtless insect.

EXTRACT FROM
OUT OF OUR MINDS

George O'Brien

'Wuzzis, wuzzis?' they cried, and, "Ere, 'ere,' deafly, clamouring for a hearing, all pissed out of their minds except little Jack Worrell. And when I'd served him another few light ales he too would be weeping and shouting for snob drinks with the rest. Because this was the day Sir Winston Churchill was being buried, and this was the belated wake put on for him by the regulars of the public bar of my new home, the Jolly Gardeners, Black Prince Road, by Lambeth Walk, behind Decca on the Embankment.

If wake was the word. I needed the notional stability of proper naming. But for all I knew both word and practice were foreign to Jack and co. I didn't like to ask. I'd got strange looks in my three weeks here because I couldn't pahlivoo Cockney proply. I still felt false saying 'Wotcher' and 'Ta-ta'.

Opening my mouth now, though, would only cause more estrangement. I didn't know their Churchill. The dinnertime ideologues of my childhood had acquainted me with a wrong 'un, the scourge of Erin, bully, boaster, and bather in brandy, not the victor and Chrysostom in whose name this epic booze-up was being staged.

Jack's wife, Betty, four foot-eleven to his five-one, was as plain and thin as a length of sticking-plaster, a material whose effect on the short hairs her manner imitated with uncanny tenacity. She usually sat facing the street door against the partition, her back as erect as a rifle. Gavel of brown ale to hand, she surveyed all who passed, vetted whoever entered, laid down the law, tore off the frequent strip. 'She knows her own mind, ole Bett does,' the men'd mutter, cowering, giggling, in the silence following a tirade. Now she swayed at pub-floor centre sloshing back whisky macs, orating on the times she'd seen. Trundling with the nippers over to the Elephant to sleep down the Tube. Old Mrs Freeman jumping out her bedroom window, an obscene firework in a burning nightie. Powdered eggs, how they repeated. Snoek, a Boer delicacy, contradiction in terms. Betty shook her head, and tears inched down her candle-yellow, candle-narrow face. All looked at her in stupor, aware of her stature. Mother Lambeth, the Madonna of the Buildings, shedding tears of milk and pearls.

'Boove's gin!' roared George. He meant the dear stuff. The real thing today, and ice and lemon too, ordered in a tone that said, I know my rights! George nodded vehemently, as though insisting that he was definitely going first class and the whole hog. His face was a plate of rare roast beef, with a wattle of scrag-end beneath the chin which continually trembled, as mute and as expressive as a weather-vane.

'Where are they now, then?' he demanded, attempting to lean far enough over the counter to see the telly, screened off from the pub by partition of the Jug and Bottle for the patrons of the saloon only.

De Gaulle, that other Dev, was entering St Paul's. Kaunda, too, and other leaders of those other Irelands.

Si monumentum requiris, circumspice.

George still couldn't see, so I called the roll to him.

'Nig nogs, eh?' George sank his snout into best bitter's froth. He worked as a ticket-taker at the head of the escalator down Trafalgar Square Tube. He came into his own when trains departed. He ordered pork scratchings, also Smith's Crisps, the special ones that came with the little blue bag of salt. Dripped into the dregs of his pint, the salt made a seething, short-lived half-life, the way the world at large worked on the man himself.

And, 'Waaaw!' went Terry. 'My guvnor's dead.'

Terry had turned up unwashed from some ungodly shift in greasy jerkin and slime-shiny boilersuit. A skull that was a

182 bucket, and starting from it a brush of crewcut hair, a night-worker's dirty-linen-coloured face. Bottle-end specs and turned eyes, head tilted as though he was looking for fight, but he was only looking for focus, half-seas over on Lemon Hart. Tattoos blotted doughy biceps, signatures of service and palmier occasions. 'My guvnor's dead. Waaw!' leaking sweat, snot and tears on neighbours' mufflers new this Christmas.

I sidled over to the saloon, where telly and decorum held the hour. Telly England I could handle. It was contained, contain-able, a nation of uniforms, a club for formidable brass bands. Life proceeded like a Churchill speech, with measured tread and brazen summons, soused in righteousness. The medieval dramaturgy of death acted out its protagonist's vocabulary – herald and postilion, horse and drum, catafalque and eulogy. Bearskin followed Beefeater's primeval plaid, and Garters joined forces with Black Rod. It was all that in Ireland seemed unhappily enigmatic or idiotically farfetched. All that the landscape had been force-fed and disgorged as ruin: it was the imperial annals of my childhood – *Wizard*, *Hotspur*, *Champion*, *Lion*: names of a daring, power and whiteness that was not ours – steadfastly upheld in panels so neat and final they might have been telly's avatars, more than adequate. Foremost of the escorts were the Royal Irish Hussars.

History was the loyal onlooker's colourful reward, not a *via dolorosa*. I couldn't tear myself away. I might have been a small boy again on Sunday after second mass in the front room of Swiss Cottage, waiting for lunch while *Family Favourites* flooded in, and wolfed down its litany of novelties – the Ox and Bucks, Signalmen and Sappers, groups with names like comic-book tools: Wrens, WRACS, WRNVS. All domesticated and dissembling – 'With a Song in My Heart' (and a particularly syrupy version at that). This was the forces' disarming theme, not with a round in my breech, which I understood was how they visited Cyprus and Malaya and those alleged beasts, the Mau Mau.

Akrotiri spoke in static. The announcer's voice was speaking (I could see) from a shack on the windy side of a mountain. There were 'terrorists' perched on rocks outside the window, dreaming of 'freedom', absent-mindedly picking burrs from their sheepskin vests. I recognised them easily. They were Apache braves. Jeff Chandler would be along in a while to point the way to them. They had just cycled in from Ballysaggart. EOKA was Greek for Sinn Fein, IRA. Grivas, loosely translated, was Griffith with a gun, and Makarios Mannix (more Irish than the Irish themselves).

Yet, even though the air was crackling and the voice of the outpost raised, everything was fine. Black Watch could pale into insignificance and Green Howard wilt and Sherwood Foresters might yet be cut down root and branch. Still would sweet Jean in London and sound Bill Crozier in Cologne spin the hits. Here's one a lot of you have asked for, it's The Platters and 'The Great Pretender'.

My grandmother and major parent, Mam, did try to change my tune every so often by reminding me, 'Huh: they used to call it *Forces' Favourites*.' But her vaguely remonstrative, implicitly ironic tone was lost on me. I'd heard her sound that way about a lot of things. It only meant the times they were a-changin'. All I cared to hear was this stamp-collection of the air, with liveries, denominations and arcane values to please the most fastidious (yours truly). And here, too, though Mam never heard it, and I could hardly bear to, my reality was named in requests to be remembered from afar, the triteness of undying love protested, the fond hope of being together again: 'counting the days, darling'; 'missing you'. Soon. Love. Naive candour and estrangement's verblessness. All putting me in mind of Dublin and my Daddy. And Dickie Valentine doing 'Too Young' did seem to say it all.

Yet, despite tuning out Mam's remark, I knew radio couldn't have the last word either on forces or on favourites. For one thing, there was that photo in the parlour. It showed the head and shoulders of a clean-cut young man. He wore a peaked cap that kinned him closer to Colbert the station-master than to Cooney the cattle-drover, and there were bright but indecipherable insignia on the shoulders of his jerkinish jacket. This was one of the Alexanders, a British soldier, son of Captain Alexander, a gruff old party with a white moustache and a spread the size of his gratuity out the Mayfield Road. We lived where old imperial retainers could manage to retain. Was it not as natural a fate for one of these old hands' handsome, bored, under-educated sons to serve the crown as it was for the neighbours, labourers, to shoulder pick and shovel for MacAlpine? It was the photo that was strange. And in the best room, too, where only priests and high insurance men sat for very long. 'Why?' I pointed to the picture. 'He was killed in Korea,' came the snappish reply. I didn't understand. (I made a memory instead.)

Then, for another thing, there was my aunt Lizzie, who joined the Royal Army Medical Corps after years of nursing in dull Colchester. It was as if there was nothing for it but to declare herself English through and through. I thought what she'd done was against our religion. And she seemed to show a convert's zeal by being posted first to Glasgow, where Catholics, I knew, were dog food. But she sent a snap. Her unfamiliarly broad smile and her rather regal blue-and-crimson cloak made everything all right. She looked no more compromised than if she had joined the Good Shepherds. It was hard not to smile back at her novice-happy eyes. Soon afterwards she shipped out for the foreign missions, first stop Kuala Lumpur, later Lagos, where she met a man – more than a man, indeed; an English Protestant banker – and married in style. So then she'd volunteered for the well-to-do as well? It was strange, as unlikely a story in its way as the non-story of young Alexander, a fairy-tale of love and wealth and warm weather. And, like the reader of a fairy-tale, I thought I was being told something about who I was, and felt exposed.

Being motherless little Seoirse in oversafe Swiss Cottage in somnolent Lismore, county Waterford, was complicated enough. Daddy was in Dublin. I was his for just a month or two a year. The rest of the time I had his mother, Mam, his brother George and sister Chrissy to protect and pamper me, more parental than parents themselves, yet unreal by being three, by being compensation. Orthodoxy was what I wanted, not complications, I loved being Catholic, belonging to a holy family, and knowing I could be good to the last drop if I tried. I loved being Irish and having as mealtime guests De Valera, Nehru and the Boers. Mam would cry, '*Jambo, Jomo!*' given half a chance. But now she had a daughter who was all God-save-the-Queen, and a husband who said 'church' not 'chapel', and was happy: one of us, yet not; different, but related; as intimate a stranger as my father, and as difficult for me to ask about. I pondered timorously the moral of the fairy-tale, families are a front for leaving home, marriages mask disloyalty, life betrays itself in a confusion of raised voices and slammed doors. And at the same time, Lizzie was living a version of my story, only hers wasn't called Lismore, but England.

And here I was – Terry, on Martell now, bawled an order, I automatically served – discovering an England of my own with memory alone to guide me, confused that there seemed neither right nor wrong to where I was, no scheme, no pattern, no consistency. Not for the first time since my boat came in I felt I'd left but hadn't yet arrived. I was cold. I was waiting. I stood stropped in an official anteroom, all vibes and echo, guilty of departure but wanting to feel innocent.

Alone, behind the bar, I tried to console myself by imagining the confusion of other. Mightn't Terry's mouth-organising 'Waaa' of him bewailing his changing times? A family favourite but dim as a Toc-H lamp, to whom National Service had seemed salvation. He took its bollockings in stride, found compensation in the boyish closeness of platoon and squad, saluting to a Heron of the Queen's Flight, in conjugating the fabulous verb 'to man'. He was born again a bulldog, and once, in Aden, went with a bint who turned his blood to sand.

186 Demobbed, he headed to the palais down in Streatham, all hair oil and hormones. This time he'd *defny* look those Judies in the eye. He twisted his neck around in its unfamiliarly tie-bound collar, feeling a momentary rush of confidence, as of blood to the head. But Carol and Heather continued to pass by on the other side, on parade to 'The March of the Mods'. They were forming a big strong line for Joe Loss. ''Ere, wuzzis Madison, then?' It's the dance sensation that's sweeping the nation, thassall. He should've gone down the pub instead, his future all at once a cold-shouldering present.

Imagining Terry's past, or trying to match myself to it, did not allay the present. I was too aware of difference, and its protection, to get beyond it. But at least Terry's rum-fired, crass delirium of the brave was more engaging than the nothing that was doing in the saloon. That was another Lismore parlour, packed with dazed stillness. Ernie and Dave and Beryl and Connie all called for their brown ales and milk stouts with surplus hush and extra 'ta's, then self-effacingly slunk back to where family, neighbours and old mates kept on the *qui vive*, as rapt and unflinching as an honour guard, heads thrust slightly up and forward at the Pye.

As had so many of his live shows, Sir Winston's positively last appearance commanded a captive audience. Once again – it was a gift he had – all were on the edge of their seats to witness this canonisation of the commoner, this last word in compensation for the mythological failure whose name sometimes flashed found in the disputatious pub, the Juka Winza.

They barely moved. They barely spoke. They waited, vague, expectant. Solemnity might yet produce a formula (as so often previously). At Ludgate the skies should still resound in brazen fanfare with one of his punchlines (*Now this is not the end. It is not even the beginning of the end*) and their beloved prisoner break the bonds of death, rise up and bid them stand at ease, stand easy. No surrender! That was what he had preached (and his father before him . . .) No better time than now to practise it.

The saloon's tense attentiveness might have been a mute call for a miracle. But it also conveyed that there was no use pretending. The onlookers knew they were at a funeral, not a wake. Theirs was a duty, not a booze-up. Their hero'd bought it. He had surrendered. Somehow they had to find it in themselves to wrestle with the concept, pin it down. This was it. Everlasting Coventry. Eternal jug. He who had delighted them by speaking their minds for them, now, cruelly, asked them to think of him. The shroud. The silence. To think was as dumbfounding as to lose.

All things considered, then, the telly was a godsend. It was a way of not talking. It made things surprisingly bearable, resembling recent Christmases. The confident chronicling that dimblebied along so imperturbably was the sound of surfeit. But sobering realisation that public life was not all Coronations and Grace Kelly weddings rendered them inert, immobilised as much by the medium as by the event. They were a mute, unwaking escort, indoctrinated with a cultural novocaine which stiffened upper lips to the uttermost and made of the soul a bowler hat. They sat like the guards on horseback up in Whitehall. Like gulls gripping a wire.

And then, out of nowhere, it seemed (out of my mind?), there came a row and a ruction. I forget which stage it was in the proceedings. The launch had arrived at the South Bank. The coffin had been entrained for Bladon. The Charon–class locomotive had already crossed over from Waterloo. There was a thunder of footsteps in the pub, and shouts of semi-recognition and other sounds of eagerness and scrambling. Jack and George and Jack's son, Pete, and Terry, and everyone, were standing on the benches under the windows, straining to look out. I don't know if they could see that South Bank wharf: I doubt it. And if the train did come our way (there was a railway bridge over Black Prince Road), would it be visible from the public bar? Perhaps it was the inverted Blitz of H M Fighters screaming by above that roused them so. I may even be imagining all this.

In any case, the scurry to the windows is one of the clearest images that day has me with, as strong as the groundless memory, or fabrication, that as the coffin was being shouldered down the steps of St Paul's one of the able-bodied pallbearers almost lost his footing. I don't know if I saw that slip, or if, either then or at some later time (though oddly, not now, actively recalling), it struck me that there should have been one. And all I can say about the Public Bar uprising is that I must need something like it to be true, something unexpected, vaguely anarchic, disrespectful of property, bad form, some would-be collective shout of 'Cheers', an intolerable raspberry bestowed upon the grim saloon. I want the pub folk to have seen something that the telly couldn't show. I want them to have imagined themselves an escort also, their mufflers and moleskins no more out of place than any other of the day's uniforms.

Soon after the clatter and rush, the show ended, the telly darkened, it was time. The sky all day was iron. Through the open door I saw the black light slide off the concrete flats and grey brick fronts, the gifts of reconstruction, bequest of peace and Labour. The regulars took hands and walked into the valley of darkness. Home.

I watch them slip away from me, needing to remember that for five indecorous minutes they had their finest hour. Otherwise, it seems like I wasn't there at all.

EXTRACT FROM THE BIRDS' SANCTUARY

Frank McGuinness

ELEANOR HENRYSON *is an Irish recluse painter, in her fifties.*
STEPHEN *is her nephew.*

ELEANOR: I will die if this house is sold. I'll stop painting. I'm
sure there's plenty who would think that would be a happy
death. A happy death. My mother's fervent prayer to that
person. In the later stages of her illness, she stopped praying.
Maria Regina Henryson. Mother. Do you ever pray,
Stephen?

STEPHEN: I did, once. It worked. I stopped then. I'm not a
pushy person.

ELEANOR: Marianne prays. She used to pray for money. That
worked too. She doesn't need to sell her share of this house.
She has plenty of money.

STEPHEN: Will my father agree to sell with her? Will they sell?

ELEANOR: Over my dead fanny. She'll be here soon. We'll
know.

Silence.

ELEANOR: It has a life of its own, this house.

STEPHEN: Built in 1843 at the bottom of Booterstown
Avenue, some say it is the loveliest house in Dublin, for
from its windows may be viewed every watery inch, every
reed and rush, all the wildness of the birds' sanctuary, that is
truly God's blessing on this boundary.

190 ELEANOR: No human hand should maim the creatures of the air nor build upon the silent wastes of the deep that protect all that make their habitation in that sanctuary. It is said when Queen Victoria visited Dublin, she stayed in Booterstown. Her carriage drove down the avenue and she saw this house and chanced to wonder at its beauty. At her command the carriage stopped, she walked up the path and knocked, but no one answered her. She stood there silent, looking in, still wondering who lived there and why they did not welcome her. My father said that those in livery attending her watched the great Queen's face and saw on it a shiver passing through her soul as if in sorrow for the wrongs done.

STEPHEN: And seeing the Queen's sorrow the woman of the house, a beautiful old woman dressed in black, opened the door. This woman said to the Queen of England –

ELEANOR: All sins are forgiven.

Silence.

ELEANOR: All sins are forgiven, so my father said in his superstitious way. Utter nonsense, of course. Completely untrue. Queen Victoria visited Ireland in 1849. We moved here in 1929. I've heard of racial memory, but that fantasy is pushing it, even for this family.

STEPHEN: I wish it were true.

ELEANOR: Why?

STEPHEN: I rather fancy you as the descendant of that beautiful woman dressed in black.

ELEANOR: I rather fancy me as Queen Victoria. The other one is utterly batty. Rabbiting on about sin. That's the kind of old fool one sees marching down O'Connell Street parading pictures of the Pope.

STEPHEN: I thought you fancied the Pope.

ELEANOR: I did find him attractive – in a Jewish sort of way.
I'm an incurable romantic. Like Marianne in her own way.

Silence.

ELEANOR: Marianne believes that story about Queen Victoria. Let her.

STEPHEN: Yes. My father believes it too.

ELEANOR: Robert would believe anything.

STEPHEN: Yes, he would. Why does Marianne believe that
story?

ELEANOR: The workings of that woman's mind have long
been a mystery to me. Three times a year we speak. My
mother's anniversary, my father's, Christmas Eve. I put
down the phone and I see her face. And I paint it in the
birds' sanctuary, my painting of the birds' sanctuary –

She begins to sob.

ELEANOR: Stephen, I am so nervous. I am so nervous. If they
sell the house over my head – if they take away the house –
for three years I've been a recluse to finish the painting of the
sanctuary – Stephen – I do apologise, don't come near me – I
do apologise. If that bitch Marianne starts to run down
Ireland and the Irish I'll kill her. She will. She has to. Damn
her.

STEPHEN: Does she love the house?

ELEANOR: In her way. Yes.

STEPHEN: Is that why she believed the Queen Victoria story?

ELEANOR: She believes it because my father believed it. She
understood him. You shouldn't pry, Stephen, and you
shouldn't bathe in that filthy sea.

EXTRACT FROM GLENAGEARY BLOODY BLUES

Joseph O'Connor

God, if there's one thing I hate it's bloody churches.

Got up early this morning. Usual performance from the Aga Queen, Said can you not give the dramatics a break, not even on the day of my father's funeral. Blamed her nerves as usual. I really don't know where she'd be without her nerves. The Aga Queen, I call her. We have one of those old-fashioned cooker things, an Aga, hot all the time. She sits there all day when I'm out, just sits there smoking, whingeing on, listening to the radio, reading articles about cancer and Elvis Presley, wandering around the house like bloody Banquo's bloody ghost stalking the battlements. She convinces herself she has it. The big C, she calls it. I tell her if she keeps on the coffin nails she will, but she never listens. Not that *you* care, she says to me. She tells the kids she has it. That used to be her excuse. She would start then, down to the shops, something for a cake, nod and a wink. Mr Robertson said to me you must have a lot of cakes in your house the amount of sherry she buys. The thing is, she says she's stopped now, but I don't any more. Care, I mean.

It's probably just as well she didn't come. He would have sat up in the damn coffin and roared at her. Bad enough as it is. Mammy's bearing up well, Cissy over the top as usual, but I can't even get upset. God, what a heartless bastard I must be.

I used to try and convince myself they didn't know. The kids. I used to get up every morning before everyone else, hunt the bottle all over the damn house, up and down, all over the bloody show. In the oven, under the sofa, out in the bushes, even in the toilet cistern once. I came home, armful of bloody library reports, floor swimming with shit, her upstairs, going on, locked in the room. The plumber found them, armful of bottles. He said have you been having a party, squire, and I said yes. I didn't want to embarrass her. Bang. Another hundred quid out of your life. What can you do?

It's no wonder I've never got promotion. It must be a damn record. Fifteen bloody years and still Assistant Librarian, grade bloody two. It's not just the worry, it's the time. That's what I say to Reynard when he starts, not that he's anyone to talk. You have to put in the hours, get to know the right professors, pull the right strings, I tell him. How could I? All I could do to put in the nine to five, come home then, not knowing whether the bloody house would still be standing. And it's me who had to pick up the pieces. Me.

I get up, try to cook Niall a breakfast when I can, try to get Johnny out of his bed. That's the hardest part. It's like trying to raise the bloody *Titanic*. I even tempt him with a lift into college but he's as fond of the bed as his darling mother is fond of the Aga. All his friends say he's very gregarious, but never a word to me. I see him across the canteen sometimes, laughing, arguing, thumping the table, and I want to talk to him. But I hardly ever do. I should make more of an effort, I know, before it's too late. Not like Dad and me. Never got over our little difference. Seems so small now. One thing about a funeral, it certainly concentrates the mind. Argument in the car. He's a good kid, but I mean he could have shaved this morning of all mornings. It wouldn't have killed him. He's bright though. He'll go far, I'm certain of it. If he doesn't get saddled like his old man. Any signs of that and I'll shoot it down fast enough.

I'm funny about a cooked breakfast. I like the young lad to have porridge. It's stupid, I know. He hates it. The faces he pulls, and God knows he's not exactly a good-looking child as it is. I know it is ridiculous, but still, I like him to eat it. It gives him a good start.

In the middle of it all I try to shave. Every single damn morning I cut myself. Before we got married I never cut my

194　face once, now I do it all the time. Every morning for twenty-one years I've emerged from the bathroom with my cheeks plastered in toilet roll looking like a damn mummy or something, crawling out of Tutankhamun's tomb. That's the way I feel too. Doesn't even bother me any more. I get the kid into the bathroom then, wash his hands. We play a little game. I say roly poly, now turn over and he turns his hands upside down and lets me see the nails. He's a good kid. So's Johnny too really. I get a kick out of them. God knows they've had to put up with a lot. They mean well.

Lately I find money missing from my pocket. At first I thought it was her, but it isn't. It's him. I say nothing much. The Aga Queen doesn't agree with pocket money. She says it spoils them. She read that in one of her damn magazines, some new theory or something, the usual. Now what I do, I leave just enough there every morning. I know he's going to take it and he does, but neither of us ever says anything about it. Silent agreement kind of thing. I drop him into school then, bring Johnny in with me. Well I mean, it's only a few sweets or something for God's sake. She has the nerve to rant about teeth, when she goes on the way she does.

I used to do that too, suppose that's why I'm soft on him. Never any money to spare, you see, in our house, not with seven children. Dad unemployed, as he put it. The day he caught me, he beat me round the house, top to bottom, and I prayed to God to kill him. Kids. Of course, what could he do? Hard enough to make ends meet. I don't know how she managed, I really don't. The woman was a saint. They could have done with my wages too, but they let me study instead, when I got the place. I sometimes think I would have been better off not. Cissy told me they used to pray every night for me, to pass the exams, down on their knees.

God, if there's one thing I hate it's bloody churches. Niall liked the big car, but he got upset as soon as we arrived. I told him Grandad had gone on to a better place but then he cried even more. Made me think. The first time I saw Dad cry was the day I graduated. Only time actually. He was so thrilled. He stood outside the hall in his uniform, tears rolling down his big red nose, arm around Mammy, handing around cigars. A bit much, but he was so proud I had to let it go. All the neighbours there as well, decked out. He told me he loved me that afternoon, and I tried to steer my friends away from them. A drop too much, I think. I was embarrassed. It's funny to think of him gone now, quiet and still. Even when he was sick he was alive to everything. Cantankerous, I suppose, but still, blood's thicker than water, I wish some people would remember that, but of course, no chance.

It's terrible, but I wish it would end. Got to be back by lunchtime, another bloody faculty meeting, into the fray. Law is acting up again, in league with Philosophy, going on about availability, seating space, classification, you name it. But we haven't the resources. What are we supposed to do, conjure it up? I said, Professor Martin, we can't squeeze blood from a stone, but he just shrugs at me. I wouldn't worry but as usual it's guess who's neck is on the line. That's right. Muggins here. I had to plead with Reynard to head off English at the pass. He said he'd see what he could do but it really was about time the learned periodicals list was updated. He said there's stuff in there predates the bloody printing press.

Funny to see Dad laid out in his uniform, cap on top of the coffin. He'd have liked that. The hymn they played, 'By the Rivers of Babylon', really not very tasteful. Apparently the parish priest told the folk group he was a sailor so it was either that or 'Bridge Over Troubled Waters'. Hobson's choice, what could I do? I hate these modern ceremonies, all analogies and pretending Jesus is some clapped out beatnik in a caftan and spotty youths strumming guitars in training shoes.

Johnny says it's all rubbish anyway, opium of the people and so on. That's his friend Charlie. He's probably right too. His mother says being a student he'd know all about opium but he has learnt to ignore her over the years. It's the only way. I think he realises that.

I wish Niall would sit still. He fidgets so much, he's a real bag of nerves. Muttering to himself all the time. It's difficult enough as it is. I didn't know where to look, arriving without herself in tow, everyone frantically diplomatic. But suffice it to say, eyebrows were raised. I suppose they all know anyway. No point in fooling myself, but still I do wish.

God Jesus, I wish they'd get on with it.

Johnny says I talk about his future as if it was a rare skin disease. He has a way with words. Something has to be done about my future, we'll have to see about my future, we must get my *future* seen to. He's funny about it really, I have to admit it. He's quite sharp too, like his bloody mother, I suppose. That's what makes it important though, I know he's got the brains for it. His future I mean.

Went for a drink with him last night, had a great chat in the bar. We're really getting on fine these days, considering how things are at home. Saw him in the canteen yesterday at lunchtime, with that Charlie character and a girl I haven't seen him with before. One of his students Reynard told me. Strikingly attractive girl actually, even though her hair was blue. Nice hands, I noticed, very expressive. Was going to go over and pay the captain's compliments as 'twere but well, Reynard was in full flow and when he gets like that he can be a bit of a liability. So I pretended I didn't see them, and just went up to lunch. Chicken à la King again. Reynard says anything with a foreign name should be avoided, because it means it's yesterday's leftovers tarted up. I didn't feel like eating much anyway. Not after the morning's performance.

Reynard was absolutely cock-a-hoop because he's just got a poem published in the *Sunday Tribune*. Hardly anything to write home about if you ask me, especially as it's a poem he wrote four years ago, but I suppose beggars can't be choosers, so I splashed out on a couple of congratulatory rum babas. I do feel for him. I mean, it can't be easy, what with the other business still bubbling below the faculty surface. He says they've really got it in for him, another night of the long knives on the horizon and so on, and I can believe anything of those bastards. I mean, the sickening thing is, they're all at it. Poor old Reynard though, got himself caught, as they say, *in flagrante delicto*. That's the big crime around this place. Getting caught. Still, togs round his ankles, going at it hammer and tongs, my God, the mind boggles. He tells it well, but I mean, it can't have been easy, Dean of Arts walking in, girl spreadeagled on the desk, dress around her ears, Reynard in the throes. Apparently the Dean said I thought this was supposed to be a tutorial on James Joyce, Reynard said would you believe it is or says he did when he tells it, which I suppose is pretty quick, but a little too quick to be believable for him. He embellishes everything. That's the poet in him, I suppose. That's what *he'd* say anyway. That's Reynard's excuse for everything. He seems to think we're great pals as he puts it, but in fact we really don't have much in common.

At lunch he told me he still *loves* Margaret, but it's the passion he misses. He says there's no problem with the sentimental side of things but Margaret just isn't interested any more. I get a bit embarrassed when he goes on like this. I mean, a man of his age. He says he has his needs and he's only human, but I mean, it really isn't as simple as that, these are students we're talking about. Sometimes he asks about myself and the Aga Queen, how things are going in the connubial bliss department. I've never told him. I just don't think it's right, that's all. That's one subject I just don't want to discuss. Reynard, I told him, that's right off the curriculum, if you don't mind. So he said he didn't, and he asked about Mother instead. He can be quite diplomatic.

Mother's looking well since she came, considering. Funny thing is, she gets on best with Niall. He gets a big kick out of her, all her stories, tall tales. Sometimes when he comes home from school it's straight up to her room, talking away, nine to the dozen, like the United Nations or something. I'm glad he's not around the roads anyway. It's good for her, I'm sure. She's missed him over the last few years. Good for him too, I suppose. The thing is, I'd like him to know about where he comes from, in a way. Him and Johnny, they really don't have much idea what it was like. I mean, it's all very well for Johnny, the working class and so on, morning noon and night, the proletariat and such, but still he's got no real idea. I mean I never even *heard* the phrase working class until I went to college. Neither did he.

Money's tight, of course. I mean, she doesn't eat much, not at her age, but everything counts. And there's her prescriptions and things, and she needs a little something just to keep her going. Oh well, just have to batten down the hatches, no other option. This is Johnny's big excuse, money and so on. I mean, I've told him there are all kinds of scholarships, grants, exchange schemes, you name it. That isn't an excuse at all. I tell him that's no answer. I've offered to get someone to look them all up, we have lists in the library, but he says he doesn't want to do a doctorate and that's it. He says it's selling out, however he reaches that conclusion. That does hurt me I must say. Anything else I can take, but not that. I say nothing, but he doesn't realise what it means to me. Still, I suppose for the moment I have to play along with him. A phase, no doubt. He rolls his eyes when I say that, and he looks like his mother used to. Oh yes, he says, everything's a phase, isn't it? He makes me laugh. Never mind. He's still got nearly a whole year to finish, maybe that will give him time to come around.

The Aga Queen and I are actually at one on this, a very rare event. I mean, she puts it all the wrong way, sinful to waste the talents that God has given you and all that nonsense, priceless coming from her, but still, at least it's a two-pronged attack for once. That's something, I suppose. Something to be grateful for.

Big showdown today at work. Mrs Delancey launching another one of her pogroms against the evening staff, cutting down overtime, cutting down everything, mutiny brewing amongst the mature students, Mr Bridport for the Union gloriously ineffectual as ever, camping around Enquiries like Quentin bloody Crisp in a pin-stripe. I said the temperature in the library had just been reported by the World Health Authority as an official danger-level and that if it went up one more degree non-severe brain damage would occur. Mrs Delancey said that wouldn't make much difference around here. I said, Mrs Delancey, I resent that remark and she told me I could resent what I liked but air-conditioning was Maintenance's problem, not hers, she had a library to run, take it up with them. She knows very well you may as well be taking it up with a brick wall. Reynard says if you're flying over UCD and you see two black dots, one moving and one static, the one that's moving is a crow and the one's that's static is a maintenance worker. He's bloody right too. The damn place is falling apart at the seams.

I really noticed it last night. Johnny came down to see me, studying late for a change, pleased although I said nothing, asked for a lift home. While he was out getting his coat I went upstairs, walked around switching off the lights, putting books back on the trolleys. Seeing it empty like that, all the half-empty shelves, it really did bring a lump to the old throat. All the seats and desks, deserted, graffiti carved in, the humming of the damn airconditioning, strange. I don't know what I was expecting, but it made me feel downright funny. I stood in the dark, just for a few moments, looking out at the lights down by the lake, thinking. Then I came down and locked up. Unusual for me, but there you have it. Biorhythms or something, perhaps. Reynard swears by them at any rate.

All I hope is, when Johnny does his doctorate he doesn't end up back here. He'd be better off leading the bloody revolution than doing that. He really would. Although I suppose if it came to the crunch, I wouldn't admit it.

ARK OF THE COVENANT
Ciaran Carson

1

They palmed it in and hid it in a bog, invisibly, between
    the Islands of Carnmoon
And Island Carragh South: a strange device, concocted from
    the inner workings
Of a fertilizer bag and someone's fertile brain – gyres
    and gimbals, wires and moans.

A vulgate apologia was on the cards already, the orchestra
    of palms upturned and weighed.
It would be interpreted, dismantled, in iodine ablutions
    of The News
Which comes before The Weather: thunderclouds that move
    in symphonies of woad.

Soldiers painted like the palm-and-finger paintings of
    a child, smears of black
Which underline their eyes like eyebrows, so's the light
    won't blind them: they are
Egyptian, mummified and profiled in the *ignis fatuus*
    of check and road-block.

Scrawled hieroglyphs elaborate the black slick of the road.
    Witnesses
Are called upon, but the ink has lightened into amethyst,
    and soon its blue will be
Invisible, as new ideas dawn across the moss. A great panjandrum
    will construe their whatnesses.

They Trojan-horsed it in and stashed it in a bog, intentionally,
    between the Islands of Carnmoon
And Island Carragh South: a palpable device to suit the
    nomothetic military,
Their *sotto voce* Blacks and Tans; to second-guess the language
    of their brief campaign.

They read it in the Vulgate, words which spoke with high
    authority of semaphore
And palms. And psalms were evident in thunderclouds as
    pyramidal rays of light
Engraved in bluish tints, when God's eye glitters through
    the cloudy hemisphere.

He is painted like a waterfall or thundercloud of beard
    and ikon, topaz
Frown that condescends to Bethlehem, where shepherds watch
    by night across
Carnmoon, hunched carmine in the lanternlight, as they
    rehearse the day's momentous topics.

They are the witnesses of snowflake-lazy galaxies, who
    prophesy the moon,
Blue moon that indicates a Second Coming is at hand. It is
    a trip that might be
Wired or not, a trap of wired-up jaws from which ensues
    the Vulgate moan.

3

They hushed it in, in its impenetrable black: a bag, a
      coalsack isolated in Carnmoon.
It seethed with good intentions of its maker, trickling
      microseconds slow
As syllables which tick their clock like condensation drips
      in mushroom mines.

The dead black Vulgate of its text is barbed and gothic,
      and is inspired by Yahveh.
Its circuits have been dipped in the blackletter font. They
      have named it, *Proclamation*.
And whosoever does not take the word on board will be for ever
      called Yahoo

Who are doodled like the antlered stags and men in glyptic
      caves, ritual ochre
Hands imprinted there. The rubric of discarded bones has
      made it difficult to tell
Humerus from humus, as the sheep enact a huddled parliament
      on Carnmoon's snowy acre.

The animals were nodding witnesses, plumes of breath
      illuminated by the birth,
The icy straw. The frankincense and myrrh have taken on
      a cordite odour;
The movable star is relegated to the black bag, where it
      weeps amidst the weeping broth.

4

They'd bound it in a mock book buried in the bog between
    the Islands of Carnmoon
And Island Carragh South, and sniffed the glue and ichor
    of its perfect binding
And its veins. The dope-black seeds of its brain they
    wrapped in husk of cardamom.

Black Vulgate barbs and verbs were conjugated there
    with wired-up quips,
Hosannahs subjugated by the nomothetic tablature. It's
    writhing into future
Tense just now, elaborated by its wish to be, to match
    the pro quos to the quids.

Soldiers, camouflaged as hedges in the hedgeless bog, flit
    through the Islands of Carnmoon.
Their palms are blacked as if for fingerprinting, and
    the blue whites of their eyes
Illuminate the rubric of their Yellow Cards. They slant
    Egyptianly with dog and carbine.

One dog was witness, moaning through the scattered codices
    and hieroglyphs.
The alphabet of troops was learned by rote and entombed in
    the black aplomb
Of a police notebook: an abecedary *sans* eyes, *sans* teeth,
    sans everything, and sans serifs.

THE ORGANIC GRID:
NOTES ON WILLEM DE KOONING

Aidan Dunne

He continues to paint every day at his home on Long Island, despite the Alzheimer's disease, but remembers nothing. He will not begin a painting on his own initiative. Each morning he is led to the studio. 'Assistants' prompt him into painting by inscribing marks on canvas which he then responds to and develops. It is a strange, ironic fate for a painter.

A lot of money is tied up with the question of his continuing productivity. He is the holder of the record for the highest price paid at auction for a work by a living artist, his mere signature on a canvas guarantees value. Examples of the works produced under these conditions do not inspire confidence. They contain stylistic touches alien to most of his output and are untypically tentative, slack, even vacant. But that is merely consistent with the conventional view of his work of the last twenty or more years, even though until the early-eighties he was clearly and forcefully in control of what he was doing.

'Behind the current de Kooning there is always a better one who has faded into the past,' as Harold Rosenberg commented sardonically as early as the mid-sixties. A talent in decline, indulged but past it, eclipsed by successors, a dinosaur. Except that it is not true. *Pace* the young Turks of the New Wave, painting is still an old man's art, experience bears fruit, and the de Kooning of the seventies was a painter at the height of his powers. His mistake was to be a painter at all when paintings had become, for the arbiters of style, not so much irrelevant as invisible.

'There are as many images as there are eyes to see them,' Sam Francis once wrote. Never more so than now, when images proliferate in every available medium, exponentially boosted by technological developments. There have been many excited commentaries on contemporary western culture as an arena open to the free play of signifiers cut adrift from any notional signified. Without endorsing the more extreme forms of this view, it is clear that meaning must be degraded through sheer excess, and that paintings are but mere images fighting for attention among a virtual infinity of images. Great paintings, even the very idea of great paintings, paintings as demanding, significant repositories of thought, are more and more like lost cities in the jungle of images, overgrown, buried.

In addition, the very premise of painting as a complex, multi-dimensioned activity has been periodically under assault since the sixties, whether because it is viewed as 'a vast but finite quarry', as Ortega y Gasset said of the novel, at the point of exhaustion, or because it is technologically bypassed and no longer equal to the complexities of contemporary life.

There are two major fronts in this campaign against painting. One is the reductionist argument that a painting is no more than the sum of its concrete elements, that its truth lies in its mute, factual thereness. This line of approach leads from Cubism to a true Minimalism, though there are numerous variants of it. Less obviously perhaps, it also, in its exclusive formalism, leads inexorably beyond painting, beyond the mere object, to Conceptualism.

The other is essentially a related argument which suggests that truth is in materials. The lineage here is *arte povera*, Joseph Beuys, Neo-Geo, Object Art, again linked to Conceptualism and the kind of art that almost every art-school graduate is making now, and that almost every curator is bagging and making pronouncements about. This kind of art is honourably seen as a workable way for art to take on the world, but it lacks, almost by definition, precisely what painting can possess, a set of coherent formal criteria.

There is as well a relativistic undercurrent which promotes the view that painting is amenable to some manner of

206   rehabilitation if it renounces its heretical, hegemonic past, accepts an orbit within a diminished sphere of possibility and subscribes to the kind of system of meaning that is typical of the representational image. If, that is, it has a form and a content that can be interpreted and dissected in representational or quasi-representational terms (that is, if its style is worn ironically, so that abstraction ironically employed is no longer abstraction, it is 'abstraction', a representation of abstraction). That a painting should be straightforwardly about its own sets of internal formal relationships in the light of other, contemporary and previous compositions similarly preoccupied is anathema to current conventional wisdom. Such formal considerations do not rate in themselves.

Surprisingly, painting, having been out of critical favour for more than a decade, enjoyed a resurgence in the late-seventies and early-eighties. (At the same time it should be said that there is something unreal about this statement, passably accurate though it is. While the spotlight of critical or curatorial interest falls on relatively small areas of activity, painters still paint and people still look at, care about, buy and discuss paintings.)

In any case, here was painting meeting the epoch of the image on its own terms, fiercely fighting its corner with all the paraphernalia of the entrepreneurial eighties, including aggressive commodification, spirited media hype and a concomitant celebrity status for the (usually male) artists. Art as a continuation of business by other means.

The New Wave painting was, typically, figurative, Expressionist, brash, big, international (with manifestations in Europe, New York and, to a lesser extent, Tokyo) and Postmodern. Any all-encompassing dreams of the Modernist project had been discarded. Style was something you fed into the blender. Artists who had been painting away for many years, like George Baselitz, profited from this swing in popularity, together with many younger figures who came to it fresh.

The proliferation of younger talents was particularly notable, heralding a new epoch.

Or perhaps not.

Much, even most of the talents thrown up by the time proved short-lived. Many of these newly fashionable painters, particularly the Germans like Hödicke, Baselitz, Lüpertz, Fetting, Koberling. Salomé, Penck, Fetting and Middendorf, took their bearings from just a few aspects of German Expressionism (Kirchner, notably, and perhaps, though superficially, Beckman), turning out, typically, rudimentary images in ejaculatory bursts of pigment.

When the Royal Academy staged its benchmark 'New Spirit in Painting' exhibition in 1981 (a more internationally balanced show than the following year's '*Zeitgeist*' in Berlin), it naturally cast around for precursors of the New Spirit, lighting not on more distant historical exemplars like Kirchner or Beckman, but, reasonably enough, on Picasso, Bacon, Balthus and on the Americans de Kooning and Philip Guston. And, at least on the face of it, the two Americans were an obvious choice.

The case for their inclusion went something like this: de Kooning was the Abstract Expressionist who originally committed the heresy of reintroducing (and with a sense of humour, too) the figure into a purist abstract arena with *Woman I* in 1952, thus demonstrating that figuration had a future. Something comparable happened eighteen years later when, in the teeth of the new painterly orthodoxy of Post-Painterly Abstraction and Minimalism, Guston flabbergasted the art world by exhibiting cartoon-like figurative paintings. Their example paved the way for Baselitz et al. All, in a sense, true.

First of all, though, the differences between the two. In his later paintings, Guston slides into an idiom. In relation to his previous work, his figurative paintings and drawings have stopped trying. They accept a particular language and make representations within it. The language is derivative of elements of popular culture, comic books, cartoons, with con-

208   notations of narratives. What counts is his gesture of conflating low with high art, and that is implicitly a gesture of capitulation. If you can't beat 'em, join 'em. Painting can play that game too. And that is essentially the strategy adopted by the New Wave painters.

De Kooning also makes references to elements of popular culture, cannibalising advertisements, drawing on the sex goddess mythology of Marilyn Monroe. But he does not slip into an idiom. From its beginning to its decisive, liberating lack of a closed, finished conclusion (in fact, in the artistic community, de Kooning was infamous for his difficulties with 'finish'), his *Woman I* is not only a representation of a figure, it is about the difficulty of representing the figure.

It draws on Cubism, not as a style or an idiom, but as a necessary apparatus for dealing with the world in paint in the twentieth century. It even significantly advances Cubism without taking it down the road which, as orthodox histories have it, is signposted straight on to Conceptualism. 'Cubism,' Charles Harrison has noted, 'could never cope adequately with spherical forms.' Such forms are rendered as a series of silhouettes. The formidable breasts of *Woman I* are swathes of pigment, and swathes cut through pigment, that scoop up the reality of flesh and dump it, like Courbet's tree, in front of us. De Kooning describes form without illusionistic modelling.

The figure was, in 1952, no stranger in his work. For one thing, he had grappled with *Woman I* for about two years, continually repainting and obliterating the image. Then, *Woman I* is an icon of twentieth-century art and her explosive genesis is a myth of twentieth-century art. In fact figuration and abstraction coexisted easily in de Kooning's output, not alternately but consistently. There is no real lapse from figuration in his work throughout the forties. He works towards *Woman I*, not away from her. Figures had long been a staple subject for him.

Looked at from this direction, from the direction of his own earlier figurative work, *Woman I* represents not a perplexing return to an abandoned line of possibility but a radical stage in a continuing deconstruction of the figure. That is to say, what is surprising about the painting is not its figuration but the difficulties it perceives in figuration, its ferocious engagement with the brute fact of the thing itself, the figure's palpable forms, masses and spaces.

'In the end,' he remarked himself, 'I failed. But it didn't bother me.' Or, as Harold Rosenberg put it, 'Painting the *Woman* was a mistake. It couldn't be done.' In an exchange with Clement Greenberg, who told the artist that it was impossible to paint the face nowadays, he agreed but said that it was also impossible not to. What makes *Woman I* a great painting – though by no means de Kooning's greatest – is that it's an account of this failure. The real act of defiance came subsequently, when he continued to address himself to the figure even though his dealer couldn't shift the pictures and begged for abstract works.

Were de Kooning to succeed in his aims, one commentator suggested, all ambitious painting would have to cease for the succeeding decade, because, given his grandiose scope, the centrality of his concerns, he would wrap it all up. Clement Greenberg, too, the apostle of flatness whose Satan was the third dimension, before he did a volte-face, dismayed at what he saw as de Kooning's inadmissible employment of a Cubist scaffolding, was fulsome in his praise, seeing in his work ambition of the 'most profoundly sophisticated' kind ever seen in a painter based in the United States, one 'painting in the grand style . . . whose gifts amount to what I am not afraid to call genius'.

Yet this is the painter who, as has been noted, was notoriously unwilling or unable to complete a painting, chronically so until about 1947. For the following six years, any finished painting was as liable to be destroyed as released from the studio. Many works of the time owe their survival to chance visits from friends or colleagues, or to forgetfulness on the part of the artist who had lent out pictures. He continually

210 postponed finishing a picture, either scraping it off and starting again (often repeatedly) or devising ways to slow the drying of the pigment and keep it workable.

He was extremely taken with the story of Balzac's fictional artist Frenhofer, whose unintelligible masterwork forms the subject of *The Unknown Masterpiece*. Frenhofer, Thomas B. Hess noted, 'painted a de Kooning (*Woman I*) almost exactly a hundred years before the fact'. On more than one occasion de Kooning said that ideally he would like to work on just one painting for the rest of his life.

Many key works betray just such an ambition. One of them, *Excavation* (1950) (directly comparable with its equally impressive precursor, *Attic*, dated a year earlier), a big, eight-foot, close to monochromatic canvas with intermittent flares of primary colour, patterned with interweaving, incisive lines, was finished, he felt, when he'd painted himself out of the picture, and that holds true for all of his best work. *Excavation* is finished, but not closed off. It is indeed like the site of a half-completed excavation that might well continue indefinitely.

Significantly, it exhibits another trait characteristic of Frenhofer's imaginary masterpiece. It is exhaustive. Like Picasso's *Les Demoiselles d'Avignon*, it is an inventory of possibilities, an aggregate, compendium piece into which everything is crammed, nothing left out. There are layers and layers of forms, worked over and over, lost and found, buried and revealed, reflecting, Harold Rosenberg remarked, a 'density of experience more often found in poetry'. Many of these forms suggest bodily parallels, but not specifically. 'Even abstract shapes,' the painter said, 'must have a likeness.' The spatial framework of the painting, as well, its free-flowing interconnectedness, is as important as the forms it contains.

Like certain other paintings, and certain pieces of music, it is a world unto itself. In an essay on devising his concert programmes, Alfred Brendel wrote that certain works demand specific conditions in performance. For example, he cites Beethoven's *Diabelli Variations* as a piece that must always come at the end of a programme because the notion of entering another sound-world after something so totalising is inconceivable.

De Kooning was wary of articulating artistic ideas largely because, he felt, artistic ideas sounded simplistic or downright odd when spelled out, and painting was very much a directly physical activity. He was similarly cautious about admitting any connection with Cubism, yet if we go to the work the link is obvious to anyone with a pair of eyes. Canvas after canvas presents us with wrenchingly reconstructed worlds. His subjects are, archetypically, spaces and figures. His paintings repeatedly address themselves to two fundamental and overlapping questions: how do you make a figure in painting now? And how do you make a space in painting now? That is, complex spaces and palpable, sculptural figures (he eventually did turn to sculpture), and sometimes desperate attempts to reconcile figure and ground. Most of the latter paintings, particularly, are records of lost or inconclusive battles. Arguably the problems are never resolved, but the debate is perpetuated.

Frank Stella, whose artistic evolution, from Minimalism to increasing complication and surface activity within strict abstract precepts, reversed the conventional progression (and bravely so), sees the issue of space in painting as crucial, but opts firmly for an exclusive approach. De Kooning and Jackson Pollock he sees as being 'subjected to threats from the representational painting of the past', as they 'struggled with the stubborn armatures of Cubism'. Abstract art, for Stella, allows a vital 'working space'. The world must be decisively excluded.

Yet his own later, busier work, with its relief constructions and frenetic colour patterning, doesn't really allow the spectator access. In this he is closer to Pollock than de Kooning. Like Pollock, whose earlier images were progressively edged out by the sheer business of laying paint on the surface, by all

212   that was happening on the surface, Stella ends up working hard to repel, enjoying a more or less illusory freedom. Whereas de Kooning, as Conor Joyce puts it, does succeed in his later work (consistently, in fact, from *Excavation* on) in breaking through the surface and creating his own space: taking a walk in his own landscape, to paraphrase the painter himself.

In art at the beginning of the century, science and technology are Euclidean, hard-edged, regular, logical, reductionist. Just as they are in the classical Cubist grid, a framework for the quasi-rationalist breakdown and reconstruction of perceived reality. But the enraptured enthusiasm for technological progress that informs certain aspects of Cubism and more particularly Futurism foundered on the killing grounds of the Great War and was extrapolated to a nightmarish degree in the death camps of Nazi Germany. Technology without a conscience goes hand in hand with a sickness in the soul.

In de Kooning's work the hard-edged, right-angled grid of classical Cubism, no longer sustainable, is gone. In its place there is what might be described as an organic grid, something that is intermittently developed throughout his career, and finds its most accomplished expression in the stunning series of paintings made throughout the seventies.

After the *Woman* series of the early-fifties, he became preoccupied with spatial questions in another remarkable series of paintings, from, typically, the dense and clotted manoeuvring of *Composition* (1955), with its plethora of 'likenesses' that never become subjects in the way that *Woman* does, to the starkly architectonic *Rosy-Fingered Dawn at Louse Point* (1963), one of many rural landscapes that some critics found too empty for their liking. Here he came to a dead end, the same impasse evident later in a crisis picture, *Two Figures in a Landscape* (1967).

Then, in the seventies, he embarked on a magnificent series of paintings, mostly untitled (though some, like . . . *Whose Name was Writ on Water* or *North Atlantic Light*, were titled or acquired titles), to all intents and purposes abstract. The handling of pigment in them is vigorous, they are fantastically mobile, there is a tremendous sense of freedom about them. No angst, just endless and apparently effortless invention.

What these paintings manage is to find a way out of the impasse, via the harmonious marriage of his repertoire of biomorphic forms, Rosenberg's 'abstracted metaphorical shapes', pioneered by Arshile Gorky and influenced, if indirectly, by Surrealism, and what might loosely be called the landscape, albeit a landscape of pervasive flow, a protean, dynamic, watery domain. Figures are not placed in these works, simply because the spaces they embody are both inside and outside. Adjoining areas of the paintings – always a matter of decisive importance – link up via a transformed, elastic but recognisably Cubist grid. Each painting from this period is a sustained and often brilliant attempt to hold contradictions and oppositions in check: in and out, figure and ground, form and space, one area and another, drawing and colour.

They are paintings 'about' space, yet they are also replete with likenesses – in the fall of light, snatches of line, sweeps of movement. They evade the trap of becoming representational images while remaining completely open to the world, avoiding the constraints implied by self-imposed rules about formalism and abstraction. They manage this because they are worlds of their own. You could read this persistent refusal to plump for either option – abstract/representational – as mere equivocation, another symptom of de Kooning's penchant for postponement, his dislike of closure. But it is a liberating irresolution.

For their time, and ours, the later paintings, the paintings of the seventies, are awkward customers. On a superficial level at least, you can see the logic of juxtaposing *Woman I* with the expressionist outpourings of the New Wave. But the paintings of the seventies that did find their way on to walls adjacent to the work of the likes of Hödicke and the rest are a million miles removed in tenor and concerns. It is ironic that just when everything came together, just when he looked ahead, de

214 Kooning was fêted for qualities largely peripheral to his actual achievements.

By then he was indulged rather than understood. So shaky was faith in painting that no one really dreamed there were significant advances to be made within such a traditional framework. Better to settle for the excitement of the moment. Hence the authority imputed to the seventies works is purely hieratic. Because they have the Midas touch, the celebrity signature, they're worth looking at. They're worth looking at, again and again, because they are great paintings, central to any consideration of the subject in the twentieth century. They're difficult to write about, not amenable to academic analysis, not demonstrably Postmodern. All good reasons why we shouldn't accept conventional wisdom about them too readily.

EXTRACT FROM THE FABULISTS

Philip Casey

Tess was not political, but it seemed appropriate to join a Parade of Innocence, a march in the name of freedom for six men. In a way, she too was blameless and imprisoned, if it wasn't stretching the comparison too far. At first she hadn't known what was happening, with the commotion, and the deathly beat of drums. It could have been a bizarre funeral.

She had come out of North Earl Street, *en route* to her flat, and was intent on leaving the demonstrative to demonstrate. As she crossed over to the O'Connell Street median, amused by the woman who danced with her cross, a large colourful bird caught her attention, its neck lunging this way and that, and intrigued, she joined the crowds that lined the pavements on either side of its path. It was then she heard the collective name of the men who the parade supported. Several times in the long months before she left, she had heard their names on radio, had seen their brutalised faces on TV, and wondered if the assaults on her and her feeling of being trapped could be set beside their experience. In truth, she hadn't thought of them unless they were mentioned, but for the moment their faces occupied the screen she thought of them as her patron saints. Odd, that. The idea had slipped into her head one night, and she had never questioned it. And now, by chance, she could honour them.

Behind the bird, propelled on a platform by bewigged men of law, came a caricature judge, rolling demented eyes and slowly waving his hand. In their wake were squads of baton-waving police, whose shields were festooned with the tabloid venom spewed on the framed prisoners. Men prowled in cages; behind them came black-clad ranks, in cowls or Venetian hats

216 — black faces, white masks — carrying flaming torches. Behind them again, singers in red-and-orange cloaks. Unused to carnivals, Tess was mesmerised as one scene displaced another. It was like Venice in Casanova's time, or the pre-Lenten German carnivals, except they were not so solemn, so mannered, so . . . macabre, maybe. There was a hint of plague.

Perhaps it was the drums that made her uneasy. She was relieved when they receded as the support groups began to pass, carrying their placards and banners, and as once upon a good time she had a job and union card, and despite the ache in her belly, she slipped in behind a union banner and felt the warmth of being part of something selfless and noble.

By O'Connell Bridge the groups had become less disciplined and more sociable. A lot seemed to know each other. She knew no one that she could see, but out of the side of her eye she noticed that, although he was in company, a man was idly watching her. She had noticed him as she joined the parade, because he had a stiff arm, but now he was lost in the shifting mass of the crowd. There seemed to be mythic animals everywhere you looked, weaving in and out of the straggling groups, urging them on, slagging friends from the anonymity of their masks. Darkness fell quickly as they marched on.

At the Central Bank Plaza, the Parade mustered under a moon in a clear sky, and the crowd spilled over on to Dame Street. By the time the end of the march arrived, the speeches were coming to a close, Christy Moore had sung his song and there was one last song from the red-and-orange singers as a wire sculpture of a large victory fist was set on fire. Tess had got herself close enough to feel its light dance on her face.

She turned to leave, and saw him looking at her again. He averted his gaze, but taken by surprise, she felt herself redden, and she scurried behind the Bank and through Merchants' Arch to the Ha'penny Bridge. As she waited for the lights to change, he arrived beside her. In the steady flow of traffic, a bus and then a lorry passed, leaving clouds of diesel smoke in their wake. By now he was one of many who had come from the

Plaza. The lights changed and they streamed across. The yellow bulbs of the bridge lamps were flickering in their black casings. You could taste the sulphur in the air as coal fires burned across the city. There was something nineteenth century about it all. Perhaps it was an innocent coincidence, but he was still walking beside her and she was uneasy. On the other side they had to wait for the lights to change once more. When they did, she walked quickly, and pretending to look into the security gate of the Winding Stair, she could see he was following her. This was ridiculous. She hurried along Ormonde Quay, her heart pounding, and as she crossed the junction at Jervis Street, she broke into a run until she reached her door. There was no sign of him, but her hand shook as she unlocked it. She ran up the stairs and, out of breath, slammed the door of her flat. Not daring to turn on the light, she went to the edge of the window. It took a few moments, but then he came into view, walking at a leisurely pace, his head bowed. She didn't think he looked like someone following a woman with intent, and to her relief, he didn't check her door as he passed, but you could never tell. She pressed her cheek against the cold pane and stared at the floodlit bridge. Now that she was calm, she felt very tired and empty. 'Fuck him,' she said out loud. It was addressed to the stranger, to Brian, to anyone, mostly male, who deserved it. Arthur excluded, of course. Once again, she realised how she dreaded him becoming a man, however unlikely it seemed he would turn out like his father.

She lit the gas fire and went to the bathroom to change a sanitary towel. A fungus had formed on the wall where a chronic leak had left its tracks. It would have to be seen to but right now she hadn't the energy to think of such things. In the living-room, she drew the curtains and put on her cassette of Schumann's *Fantasia*. Turning off the light, she nestled into the scruffy armchair and closed her eyes, her hands on her belly.

When she woke, her neck ached, and, confused, she stared at the red light on the cassette. The air was dry and her mouth was parched. She turned on the lamp. The clock on the mantel ticked around midnight. Grumbling, she looked through the curtains at the street below, wondering if she might get a takeaway. The Chinese would still be open, and it wasn't too far, and her mouth watered at the thought of a beef curry – but it was too damn late. With her luck she would take a collision course with the only drunk on the quays looking for a woman to abuse.

Her kitchen was so narrow that if she bent down her head could brush one wall and her heels the other. In a box on the floor were carrots – a little dry but they would do – Brussels sprouts, an onion, some garlic and a suspect potato. Cut up fine, they would boil in a few minutes. Her mouth was watering as she watched the vegetables boil, so she turned out the light and gazed at the flame under the pot and listened to them bubble away instead. Her mouth still watered, but she stayed by the cooker for warmth.

She put on the other side of the *Fantasia* as she ate. The meal revived her, which she appreciated as food often made her feel bloated and uncomfortable, especially at this time of the month. Poverty had some good points after all. There was a screech of tyres as a car sped against the flow of traffic outside. Later, she lay awake, listening to the music until after four, her only light the red eye of the cassette.

There was grey light between the curtains as she woke. Closing her eyes again, she lay still for a time. There was something important she ought to think of but it didn't matter right now. She stretched out and brought the clock to her squinting, rheumy eyes. It was two, and she had to be at the dole office at half past. There was just about enough time for a cup of strong tea, and a quick wash and change.

The queue had stalled because of an argument at the hatch, and several women were already grumbling and restless. There was a light steam rising off their coats, and one woman's hair was stringy from the rain. Tess took off her knitted cap. Small mercy, her hair was dry. The young woman was still arguing, her voice rising and her face red. She turned sideways, shouting from an angle at the unfortunate clerk who was now exposed to the queue. Out of curiosity, Tess stepped a little to the right so she could see everything. The woman's feet were planted solidly on the ground, but her hips were working like pistons, as if to keep her tirade at full steam. The clerk answered coldly, retreating behind an immovable bureaucracy, but Tess could see she was upset.

'Fuck this for a lark,' the woman in front of Tess swore. 'I've a kid to collect.'

'Me too,' Tess said.

The woman glanced at Tess, then called at the clerk, 'Would you not get her a supervisor so we can get out of here today?'

Tess gnawed on her nails, and stared at a big rubber plant as she automatically shuffled along. Her turn came, and putting her cap firmly back on, she signed the docket and brought it to the pay-hatch queue. The notes were fresh and before she put them in her purse, she flicked them for the pleasure of it. Outside, she hesitated, longing for a cup of coffee, but she would have to get the bus to Fairview.

She arrived outside the school on the stroke of three, and heard the faint bell and then the clamour of the children as they rushed out, lusting for freedom. Tess glanced at a woman who nodded and they smiled at each other. There were a few men waiting too, aloof – embarrassed, she supposed. Only one spoke to his children; the others turned as the children came up to them and one walked away as soon as he saw his girl, letting the child catch up with him along the street. He was the surly one who eyed Tess most days but always turned away as if she embodied all his humiliation, and she hated him. It wasn't her fault he was unemployed and humbled like this in front of women. Damn him, he was employed bringing his child home, like everyone else here!

Arthur as usual was last, holding his satchel in front of him, his knees bumping it forward as he walked. She always meant

220 to reprimand him for dragging his feet out of school as if she was the last person he wanted to see, but as soon as she saw his dreamy brown eyes, she forgot. They stayed on her until he had almost reached her, and then his face would come alive, in a mischievous, embracing grin which made her gasp. Like an actor with perfect timing, he left it to the last moment, keeping her sense of expectancy flickering.

'Hello, Tess.'

'Hello, Arthur.'

She gave him a quick, sideways hug. Arthur was a loving child, but she had discovered that boys no less than men disliked being embraced in public. They walked happily through Fairview, oblivious to the constant roar of traffic. She glanced down at Arthur, who seemed completely at ease with himself, and while envying his self-possession, she was grateful for it too.

He was obviously happier since she and Brian had split up. There was peace in the house and he could be with both his parents for some of the day, most days. How had two people, who had been at each other's throats for most of their marriage – how had they produced a placid, contented boy like Arthur? She often wondered, and supposed it to be one of those conundrums that make one get up in the morning because life is still mysterious, even religious.

'Can I invite Annie to tea?'

'Who?'

'Annie. She's been sick.'

'Annie. Oh yes, of course . . . Yes, of course, invite her to tea! That's a very nice thought, Arthur.'

And to think she hadn't even missed Annie. He retreated back into himself, with a hint of a smile, content. He looked as if he had his life plotted out, and his asking permission was only a polite formality. Whereas his mother was in disarray, feeling superfluous and not at all an adult in control.

She steered Arthur into the playground in Fairview Park and sat down, holding him before her and looking earnestly into his eyes. 'Arthur, do you miss me not being at home at night?'

He thought about it for a moment. 'Would you come and tuck me in more often? Daddy's not very good at telling stories. He reads through a book at a hundred miles an hour and turns out the light as soon as he's finished.'

'Do I tell good stories?'

'Well, you don't rush, and they come out of your head, and your eyes go all wide when you think of the good bits.'

She laughed. 'But apart from the stories, is it all right?'

'I suppose so,' he shrugged, and dropping his bag, he ran off to the slide. She watched him climb and slide several times before calling him, and he immediately trotted to her, satisfied. She wanted to get some mince.

Annie was Arthur's age, but taller with red hair and freckles. After tea, they went into the garden, playing under the naked tree in the precious minutes before nightfall. Tess grinned. Annie was under the impression that she dominated Arthur, not realising it was impossible. What would become of him? He seemed assured of his rightful place in the world, something special and fulfilling, if he wasn't hurt along the way. She gnawed at her knuckles, watching him for a while, and then set to making Brian's dinner.

Half-way through making it, she remembered that Shepherd's Pie was his favourite dish, although she hadn't made it since coming to their arrangement six months before. Then, having been out of work for two years, he landed a job in a warehouse in East Wall. It had relieved much of the strain. Even though she had left him six months before that again, she had felt the resentment of a man cooped up in a house, blaming his wife for everything. She'd had a job which kept the house in groceries and had somehow managed to pay the mortgage. It seemed ludicrous paying the bills for a house she didn't live in, but it maintained her right to Arthur. With money in his pocket, Brian was civil to her, in speech at least. His body language bristled with amused contempt, especially after drinking, but she didn't care as long as she could see Arthur. It was, as her father put it, a queer set-up.

222   In a way, Brian had it made: his meals prepared for him and a free babysitter at least once a week. No sex, of course, not from her anyway. She stood on a chair and took down his porno videos, carelessly hidden as usual on top of the kitchen unit. What did he have out this week? She examined the titles and faked ecstasy of the cover photos, without emotion. It wasn't so much the pornography or even the violence she minded. What she minded was that he never got out anything else. All he seemed to be interested in were anonymous, gaping fannies and gouged eyes. In one, a hypodermic needle plunged into an eyeball . . . She hastily replaced the videos and leapt from the chair to the sink. Nothing came up, but her head thumped painfully, a clammy sweat on her forehead for a while. Of all the videos she had watched with Brian, that was the one thing that made her sick. And now he had it out again. Apart from the sadism, at which she squirmed, all those things she would never have dreamt of doing with Brian or any man – and certainly not with a woman – all that appealed to the voyeur in her for a while, but then its repetitiveness and cold athletics bored and finally repelled her. She saw that the videos protruded over the kitchen unit, so she pushed them back out of sight with the brush.

Over dinner, Brian was in a good mood. He even repeated a joke one of the men had told him during the day. It was actually witty for a change, and, laughing so much, he wasn't put out when she didn't respond.

'I see you've got more of those videos,' she said, looking at the floor.

'So?'

'So you've got a seven-year-old son.'

'And you don't want him to see nude women, is that it?'

'Seeing nude women is one thing; crude sex and torture is another.'

'He sees all that on the six o'clock news – OK, OK!'

She had been about to protest.

'I'm not going to let him near them, don't worry. I'm not a monster. I look after him, remember. I'm here six nights out of seven. I put him to bed, and get him out to school in the morning –'

'I know what you do!'

'But I don't know what you do, six nights of the week, unless you're walking the streets.'

'Fuck you.'

'And you. Though I wouldn't. Not now. Not never. And I'm sorry I ever did.'

She pushed the table away, upsetting everything on it, and ran into the short hallway. She was furious, mostly with herself for leaving herself open. In the kitchen, his fork grated across his plate. Breathing heavily, she felt as if she were breaking in two, trying to cope with her fury and hurt. She wanted to shout that she wasn't going to be his skivvy any more, that he could make his own slop in future, but biting her lip, she remembered Arthur. Drained, she leaned against the sitting-room door. Arthur knelt before the television, absorbed in a loud cartoon. Tess watched him for several minutes, but he didn't move, apart from when his shoulders shook in mute laughter.

The cartoon ended and she knelt beside him.

'I've got to go now, pet.'

He looked at her and leaned in towards her and she held him close, rocking him, moved as ever by his spontaneity.

'I love you very much,' she whispered. There was no reply, but she could feel how he bathed in her words, and gave himself completely to her, and she knew she would die for this, if she had to.

She looked around and saw that Brian was watching them. He looked empty and lonely and beaten, and for a moment she felt sorry for him and yearned for all three of them to be together in a warm embrace. But it was a wild fantasy, and, breaking the spell, he turned and went into the kitchen to put the kettle on for tea.

224   'I'll see you tomorrow, OK?'

Arthur looked up, nodded and rolled away on to his knees to watch a new cartoon. She went to the door, then turned.

'Bye.'

'Bye,' he answered, without taking his eyes off the TV.

She walked back to her flat, her cheeks streaked with tears in the cold evening.

PHOTOGRAPHS OF MY FATHER

Tony O'Shea

These photographs of my father were taken in
the last years of his life
(Tony O'Shea)

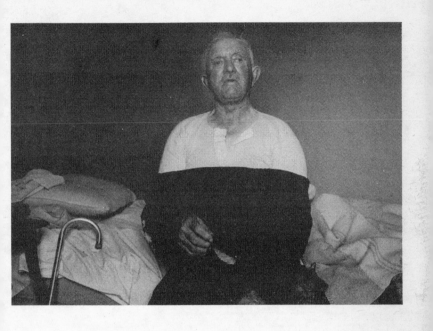

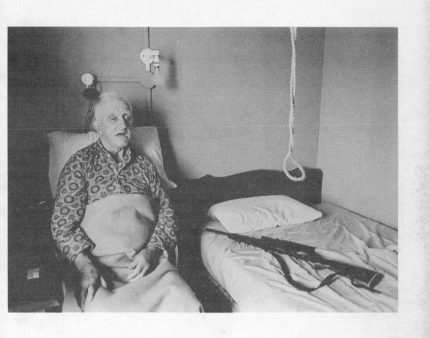

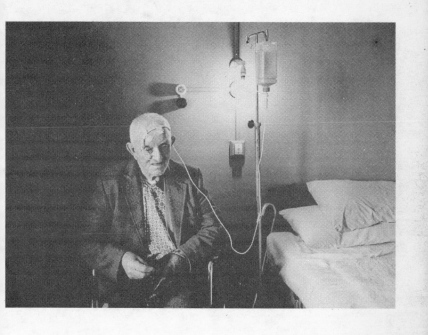

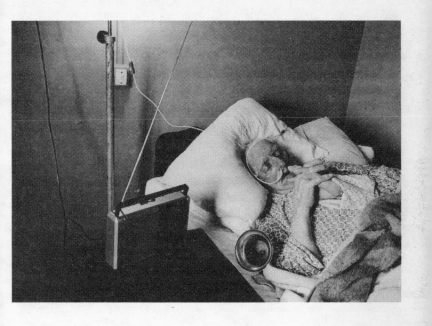

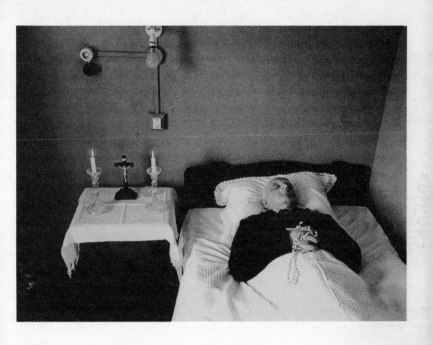

EXTRACT FROM A NOVEL-IN-PROGRESS

Mary Leland

The telephone was ringing. Geraldine could hear it as she walked from the drive around to the conservatory. She heard the trill cease in mid-peal, cut off, she supposed, by Anne's hand on the receiver. Closing the door carefully against the tinge of frost in the garden air, Geraldine heard her own name, an urgent shout, from the drawing-room.

'From your mother,' Anne said, as Geraldine went towards her.

To the consternation of her silence Anne said at once, 'No. It's about your mother. Your mother's solicitor, in Cork. He wants to – '

Geraldine turned away, mounting the stairs to her room. Without moving her body, the Labrador bitch at the foot of the staircase raised her quizzical brown eyes as Geraldine stepped over her.

Anne said, 'Geraldine!'

She answered without pausing, each step a deliberate rhythmic act. 'Tell him it was not I who came in. You do not know when I'll be back. Of course, you will give me his message.'

She heard Anne go back to the drawing-room. Closing the door of the small lavatory on the landing she rested her hands on the cold green edge of the washbasin.

The long mirror above it was frosted at each corner in the design of a water-lily. Between these brackets Geraldine saw her own face framed, the eyes blank, the mouth set, a face of negation.

The towel from the heated rail comforted her hands, she pressed a perfumed cream in a coil on to her skin and rubbed it

244 around the knuckles, the cuticles, the pleats which her fingers
smoothed briefly from the back of her hands. She was ready for
Anne, for the terror of coincidence.

In her room she changed her walking shoes for a lighter pair,
hung her jacket in the wardrobe, found her reading glasses and
her book, all without turning on the light, without looking at
herself again. Walking along the landing she passed the bedroom shared by Anne and Guy. The door was open: 'Twin
beds,' Anne had told her several years before, 'make life more
possible. There are no enforced intimacies. There need be no
pretence. It's a kind of separation, but it allows privacy without
distance. And it works, for us.'

Had Anne said all that, with such collection? Such defiance?
It would not have been characteristic, but Anne was always
capable of surprise.

From the door Geraldine could smell the pot-pourri Anne
made herself and piled in little china bowls throughout the
house, more here than elsewhere because, she said, and Guy
did not object, it brought the garden into their room. The tall
windows, curtained with lace and damask, threw broad bands
of lighter dusk across the beds immaculate under their damask
quilts. Filaments of that dusk caught the gleam of the picture
frame above the unjoined beds, where a McGonigal of rocks
and shadows deepened into its nightly oblivion.

They shared so much, Anne and Guy. They shared this
room; Geraldine knew it well in daylight, or in the roseate
softness that accompanied Anne's illnesses, or in the clear, fresh,
luxurious light of those mornings when Guy had been called
out early to the hospital and Anne had beckoned the visiting
Geraldine to a breakfast laid across the sheets.

There had been one bed only, then. Yet even in the dark
this room spoke of them both, and not separately.

Downstairs Anne had brought the tea tray to the low table in
front of the fire. Both seventy-year-old women sat one on
either side of the fireplace where the logs cracked. Light fell on
them from the standard lamps above each armchair. At the

right hand of one, the left hand of the other, were shelves of books; a small television screen – which, however, could accommodate sixteen channels from which Anne and her husband occasionally looked at one – was discreetly angled between the bookshelves. Equally adroitly placed were the combined turntable, tuner and compact disc player, cased in the mahogany shelving which also housed the records, discs and tapes.

The dog snored under the piano. If Anne's hand shook as she poured the tea from the china pot into Geraldine's cup, if the spoon rattled in the saucer she passed to Geraldine, it was because she was seventy, not because she was afraid of what Geraldine might be going to say.

Geraldine said, 'Do you remember my father at all, Anne?'

'No,' said Anne immediately, as if taken aback. Then she said, 'Well, you know I remember something of him. And I mean, I remember my parents talking about him – you know all that, Geraldine. You know – Mama knew him well, it was herself and Lady Windle who got him appointed to the university. I remember, I think I remember, that he visited us in Dunmahon. I remember once, I think.'

'I think I went there with him,' Geraldine said. 'Sometimes what I remember is not what happened, not what I did. But I do remember that big house, it seemed enormous to me. And the voices of the children, somewhere in it. I heard them before I saw them, saw you.'

They had spoken about this before. Often enough for their separate memories to coalesce. Which of them now could be sure that her memory, or hers, was accurate? The truth?

For Geraldine to call up the image, the memory, of her father she had had to depend on Anne's recall. Anne had done her best on previous occasions – there had not been many; a query in young womanhood shocking because it related to nothing in their lives as they knew them; a demand, fierce, imperious, sudden, in those days when they had come to know

246 one another again, marvelling at coincidence, as young
women.

On those occasions Anne had done her best to supply the
recollection Geraldine craved.

'You wore a pink coat,' Anne said. 'With a bonnet, it had
rosebuds on it. I remember that, they were like something off a
cake, I'll never forget, I never have forgotten, thinking that. It
must have been winter time, the coat was a heavy material,
long. There was, I think there was a little muff.

'Do you remember the little muff?' Anne looked directly at
Geraldine under the lamp on the other side of the purring fire.

'I remember the house.' Geraldine shifted in her chair,
putting her tea cup on the tray. She leaned back, slipping
her feet out of her shoes, drawing her legs under her on the
wide seat in a pose which she knew her stiffening muscles
would soon force her to abandon.

'That house – it's the feeling of it I recall. It's the feeling of it
I try to capture every time I come here, to you, to your house.'

'It was such a long time ago,' Anne said, half-smiling at the
fire. 'Do you think I tried to recreate it in some way when I had
a house of my own? I always thought that this house showed
something of Guy as well as myself. I don't think I consciously
tried to recreate something of Dunmahon.

'Although,' she added, 'I did hope that this place would
please Mama. I do remember that, hoping to impress her. Do
you think I ever did?'

Geraldine smiled herself, acknowledging the rue in Anne's
voice. It had not been easy to impress Mrs Stockley, Madame,
as she had been known.

It was more likely that she would have been relieved, rather
than gratified, when Guy's preferment to a consultancy in
Dublin brought Anne back from the English hospitals to the
kind of life, the kind of neighbourhood, she considered as
Anne's birthright.

'It was in Dunmahon that I first saw lights shining
under pictures, shining up, showing what was in the frame,'

Geraldine said. 'I remember the little bathroom on the half-landing – it was the first time I saw plants in a bathroom. A maid took me up to it. Coming back down I got a sense of passages, of rooms beyond what I could see, and voices, children – you, probably – in those rooms. I came down the stairs slowly, holding the struts of the banisters because I couldn't reach the rail. There was no one in the hall, so high, tiled and white and with flowers in the brass urn by the door, and the looped curtain across it.

'And then I heard my father's voice, and knew where I would find him. I felt a sense of him, a certainty that he was there, the door was white and open just a little crack, just enough for me to hear his voice, to know where he was.

'Do you think,' she asked Anne, 'that that's what I'm looking for, when I come here with so much anticipation?'

She saw Anne's open, unhurt smile, and laughed her apology.

'Ah, I'm sorry. Of course I come because I love you, I love to be with you. The reason, I suppose, why you come to me. We deserve each other, the way we sustain one another, and we enjoy one another. Forgive me for taking that as read.

'But isn't it possible,' she said, stretching her legs and flexing the ache away, 'isn't it possible that something in me sees that you know more about my past than I do? I mean, about my childhood, my youth? And resents it? Isn't that possible?

'And isn't it possible,' she said, leaning across the little table, eager to reach Anne's eyes, 'isn't there a possibility that I want to be able to find that door again, that little open crack through which I heard my father's voice, his voice in another room? That's all I have of him, Anne, that little gap with his voice in it, and the knowledge, the conviction, that he was waiting for me.

'I have no recollection of opening that door, which I must have done. Think of the things that must have happened – I must have gone back into the room, I must have spoken to your mother, even to you, Anne. He must have taken my hand to bring me home again, I must have gone with him, but to

248   which house? His sister's house? I must have been put to bed. I remember none of that. My mother must have been there, somewhere – not in Dunmahon, but where I was living. Where was I living – with him, or with Beata? I remember none of it; only the bathroom, the maid's striped dress and smell of starch, the brass urns, the fact of my father's presence, his cough.'

Anne sat quietly, waiting.

'You know Branscombe,' Geraldine said. 'I love it, we've been happy there, I think we've been happy. It's my home. And it's simple – I married into it. It has no ghosts for me, no ghosts of its own past. My part in it only began when I married Lionel.

'I'm not saying' – she felt Anne stir – 'no, I'm not pretending that Lionel and I haven't laid down some atmosphere, or that his children didn't carry with them some echoes, echoes that he shares, of course he does, of their past with him, and with their mother. But I only have to acknowledge that and be sensitive to it in them, especially when they're all together, which will happen more now, I think. But I don't have to carry it for myself.

'It's here. It's here I realise that I'm searching, more and more with each visit I'm looking for something. I stood on the landing upstairs just now as though I were listening for something. In Glencree – it was as though I wanted those dead men to speak to me, as though I could hear their voices. And things that I have heard, real things that happen to other people, they stay with me.

'As if I've borrowed them.'

A thought spurred her on.

'Like that cocktail dress of yours, do you remember, the black-silk embroidered one? You bought it, but you never felt right in it, and when I tried it on that time you came to us for Christmas, do you remember, it looked so good on me? That's what you said.'

'I left it with you,' Anne said, amused at the memory of Lionel's praise, and Guy's inability to recognise the same dress on a different body.

'Yes, you left it with me. And I wore it. But you had bought it thinking that it suited you, that it said something about you. When in fact it was for me.'

'It was a dress, only a cocktail dress. You're not going to get metaphysical about a dress, for God's sake!'

'No.' Geraldine spoke quietly, looking at the tiny, meshed hairs of her tweed skirt, the way the pleats cut the squares of green and purple on the russet fabric, chosen because its colours were the colours of moorland and bog, of heather and mountainside and the cold, brown streams.

Come away, O human child!
From the waters and the wild
With a faery, hand in hand . . .

Her thoughts were straying. She had not told Anne about the flowers, the card in the German cemetery. When she had come in there had been the sound of the telephone, the shock of the message she refused to hear. The coincidence. But it had been coincidence only to her. Anne could not know about it.

'That phone call. What was the message?'

Anne bent down from her chair to take a log from the basket. She poked the fire to make a hollow in the vivid ash and placed the timber there. Sparks gushed to extinction in the chimney.

Night cloaked the windows where the curtains were still drawn back. No one would see inside. The roadway was beyond the gravel, the lawn, the trees and shrubs clothing the walls. The two ageing women sat secure in the warm well of the house, in lamplight and firelight, the only sounds the far-off swish of cars on the road, the grunts of the sleeping, dreaming dog, the sizzling hearth.

'It was that man Brophy. His son, rather – although he must be elderly too, by now. He said he was ringing on behalf of your mother. I was surprised, that's why I blurted it out like that. He knew where to find you – it must be serious if he went to that kind of trouble.'

'And was it serious?' Geraldine's voice was low.

'Well, yes. I mean, she's dying. He said that she really is dying. This time, I mean. It's really happening.'

Anne began to flounder, hearing herself turn this news into some kind of comedy, seeing Geraldine smile.

'Well, he said if you wanted to be there. He left the hospital telephone number, he said you could ring him at home if you wanted. I just told him you hadn't come back yet, that I'd tell you he had rung.'

'So, she really is dying. This time, really. Did he say of what? What has she succumbed to?'

Anne didn't like the coolness, the disparagement in Geraldine's voice. She understood the response, but she didn't think it appropriate.

'You could go down,' she suggested. 'Easily. You're not due home until the weekend, this is only Tuesday. You could drive down and be back here for the ferry by Friday. I'll go with you if you like. Or you could fly, and just spend the day there, or even on the train you'd be there and back in one day. It's easy, really.'

Geraldine was looking into the fire. Her voice was still cool.

'Did he say what has stricken her? It must be something massive. The last time I heard of her she was trotting around like a three-year-old.'

'The last time you heard of her,' Anne said with acidity, 'was five years ago and she had cancer of the uterus. She had the hysterectomy, but there were secondaries and now her lungs have gone. He said there was no time to lose, if you wanted to see her.'

'Ah,' said Geraldine, her voice bitter. 'That's Mother all right – the ultimatum. Do this – do that – or else!'

Anne knew better than to say anything more. Seconds ticked in the silence, there was a whirr as the grandfather clock in the front hall prepared to strike the hour. Seven o'clock.

'Is Guy coming in for dinner?' Geraldine realised that they had made no move towards the kitchen, had not put away the tray, the tea things.

'No,' said Anne slowly. 'His rooms rang. He has a meeting this evening, so he's going to eat in town. They said he'll be late. Not to expect him. We can eat later, ourselves, if we're hungry.'

Geraldine understood the little undertow in her voice. Life is full of messages, she thought. We must make what we can of them.

'I wasn't going to get metaphysical about the cocktail dress, Anne,' she said. 'It was the other things we were talking about. Dunmahon. The pink coat. The rosebuds on the bonnet. The little muff. Real things – or do we only imagine them? Did they happen as we remember them – did they happen to us? What is memory, after all, to be exclusive? I know another story, the story of another child. It fits me, better than the pink bonnet and the rosebuds. Better perhaps than it fits that other child, because I can bear it.'

Anne settled back in her chair, fitting a cushion under her shoulders. She enjoyed Geraldine's stories. Perhaps this news, whatever she decided to do about it, would spark some more before the week was out. A relief, after all, that Guy wouldn't be home.

She wouldn't think too much about that now. Better to do what she had always done: look on the bright side, the side with the silver lining, the ill wind blowing somebody good. She listened to Geraldine's voice.

EXTRACT FROM
THE SEDUCTION OF MORALITY

Tom Murphy

. . . he slipped out the back way, got over the fence, went down to the railway cutting and crossed it. He knew where he was going. There was a heavy dew coming down with the dusk and he felt it getting in through the cracks in his shoes as he crossed the Nuns' Field. If he was not mistaken, there was rain on its way. He was making for Church, Lar Begley's.

Lar's was a strictly no-credit-given pub. It was a strictly no-conversation pub also. There might be a whisper now and again, but it was a rarity, an accident, and no one passed a remark on it. If a conversation was going in your head, that was your own business. Likewise, if you wanted to let your mind coast, or have a break from yourself and not think at all, you could do so while still remaining, more or less, part of the human race and, because of that, because you weren't in a vacuum like you might be, sitting on your own at home, it was the one place in the world where a man with a problem could think straight. There were only six or seven people in the town who went in there and it was doubtful that they had ever attended all together on the one occasion. Some of the six or seven were known to hate each other in the outside world but they were safe under Lar's roof. In any case, people rarely smiled in Lar's because smiling, if you think about it, is idiotic. If another customer was present when you entered, even if he was your best friend, you just nodded and you left the man alone. Finbar hoped that the amateurs never got hold of it and came in to desecrate it with their innocence and ignorance. He hadn't told a soul that he called it Church. He went there about once a fortnight. He'd

TOM MURPHY

be lost without it. All you needed was money. The rest was   253
simplicity.

Lar was deaf and, though it was known for certain that he
was able to talk, he would not speak a word to anyone. For
reasons known only to himself he wouldn't have a hearing-aid.
Maybe he was stone deaf and it would be no use to him or
maybe he felt, in keeping with the vow of silence, that as he
spoke none, he didn't want to hear any more shite-talk. No
one knew what, if anything, was going on in his head. The idea
of Lar made Finbar remember that he used to think that God
was a submarine, coursing slowly for ever the silent deep forty
fathoms down and that, every now and again, when the eyes
blinked, it meant that a ping had gone off inside in response to
one of Finbar's prayers. 'He's better than the word,' said old
Stephen one night, taking the pipe out of his mouth, musing to
himself. But theorising on the nature of Lar had ended years
ago. It was enough for the seven who got drink there to believe
Lar to be intelligent. Maybe they even loved him because, as
Finbar read it, deep down there was a fear that somehow, some
night, carelessly, someone of them would offend him and be
punished. Which was a strange apprehension, because Lar
neither liked nor disliked any of his customers and he couldn't
be said to be happy or sad. He was out on his own.

The light, a single pendant, was on in Lar's and Finbar went
in. There was no one at all in the place. Lar, as usual, was
pointed in the direction of the street, leaning his left hip against
the counter, the knuckles of his left hand pressing down on it,
giving the upper part of his body all the support it needed.
Below, in the gap cut in the counter, his right shoe was folded
around his left ankle. Because he was very big he had to hang
his head into his shoulder and this made the eyes screw
upwards, giving him an unintentionally baleful look. That
was the way he stood unless he was serving a customer. But
if you ever saw him pointed in the other direction, that is,
standing on the two feet and without any support from the
counter, looking in the direction of the screen of coloured

beads that his mother had put up across the opening to the living-quarters one time, you knew that he was thinking of bedding-down for the night and you had ten minutes. A child would understand it.

Finbar put himself in Lar's line of vision, showed his money and waited for the blink before putting it on the counter. If he didn't blink, you left. There was nothing to appeal to. He wouldn't ever serve a woman or any member of the Donnellan family, who were only blackguards anyhow, who came in now and again to see if they could win in some kind of silent contest against him. He always blinked for Finbar but Finbar believed that you should not take it for granted that he would.

Lar blinked and came-to. Finbar put down his money, made the seven-inch-gap sign between hands held horizontally for a pint of Guinness, pointed at the bottle of Paddy, followed by the three-eighths of an inch gap between thumb and fore-finger, for a small one as well, so that he'd have something to be doing while the pint was settling. Lar wasn't very clean but alcohol was a disinfectant.

So, was he happy enough with what he had realised on Vera to date, should he explore the matter further, to its full potential, was his heart up to it or, left to his own re-sources, what were his prospects? He had gone the other side of the pot-belly stove and taken his usual seat in the alcove of a blocked-up doorway. Lar was pointed at the street again, his knuckles and hip using the counter. The pot-belly stove wasn't going that long but the puffs of smoke that it was making through the joints were diminishing as it heated up. Finbar nodded at the stove his awareness of how conducive the atmosphere was becoming to clear thinking.

Pre-Monday night, his life was the same as that of most other men going, with financial ups eventually being balanced by downs. His sexual arrangement with Florrie Delaney, he admitted, was primitive but you had to remember that he was a very simple man. Faint heart never won a fair lady, and so say all of us, but what if you lost your senses in the winning and

had to be carted away? Since Monday night, when Vera
O'Toole arrived, a complex of emotions had him questioning his very identity. The extremes of mood-swings he had
experienced were only short of being incredible and wasn't
the prospect of their continuing too much to endure? He
had nothing but praise for the drink and the sex while they
were happening, and the bit of money, but the hangover
from all three filled him with dread and remorse and free-
floating anxiety that were impossible to understand, not to
speak of his terror of the authorities taking sudden revenge.
To rival it, a man would have to return to his time with the
Christian Brothers in Letterfrack, where there was a graveyard with one hundred children, but Finbar was not
prepared to go back to that. So, would he give Vera the
gate, was that what he was saying? That was exactly what he
was saying.

All at once it was as if a weight had been lifted from him.
The brown-ochre paintwork seemed to glow and he noticed
that the flagstones had been swept. The door rattled and he
craned his head to see past the stove-pipe who was in it. Dixie
Shaughnessy was coming in and, without thinking, Finbar
winked, how yeh, at him. Dixie looked through him. Finbar
watched the ritual of the money between Dixie and Lar and
Dixie giving a light downwards rub to an imaginary four-inch
pole in front of him for his usual. Then, when he saw Dixie
go to his corner with the pint of ale, Finbar went up for
another round before Lar settled back again. You wouldn't
ever want to overwork Lar and you avoided putting him
through unnecessary coming-to motions. He felt safe for the
first time in three days and, to celebrate, he had a double
Paddy with his pint.

It was true that, if you forget for a minute the money he was
making on Vera O'Toole, he was broke. It was true that the
year so far could not be called spectacular but, wait a minute,
that was not to say that he was reconsidering the decision about
Vera of a minute ago. The year so far had not been without a

256 few successes. The bent-wood chairs. He had pointed John-John McNulty in the direction of a pair of mirrors he'd got wind of, in a place no one would ever think of, and for the tip-off he got a hundred and seventy bent-wood chairs. He had spotted a man at the back of the dogtrack an hour before the race, feeding a Mars Bar to Stella Maris, the favourite, and he had put his shirt on Hearts are Trumps, the second favourite, No. 4, and won. He backed No. 4 in the next four races and it came up twice, leaving him two hundred and forty-four pounds to the good on the night. He invested a hundred of it the following morning in a pub in Cabra in medals.

The scam with the ham rolls had only done middling but that was because he didn't have the readies at the time to finance the size of batch that would make it worth your while. If he let the cast-iron urn, which, he believed, was an original, go to your man who was pretending to be interested in the fire-place, he would have a right rake of rolls for the big match, Saturday week. He had his copy of the Almanac to consult for the dates of race-meetings, holidays, Holy Days, fairs, fleadhs, football matches. There were any number of scams he could think of and work out, not even including his furniture. Hats, T-shirts, Lucky Dip, scarves, rosettes, official programmes for any event, his camera for the seaside, lino for the buffers out the country, broom-handles for the pilgrims at Croagh Patrick, bodhrans, shillelaghs for the Yanks, from Taiwan, not even including his ham rolls and his medals. And if he hadn't done anything about getting them to reconnect him to the electricity, it was because they were saying that a sudden General Election had to happen and if that was the case there would be amnesties flying for everyone for anything from Mephisto O'Flynn. Something always came up! O, Mephisto O'Flynn, you've a wonderful way with you! Inside, he was singing to his prospects. And he was realising now that the three-day adventure had the beneficial effect of shaking him up, making him eager to return to the familiar problems, to solve them and make money out of them and it was good to have the feet back on old terra firma.

The door rattled. That was Dixie gone out. Thursday night, he'd only have been having the one, all right.

Finbar realised that what he was drinking now and what he had drunk last night and the few he had today to settle him, after the Guards called, had started the ferment, making him prematurely drunk, so, in case he might forget them later, he would call a bottle of Paddy and a six-pack to take home when he called the next round in a minute.

He checked on Lar. Lar was chewing something. Sometimes, all right, you saw him put a handful of something into his mouth. Meal, Finbar reckoned, and that he had a bag of it beside the bed, inside. He kept a few things by him on a shelf under the counter that his right hand could reach without disturbing the rest of his body. He kept three or four mugs there, all of them brown on the inside. But one of them had a picture of a robin on it and if he ever put it on the counter, whether he was using it to drink from or not, you didn't go near him until he put it out of sight again. You could approach him, however, when he was chewing and Finbar got another round and his takeaways. A twelve-inch vertical thread for the bottle of Paddy, the open jaws of pincers pointing downwards for the six-pack.

He thought of his earlier beleagured state of mind and his present happiness intensified. Something always came up! He signed for another round. What harm, hadn't he the place to himself! His mood was self-congratulatory now, in conversation with himself. D'you know what I'm going to tell you? No. Wait'll you hear this. Finbar was looking for a hammer under the sink and he found a medal. It could have been there since his mother's time. He didn't bother to look at the image, he just assumed that it was the Blessed Virgin. He hadn't planned to do an experiment that day so maybe he didn't follow the procedures of last year's procedures to a 't', which was what he wanted to do. But he'd found the medal, anyway, and it was the only one in the house, as far as he knew, and he thought he'd see. Wait'll you hear. He drilled a bigger hole for the chain, he gave it just a lick of emery on the face and a good rubbing to the back and all around and over the rim. He hadn't used the emery last year, he let strong vinegar do the job, but he was out of vinegar.

He threaded the medal on to a string with the tweezers and dipped it in flux, to promote the fusion, yeh see. *Dominus vobiscum*! Where's me grease gone, he says. Dab of grease from the sprocket-wheel of the bike on to the face of the medal. *Et cum spiritu tuo*! Now, lo, he baptises the medal in molten solder, dips it, one, two, three times. I will go unto the altar of God, to God who brings joy to my youth! See him, how he floats the medal on the silver waters of Babylon! He's after a shape, something like a tear, a sort of a globule. Lift up your hearts! We have lifted them up! Here's where it gets interesting. Kyrie, Kyrie, he's twisting the string, he's watching the transformation, Kyrie! He's thinking, there once was an ugly duckling, when, hello, what's this? There was something going wrong. Lo, the solder was not falling from the greased and only partly cleaned face, like it was meant to do, like last year. Christie-Christie-Christie! The shape of a globule, yes, but where was the Virgin Mary's face peering out at you, as from a silver cave? The medal was disappearing into the stone, becoming engulfed, it was gone. He hardly knew which was the face side now, it was like a small fruit, and he took it out. *Ora pro nobis*, he poked the string out of it and, as last year, there was a beautiful dimple, convexing smoothly to an orifice for a chain, unlike the mean, burred hole of the original but, so what, what use to anyone was a little silver pear? *Dies irae*! He was about to see if there was another one, by any chance, under the sink when it started to happen. What's this, he says? Lo, two small black dots came appearing in the stone, appearing to come from the inside to the surface of the stone. They are growing inside the stone, darkly, and coming to the surface. It was like an X-ray that you'd started to hold up slowly to a light. Lo,

TOM MURPHY

what can these be, he whispers? Impurities? Or can it be a skull? 259
The banshee is out tonight, go down on your knees and say
your prayers! The line of a mouth had formed, the dots had
become sockets, light and shade were creating strong brows
over the sockets, eyelids, a chin, the high points of cheekbones
and deep creases curving down the cheeks from a strong nose.
Wait on, he whispers, oh, not without fear of what he was
witnessing because this was not the track of the Virgin's face
and, as true as Christ in the shroud of Turin, it was the Pope
was in it! What did you do? What did I do? What could I do
but laugh and say, can this be another sign, because, that very
instant, I remembered I'd seen the same man shot the night
before in a dream.

But, listen, it isn't right to be smiling in here and maybe it's
nearly time to gather up and go. You may think I'm drunk and
I'll answer you back, I am. You may say dreams have let you
down before and I'll say so has everything else. You may tell
me that signs are only wishful thinking but I'll tell you, the only
thing likely to shake the Medal Man's conviction of ten
thousand pounds out of medals alone, this year, will be a
bigger and a contrary sign to the ones he's getting . . .

The hair was standing on the drunken Finbar's neck. Even
before he looked and saw the way that Lar was, he had sensed
the change of atmosphere in the place. Not if it was a stone that
was doing it could he have been more astonished, not if you
had locked him up in an empty church at night and tied him to
a pillar and a forest of statues was moving and coming towards
him with bleeding outstretched hands could he have been
more frightened and awestricken. Now he understood why the
tinkers never came near the place. Lar was standing inside the
counter, head hung, facing the screen of coloured beads,
crying. Finbar felt himself go pale, his eyes widening. 'Oh
God!' he said in an unnatural voice. And though he could feel
an intense heat and he could hear something singeing and he
could smell burning hair, his feet were stuck to the floor. 'I'm
sorry, Lar, I'm sorry,' he said and, again, the voice did not

260 sound like his own. There was nothing to appeal to. Lar
continued there, dumbly, head hung, facing the screen, with
one big tear after another running down the side of his face.
How long since he had reversed the stance to indicate that he
was for bedding-down would never be known, but even if
Finbar had exceeded the permitted ten minutes' drinking-up
time by as little as five, he knew that Lar's was finished for him
now, for ever. Then he realised that in the horror of the first
moments of the experience he had backed away and the
intense heat behind him was his coat, burning against the
stove . . .

Michael Longley

CAVAFY'S DESIRES

Like corpses that the undertaker makes beautiful
And shuts, with tears, inside a costly mausoleum
– Roses at the forehead, jasmine at the feet – so
Desires look, after they have passed away
Unconsummated, without one night of passion
Or a morning when the moon stays in the sky.

THE GHOST ORCHID

Added to its few remaining sites will be the stanza
I compose about leaves like flakes of skin, a colour
Dithering between pink and yellow, and then the root
That grows like coral among shadows and leaf-litter.
Just touching the petals bruises them into darkness.

THE FISHING PARTY

Because he loves off-duty policemen and their murderers
Christ is still seen walking on the water at Lough Neagh,
Whose fingers created bluebottles, meadow-browns, red
Admirals, ladybirds, glow worms, and are tying now
Woodcock feathers around hooks, lamb's wool, badger fur

Until about his head swarm artificial flies and their names,
Dark Mackerel, Gravel Bed, Greenwell's Glory, Soldier
Palmer, Coachman, Water Cricket, Orange Grouse, Barm,
Without snagging in his hair or ceasing to circle above
Policemen turned by gunmen into fishermen for ever.

Eavan Boland

THE DOLLS' MUSEUM
IN DUBLIN

The wounds are terrible. The paint is old.
The cracks along the lips and on the cheeks
cannot be fixed. The cotton lawn is soiled.
The arms are ivory dissolved to wax.

Recall the Quadrille. Hum the waltz.
Promenade on the yacht-club terraces.
Put back the lamps in their copper holders.
the carriage wheels on the cobbled quays.

And recreate Easter in Dublin.
Booted officers. Their mistresses.
Sunlight criss-crossing College Green.
Steam hissing from the flanks of horses.

Here they are. Cradled and cleaned,
Held close in the arms of their owners.
Their cold hands clasped by warm hands,
Their faces memorised like perfect manners.

The altars are mannerly with linen.
The lilies are whiter than surplices.
The candles are burning and warning:
Rejoice, they whisper. After sacrifice.

Horse-chestnuts hold up their candles.
The Green is vivid with parasols.
Sunlight is pastel and windless.
The bar of the Shelbourne is full.

Laughter and gossip on the terraces.
Rumour and alarm at the barracks.
The Empire is summoning its officers.
The carriages are turning: they are turning back.

Past children walking with governesses,
Looking down, cosseting their dolls,
then looking up as the carriage passes,
the shadow chilling them. Twilight falls.

It is twilight in the dolls' museum. Shadows
remain on the parchment-coloured waists,
are bruises on the stitched cotton clothes,
are hidden in the dimples on the wrists.

The eyes are wide. They cannot address
the helplessness which has lingered in
the airless peace of each glass case:
To have survived. To have been stronger than

a moment. To be the hostages ignorance
takes from time and ornament from destiny. Both.
To be the present of the past. To infer the difference
with a terrible stare. But not feel it. And never know it.

THE PARCEL

There are dying arts and
one of them is
the way my mother used to make up a parcel.
Paper first. Mid-brown and coarse-grained as wood.
The worst sort for covering a Latin book neatly
or laying flat at Christmas on a pudding bowl.
It was a big cylinder. She snipped it open
and it unrolled quickly across the floor.
All business, all distance.
Then the scissors.
Not a glittering let-up but a dour
pair, black thumb-holes,
the shears themselves the colour of the rained-
on steps a man with a grindstone climbed up
in the season of lilac and snapdragon
and stood there arguing the rate for
sharpening the lawnmower and the garden pair
and this one. All-in.
The ball of twine was coarsely braided
and only a shade less yellow than
the flame she held under the blunt
end of the sealing-wax until
it melted and spread into a brittle
terracotta medal.
Her hair dishevelled, her tongue between her teeth,
she wrote the address in the quarters
twine had divided the surface into.
Names and places. Crayon and fountain-pen.
The town underlined once. The country twice.
It's ready for the post

she would say and if we want to know
where it went to –
a craft lost before we missed it – watch it go
into the burlap sack for collection.
See it disappear. Say
this is how it died
out: among doomed steamships and out-dated trains,
the tracks for them disappearing before our eyes,
next to station names we can't remember
on a continent we no longer
recognise. The sealing-wax cracking.
The twine unravelling. The destination illegible.

IN WHICH
THE ANCIENT HISTORY
I LEARN IS NOT
MY OWN

The linen map
hung from the wall.
The linen was shiny
and cracked in places
(the cracks were darkened by grime).
It was fastened to the classroom wall with
a wooden batten on
a triangle of knotted cotton.

We have no oracles,
no rocks or olive trees,
no sacred path to the temple,
and no priestesses –
the teacher's voice had a London accent.
This was England. 1952.
It was Ancient History class.

Ireland was far away.
And farther away
every year.
I was nearly an English child.
I could list the English kings.
I could place the famous battles.
I was learning to recognise
God's grave in history.

The colours
were faded out
so the red of Empire –
the stain of absolute possession –
the mark once made from Kashmir
to the oast-barns of the Kent
coast south of us was
underwater coral.

And the waters
of the Irish Sea,
their shallow weave
and cross-grained blue green
had drained away
to the pale gaze
of a doll's china eyes:
a stare without recognition or memory.

She put the tip
of the wooden
pointer on the map.
She tapped over ridges and dried-
out rivers and cities buried in
the sea and sea-scapes which
had once been land.
And came to a stop.

The Roman Empire
was the greatest
Empire ever known.
(Until our time of course).
Remember this, children.
In those days the Delphic Oracle was reckoned
to be the exact centre of the earth.

268   Suddenly
       I wanted
       to stand in front of it.
       I wanted to trace over
       and over the weave of
       my own country and read out
       names I was close to forgetting.
       Wicklow. Kilruddery. Dublin.

       To ask
       where exactly
       was my old house?
       With its brass One and Seven.
       Its flight of granite steps.
       Its lilac tree whose scent
       stayed under your fingernails for days.

       For days
       she was saying *even months,*
       The ancients travelled to the Oracle.
       They brought sheep and killed them.
       They brought questions of tillage and war.
       They rarely left with more
       than an ambiguous answer.

EXTRACT FROM A NEW TRANSLATION OF THE BROKEN JUG: A COMEDY BY HEINRICH VON KLEIST

John Banville

JUDGE ADAM (*to Martha Reck*):   Come missus, tell us, isn't it the case.

That you've come here about a broken jug?

MARTHA RECK: That's right – and here it is, in pieces, look.

JUDGE ADAM (*to* SIR WALTER):   You see?

MARTHA RECK: In smithereens.

JUDGE ADAM: Well then, who broke it?

MARTHA RECK (*pointing at* ROBERT TEMPLE):   That villain there. He broke it, he's the one.

JUDGE ADAM (*aside*):   A villain brought to book! Begob, that's rich!

(*aloud*) Clerk, write that down: 'That villain there, he broke it' –

ROBERT: Your honour, that's a dirty, rotten lie!

JUDGE ADAM (*aside*):   Oh is it, now? We'll see about that, boy.

Come, get the bit between your teeth, old Adam!

ROBERT: Don't listen to a word from that old rip –

JUDGE ADAM: Silence in court, by God! or you'll go down
For longer years than you have life. Clerk Lynch,

270   Write as directed: 'jug, well-known, etcetera',
     And then put down the rascal's name who broke it –

SIR WALTER: Your honour, please! All this is most improper.

JUDGE ADAM: How so?

SIR WALTER: There has not been a formal hearing –

JUDGE ADAM: I thought you didn't like formalities?

SIR WALTER: Judge Adam, if you do not know the way
    To run a proper trial, I can't teach you.
    If you can do no better, then step down,
    And let your clerk preside.

JUDGE ADAM: Forgive me, please;
    I did as we do things in Ballybog,
    Which is the way you said that I should do.

SIR WALTER: I said –?

JUDGE ADAM: You did.

SIR WALTER: I said that I expected
    No difference between the law elsewhere
    And here; if that is not the case, say so.

JUDGE ADAM: The fact is, sir, we do things different here.
    We have peculiar statutes in these parts
    That are not written down, nevertheless
    Are tried and true, and come to us direct
    From old traditions we in Ballybog
    Hold dear. Perhaps in London all is modern,
    The old ways all forgot, the past ignored.
    We are an ancient civilisation, sir;
    We had our Brehon Laws when you in England
    Still lived in caves and smeared yourselves with woad.
    From our old laws I have not here today
    Strayed one iota, that you can believe.
    I know the other way, the English way,

And if that's what you want that's how I'll go.
The trouble is, when you come over here,
You Englishmen, I mean, you do not see
That things are different here to over there,
And try to push your customs down our throats –

SIR WALTER: Yes yes, spare me the patriotic speech;
A little English dullness now and then
Perhaps might save a deal of trouble here.
However, let us leave these things aside.
For now, the best thing is to start again.

JUDGE ADAM: Agreed. Now, Mrs Martha Reck, stand up
And tell the court what is your grievance, please.

MARTHA RECK: My grievance, as you know, concerns this
                                                                        jug.
But let me, please, before I state the case,
Describe how much this jug once meant to me.

JUDGE ADAM: The floor is yours.

MARTHA RECK: Right. Do you see this jug?

JUDGE ADAM: We do, we do.

MARTHA RECK: Forgive me, but you don't.
You see the pieces of it, and that's all.
The fairest thing I owned is kicked and smashed.
This jug was in my family for years;
An heirloom, yes, and worth its weight in gold!
A beauteous and historic thing it was.
It told old Ireland's history, all in scenes.
See here, where there's now nothing but a hole,
The Firbolgs and the Tuatha de Danann
Were shown in mighty battle on the plain,
And there Cuchulainn swung his hurley stick:
Those are his legs, that's all that's left of him.
There's Brian Boru, at prayer before Clontarf;

272   You see him kneeling – that's his backside, see?
      Though even that has suffered a hard knock.
      There's good Queen Maeve, and Grainuaile O'Malley,
      And poor Kathleen Ni Houlihan herself;
      You see them where they stand, the three of them,
      Bawling their eyes out over Ireland's fate?
      They're legless now, and Maeve has lost her head,
      And Grainuaile's two elbows are broke off.
      Dermot MacMurrough, look, and Strongbow too,
      And Dermot's daughter, what's-her-name, that one.
      Strongbow looks like he's going to fall down:
      His sword is gone that he was leaning on.
      The walls of Limerick, look, the siege of Derry,
      The glorious victory at the River Boyne –
      Our country's history, broken up in bits!

JUDGE ADAM: All that is as it may be. Mrs Reck,
      But history lessons won't patch up your jug.
      What we're concerned with is the breaking of it.

MARTHA RECK: Hold on there, judge, and listen to me now;
      I want the court to understand my loss.
      This isn't some old pisspot or spittoon;
      There's history on it, and within it, too.
      My father's father first got hold of it
      In Enniscorthy after '98.
      A rebel there had stole it from a house,
      And granda stove his head in with his sword
      And saved the jug, all bloodied from the fight.
      My father then inherited the thing,
      And drank a toast from it when I was born;
      The story's in our family, how he filled –

JUDGE ADAM: Now missus, please, keep to the point in
                                              hand.

MARTHA RECK: – It up with ale and asked the whole town in,
      He was so pleased to be a dad at last,

For he was fifty then, my mother forty.
When I was wed I gave it to my Dan –

JUDGE ADAM: For God's sake, woman, we'll be here all day!

MARTHA RECK: And in the fire of '22 he saved it
By jumping out the window holding it,
And though Dan broke his hip, God bless the mark,
The jug survived the fall without a scratch.
In those days we were living in Cornmarket,
In two rooms over Bunty Ryan's shop –

JUDGE ADAM: Now, Martha –

MARTHA RECK: You are interrupting me!
If I am not to be allowed to speak,
What is the point of coming here, I ask?

SIR WALTER: My dear, good woman, you may speak, of course,
But only, please, of matters pertinent.
The jug was dear to you, that much we know;
These other things are all beside the point.

MARTHA RECK: Beside the point, you say? Beside the point?
Is it beside the point that I have lost
An heirloom that was in my family
A hundred year?

SIR WALTER: Of course not, madam, but –

MARTHA RECK: But me no buts, your honour, if you
please;
I am an honest woman, God's my judge,
And I demand that I should have my say.

SIR WALTER: Yes yes, dear lady, you shall have your say.
The point is, we know all about the jug;
You've told us everything there is to tell
About its history and your love for it.
But you have come to seek a judgment here,

274   And retribution, if it is deserved.
Just tell us now: who broke the jug, and how.

MARTHA RECK: I told you who broke it: that rascal there.

ROBERT: That is a lie, your honour!

JUDGE ADAM (*who has nodded off, wakes with a start*):   Silence, you! Next witness!

EXTRACT FROM
A NOVEL-IN-PROGRESS

Mary Dorcey

And after your love affair with Barbara you went in search of
men. That was the easy way to forget her. Even if it had been
possible to find another girl to whom you could transfer your
attraction it seemed too difficult and perilous a course. You
were expected to love men, expected to want them. Everything in your culture and society assured you of this. Why
should you argue? Why should you set yourself against the
course of history? And all about you boys and men offered
themselves. Everywhere you turned they were turning towards
you, soliciting, demanding, beseeching attention and sexual
pleasure from you and your girlfriends.

And why is it always winter in your memory of courtship
with boys? Black night. Rain, sleet and snow. The smell of coal
smoke in the air from a thousand chimneys, the sky sooty with
it. A cold January or December night, your back against the
schoolyard wall after a disco (and why were they always in
boys' schools? Run by priests?), your feet sore from a night of
dancing in shoes too tight, the feet of your stockings (and
wasn't it stockings still?) dirty from all the feet that had trodden
on yours, your lips bruised from rough kissing. The music so
loud, so raucous, your chest hurt and speech was an impos-
sibility which forced you to basics immediately. You sensed
someone out by their smell, their looks – the little of them you
could glimpse in a near-darkened room, pressed so close to
them you might recognise no more than a cheek or an earlobe
afterwards. And here you were back to the wall being kissed by
some overgrown boy with clumsy nervous hands, the rain
slipping down your back, and you were waiting for him to take

276   his tongue out of your mouth so you could say you were cold and wet and how about going home which would be walking together or on the bus.

By the feel of the thighs and chests pressed to yours you judged them awkward or timid, greedy or insensate. Where they placed their hands when they danced a slow one most significant – on your shoulders, your waist, the small of your back, or at once flat on your buttocks. Some grasped you by the hip bones and moved you about like a rag doll. If you got someone older there was the lift home. Which meant sitting in the front seat with your hand kept all the journey on the door handle so that you could escape swiftly if he turned out to be a rapist (which he might be because what did you know about him even if he *had* kept his hands on your waist?). And when you got home he parked the car (his father's) a few houses down from yours and turned at once to take you in his arms as though you were a taxi with a meter running. And even before he touched you his tongue was in your mouth pushing open your lips, lashing your teeth.

So many of these organs made your acquaintance in those years – they seemed almost to have a separate existence detached from their human habitat; you could imagine them rolled up and laid out in rows as ox tongue in a butcher's window. And this kissing as it was called was routine and expected by priest and family though they wouldn't have said so. The boys took it as their due for the money paid in at the door and you gave it as part-payment or in the expectation of being asked out during the week for a real date with drinks bought. And the weather played its part in deciding how long you spent in the car saying these good-nights, snow and rain keeping you captive for half an hour or more and clouding the windows so that there was no chance of a neighbour seeing and none could come to the rescue. And the closer it was to Christmas the more drunken and violent were these encounters and the more likely to lead to a cock in your mouth instead of a tongue when some older boy with the foresight to open his

flies before parking grabbed your head and forced it down on
his lap before you could speak or protest. You never saw his
sort again and considered yourself lucky to have escaped with
your life, or at least as important your virginity, because the one
impulse stronger than any other was to avoid getting pregnant.
As soon as you could free yourself you escaped from the car and
ran home and maybe spent the rest of the week in the company
of girlfriends to recover your equilibrium. And he knew, even
as he did it, that he had blown any chance of a return
appointment, but what matter? There were plenty more
where you came from – a whole dancehall of hopefuls every
weekend night and no way to get home unless offered a lift by
one of his kind.

But it was not always winter. Your legs were not always cold
in a short skirt in the rain so that the men could admire your
knees and fondle your thighs. It was as often as not high
summer – August or June. It was as often as not a hay field or a
river bank when you stretched on your back half-clothed, a
blouse pulled off one shoulder or a skirt up to your waist and
some male sweating over you, bruising breasts and lips and
cramping legs and arms.

And the scent of the grass and the flowers and trees were an
intoxicant and the smell of the water, river or sea, and the noise
of the birds and the crickets and all the thousand creeping
chirping flying things that came to life in the heat. And your
play was leisurely and sensual under the sun, with talk and
laughter in between bouts of lovemaking, sexmaking, or just
physical playmaking. And in the shimmering light of summer it
mattered now what he looked like, this partner in pleasure.
You became acquainted with the greater part of his body,
knowing the appearance now of his flesh, inch by inch
intimately, the feel of it too.

You knew if their skin was white or tanned, if their backs
were freckled or spotted, if their feet were washed. And you
had immensely more say in the timing and sequence of things
in this season, the male being more timid when exposed to the

278   light and having the open space all round you instead of the
sealed container of the father's car. Fields and beaches and lying
open to every eye and always strangers walking within earshot
and knowing you could call a halt because of their presence or
draw limits to what you would offer in the name of the hunt for
pleasure; how much of your body you could safely yield up and
in what order so that the enjoyment was greater than the risk;
the risk always in the back of your mind, knowing what you
must not do if you were to remain free of the disgrace and
calamity of unwanted, unplanned, unallowable pregnancy.
And the male being shy in daylight, the emphasis was put
not on his pleasure but on yours, you being less timid, far less,
to expose your flesh to the eye, and so you revelled in your
youth and your readiness and your quickness of response and
the bountiful harvest that was your body on the glimmering
threshold of womanhood. And because it was summer, because
birds flocked in the air and every living thing called out for joy
and lust for life and because the fruit hung on the branches and
the grass was sweet and provocative on bare arms and legs and
the sun warmed every inch of you so that you were full and
ripe and heavy with desire, you wanted perfection. You
wanted physical beauty and charm and grace. You wanted
romance. And how were you to find it with these straplings of
boys, these young men offering their first, their awkward best
with sweating hands and razor hips and elbows. How were you
to keep your mind from Barbara and the beauty of her breast at
your mouth and her yellow hair filling your eyes, falling like a
swathe of late-summer grass across your face?

And how were you to keep your mind from her and
memory of the days you spent in bed with her, that spring,
her mother's bed, lazy lying flat on your stomachs across the
double bed composing love letters to her boyfriend, a corporal
in the Army. And she described what she wanted him to do and
you wrote it down and she acted out her demands and his
responses to give you inspiration. She took off her clothes
slowly, garment by garment, so that you could study her body

and describe it to best advantage. Her tie, her tunic, her blouse
– now what would he say? she would ask – write it down
quickly before you forget!

And you wanted her so badly you were sick with it. Sick
with excitement and longing but biding your time all the same,
not wanting to ruin it, making the right move at the wrong
time and having all this lovely heart-scorching intimacy gone
for good. And she was teasing you of course because she knew
how you felt and reciprocated but wasn't ready to say so. And
you could not make out what she felt for her soldier boy that
she boasted of one minute and the next scoffed at with lofty
disdain as no more than a spotty-faced youth which he wasn't
because you had seen the photographs and he appeared all that
he ought to be, dark and brooding and a worthy rival, and she
drew your attention to this whenever it suited her.

And once when you were composing a letter she said she
would like to take him to bed and once there offer no more
than her naked breast to touch and say that he must be calm and
contented with this till dawn like a good boy and prove himself
like the ancient knights and she said write it down – write
down how you think it would feel to suck my breast and you
said no, that you couldn't, it was far beyond the scope of
imagination. And she laughed at you and said nothing was,
which was only flattery but nonetheless delicious. And you
looked at her sitting at the side of her mother's bed, sucking at
the tip of a felt pen that spilt red ink across pouting lips and her
right breast showed above the lace of a poplin slip which she
wore too tight for just this effect and you gazed at her coolly,
almost broodily, your eyes intent on hers, and spoke the bravest
words of your life – we could practise, you said – you could
show me. And she blushed and seeing the red in her cheeks you
knew you had won and though you were faint with terror you
did not regret it. And she smiled at you gravely and leaning
back on her mother's bed she offered her breast to you, holding
it between her hands, then letting it rest on the rim of her slip
that was pressed down by its weight forcing it higher and firmer

280   than it was though there was no need, she having perfect firm young breasts with beautiful nipples dark-mauve. And you moved closer and put your hands over her hands and lowered your face to her and so it was that you kissed a woman's breast before you kissed her mouth and it was the best kiss to be the first kiss of your life.

And how were you to keep your thoughts from her and your longing and make yourself content with the given, the acceptable, sources of gratification? For that you must, you knew all too well. They had separated you from Barbara, suspecting something they would not state, and sent her off to boarding school away from the bad influence that you were to each other. And you knew without their saying it that you must learn to live without her, leave childish passions behind and adapt to the real world, the world of pleasing boys and men, the boys and men that would grant you freedom, a home of your own, children of your flesh.

The love of women was a love that could lead only to destruction and loneliness – an old odd woman abandoned by the world, whispered at in the street. You knew nothing factual of women who lived with women, had never heard the word lesbian spoken. Had never seen it written. But you knew of its existence nonetheless in everything that went unsaid, in the lowered eyes and whispered pity, in the genteel shudders of revulsion for something never mentioned.

You knew that somewhere there were people who lived differently from your parents and the world they held out to you. You knew that somewhere there was desire beyond the fringe of the speakable. You recognised – in the very heat and constancy of the urgings towards heterosexuality and procreation, in the ceaseless enjoinders and encouragement to find a suitable mate while remaining of course virgin – the weight of a society terrified of some alternative. An alternative beyond mention. And you pictured this alternative as some bar in Paris or New York (of which you knew nothing at all) where strange men and stranger women crept at night with haunted eyes and nervous steps to gaze at one another with ineffable longing. The hopeless frustration of their needs forever in their eyes, with ugly hair and ugly clothes and mismatched sexual features, the women sporting beards and the men high voices. And from where this fearful image rose from you could not tell but it was as strong and clear in your fantasy as all the other shadow things, the thousand shames and warnings you heard whispered from behind raised hands. You imagined further that in the whole world there were not more than a dozen or so of these women who were born into a misconception of their function or stymied physical development. But their existence held its place in the hidden layer of your mind where all the glimpsed-at, half-seen things were stored for later exploration. And you knew beyond question that this shadow world would never be any part of yours. You could not doubt your own health, your so abundant, self-evident physical normality. You would grow surely into whatever a complete and total woman was. You need not concern yourself with this process. It was inevitable and ineluctable. It was already taking you inch by inch easily, perfectly, into what your mother and your sisters and your grandmothers were and had been. It was beyond your choosing or consideration. A natural unfolding certain as a flower or seed.

And knowing this you knew also that your love for Barbara was impossible. You must forget it. Forget the rapture of your mischievous play together between her mother's fragrant sheets when each one's body was a treasury for the other, an enchanted garden, and your play carefree and innocent. And you must forget the joy of watching pleasure travel over her face, widening and darkening her dark eyes and her body under yours like a river flowing in which you found your reflection and each movement was a response and mirror of your own so that you were making love and being made love to in one gesture, the recipient and the giver in the same instant in perfect empathic ingenuous luxurious sensuality.

This you must forget and leave behind you. Elysium. It was a memory that fitted nowhere. Had no name. It was a private

282 world of delight with no relation to any other. Assuredly no relation to those lost beings and the unmentionable tragedy lived out by their kind which you could not imagine. It had no place in the normal, the given, the expected of romance and pleasure and death and sex and marriage and children that all about you was obvious and taken for granted as fixed and inevitable. So your love for her, your lust, you learned to think, was something particular and curious to you alone. A dream sprung from the private complexity of your nature. An addition to the normal, an extra rather than a diminution, but one that had no outlet in the adult world. And so in some way **by so**me means you must turn it to account, feed its potency **and** poignancy into the accepted channel. It was a tributary you could not follow, an offshoot of your nature that was more passionate than the average. And this stream must not be dammed but guided back into the mainstream which was the romance with and love of and search for the male. The male – the man of your life. The man that would be all things for ever. The perfect one. The one of dream and myth. Legendary in his beauty and his power. Your companion and your soulmate, your one desire. The perfect expression and consummation of all longing. Your knight, your warrior, your courtier, your worshipper. The man you would love. The man you would give all your body to in one piece in one moment. The man your mother and your sisters would admire. Envy you. The man who would father your children and grow old with you. The dream made flesh. The word made flesh.

And somehow you must find him in these grapplings and clumsy explorations. You must seek him from a world of impersonators, impostors and strangers. You must find him and recognise him instantly in the first moment of your eyes meeting. You must draw him to you irresistibly and bind him to you inescapably. He must know you as the chosen one, the one born for him, the one waiting to fulfil his destiny. He would create you as a woman. And you confirm him as a man. He was out there somewhere among these hundreds that you tested and found wanting. He was somewhere on the hidden boundary of your life, just over the rainbow, journeying towards you guided by fate and instinct. You would meet him sooner or later in any one of the thousand possible meeting places, celebrated in romance – by a lake by the seashore, on a mountain top, in a crowded room, on a ship's deck, in the streets of a foreign city. He was out there searching for you, hour by hour drawing closer. He was almost in sight. And when he came into your vision he would banish utterly, obliterate thought of anyone but himself. All other desires would cease. Would evaporate as though they had never been. No name would come to your lips but his. No face wanted but his. The girl you loved would vanish from memory and longing. Eclipsed at once and for ever by him as the moon by the sun. You had only to continue your rituals of search, the ordained pattern of quest and discovery. He was making his way towards you.

And thus in this certainty you need not worry or fret that you loved Barbara above anyone – that you saw her face in every face that kissed yours, that you heard her name when your own was called, that you felt the touch of her skin and the beauty of her flesh in your hands at every touch of your skin. That the scent of her was with you always and the exact expression of her eyes when she looked into yours, laughing. That you wanted none but her, could imagine no longing but for her and no fulfilment save with her.

This you knew was what it was to be adolescent. You felt no fear nor foreboding. All would be made perfect with time. Dream and reality, longing and the allowable would one day merge. You believed in this. It was unthinkable that they would not.

For anything less would make life impossible. Unimaginable. And life then, in its sum and parts, was greater than anything you could imagine. It beckoned to you in all its glory, its radiance and luxurious promise. You were fifteen.

THE MEN IN MY LIFE
Paul Durcan

When you call me a repressed gay to my face
– To my face, I am happy to say –
I smile, gratified that you have got it half right.
But of course you have got it also half wrong.
Repressed? No, not repressed,
Embracing men on the side of the street
Full of praise, awe, admiration of them.
I am a free man at home in my own country,
An image of the gay metaphor of God.

I sleep with my woman in such contentment
We stare at one another in amazement
Where sheep may safely graze.
I seek in the course of my days
As well as her company and the company of her sisters
The company of generous, impulsive, exuberant men
Who are crazy about books, gardening, travel,
War, murder, theatre, scandal;
Who love life as religiously as they fear death.

When I have lunch with one of the men in my life
We sleep-talk the afternoon away.
Our conversation is a remote, wild beach
In the West of Ireland
Into which chased tides of sleep
Charge to and fro, dragging, foaming.
Great to be gay and not repressed
And to contemplate the men in my life
And by the men in my life be contemplated.

On a Saturday morning in September
We walk down the main street of the town
Holding hands and wearing our black gowns
That I bought in a flea market in Athlone.
Great not to be burdened by great expectations.
Great to pause under a Yield sign on the mall
At the bottom of Bridge Street
Where the river disappears off down into the demesne
And to stand chatting on the bridge side by side

So close to one another that we are part of one another.
Great not to feel obliged to murder one another.
The day is mated with its own half-light
And when night comes we will feel no need
To deceive our wives. Under pink black skies
And a solitary oak tree I will be at home
With my woman. He will be at home with his wife.
We are gay brothers and in a free Ireland
Brotherly gaiety is one of the forms of marriage.

Francis Stuart

THE GREAT

The great are not great now, the good are not good;
All who are named, who appear in the eye of day
Are touched by the rot, are lipped and lapped by the flood
Of our downfall. Black is the hidden ray
Of the good and great in our time. Unknown
Are their voices, their faces are turned, do not shine.
All that shines in this air is complacent, bone
Of the bright dry bone, and the blight of the brine
Of the desert is in them. Names in the mouths of men
Are wormy. The great are the others, are those
Gathered as though asleep, those beyond ken,
Growing by far, small streams as the willow grows.

WHAT WITH THE HIGHER PASSES
BLOCKED BY SNOW

What with the higher passes blocked by snow
And other routes unfinished or unmapped
It was getting clearer that I either go
Or spend another fruitless winter trapped
Here at the halfway house of the half-hearted,
Doubting your promise that if I departed
You'd come with me – that faith too was sapped –
So, wrenched from the memories of the past,
I fled with nothing but the household pet,
Alone, I thought, fearful, at longest last
And ravaged by regret.
But then at midnight right across the track
Authority in full array was spread;
Magistrate, Counsellor, Warder and Moralist,
The horrid lot! I thought of turning back,
As 'papers', 'passport', 'visa' crossed my head.
You pulled apart your shirt and what I'd missed
Was bared, as was the bloodstain where you'd sat,
As I drove on alone but for the cat,
Over the hill to the wholehearted dead.

AUTHOR BIOGRAPHIES

John Banville's

novels include *Birchwood*, *Kepler*, *The Book of Evidence* and *Ghosts*. He is the Literary Editor of *The Irish Times*.

Leland Bardwell

is a poet, novelist and playwright. Her *Selected Poems, Dostoevsky's Grave*, appeared in 1991. Her novels include *Girl on a Bicycle* and *The House*.

Sebastian Barry

is a poet, novelist and playwright. His plays have been performed at the Bush in London and the Peacock in Dublin. His most recent novel is *The Engine of Owl Light*.

Mary Beckett

has published two collections of stories, *A Belfast Woman* and *A Literary Woman*, and a novel *Give Them Stones*.

Eavan Boland's

collections of poems are *New Territory*, *The War Horse*, *In Her Own Image*, *Night Feed*, and *The Journey*.

Dermot Bolger

is a novelist, poet and playwright. He has published five volumes of poetry including *Internal Exiles* and *Leinster Street Ghosts*; his novels include *The Journey Home* and *The Woman's Daughter*.

Ciaran Carson

has published three collections of poetry, *The New Estate*, *Belfast Confetti* and *The Irish for No*, which won *The Irish Times/*Aer Lingus Poetry Prize in 1990. He is also the author of *The Pocket Guide to Irish Traditional Music*. He lives in Belfast where he is Literature Officer at the Northern Ireland Art Council.

Philip Casey

is best known as a poet. His *The Year of the Knife: Poems 1980–1990* was published in 1991. His first novel, *The Fabulists*, will be published by Lilliput in 1994.

Anthony Cronin's

collections of poetry include *RMS Titanic*, *The End of the Modern World* and *Reductionist Poem*. His *New and Selected Poems* were published in 1982. He is also the author of two novels, several volumes of criticism and a biography of Flann O'Brien.

Eiléan Ní Chuilleanáin's

volumes of poetry include *Acts and Monuments*, *The Second Voyage*, *The Rose-Geranium* and *The Magdelene Sermon*.

Mary Dorcey

is the author of a collection of stories, *A Noise from the Woodshed*, which was awarded the Rooney Prize in 1991, and a collection of poems.

Roddy Doyle

is the author of *The Barrytown Trilogy* (*The Commitments*, *The Snapper* and *The Van*) and *Paddy Clarke Ha Ha Ha*. He has written screenplays for two of his novels and two stage-plays, *Brownbread* and *War*.

Aidan Dunne

is the art critic of the *Sunday Tribune* in Dublin and the author of several monographs on the work of Irish painters.

Paul Durcan

has published fourteen collections of poetry. He won the Whitbread Poetry Prize in 1990 for *Daddy, Daddy*. His *A Snail in My Prime: New and Selected Poems* was published in 1993.

Anne Enright

is the author of a collection of stories, *The Portable Virgin*. She is a producer in RTE television.

Gerard Fanning's

first collection of poems *Easter Snow* won the Brendan Behan Prize for the best first book of poetry published in 1992, and the Rooney Prize.

Roy Foster

is the author of books on Parnell and Lord Randolph Churchill. His *Modern Ireland 1600–1972* was published in 1988. He is working on the biography of W.B. Yeats.

Hugo Hamilton's

novels are *Surrogate City* and *The Last Shot*, both set in Germany.

Seamus Heaney

has published eight collections of poetry including *Death of a Naturalist*, *North*, *Field Work* and *Seeing Things*. He has also published two collections of essays and a play, *The Cure at Troy*.

Neil Jordan's

films include *Angel*, *The Company of Wolves*, *Mona Lisa* and *The Crying Game*, for which he won an Oscar for Best Original Screenplay. He is the author of a collection of short stories, *Night in Tunisia*, and two novels.

Mary Leland

has published two novels, *The Kileen* and *Approaching Priests*, and a collection of stories. She lives in Cork.

Michael Longley's

collections of poetry are *No Continuing City*, *An Exploded View*, *Man Lying on a Wall*, *The Echo Gate* and *Gorse Fires*, for which he won the Whitbread Poetry Prize in 1991.

Eugene McCabe

is a novelist and playwright. His plays include *King of the Castle*, first performed in 1964, and *Swift*. His novels are *Victims*, and *Death and Nightingales*. He lives on the Monaghan-Fermanagh border.

Patrick McCabe

is the author of three novels, *Music on Clinton Street*, *Carn*, and *The Butcher Boy*, which won *The Irish Times*/Aer Lingus Irish Fiction Prize and was shortlisted for the Booker Prize. He lives in London.

John McGahern

is the author of five novels, *The Barracks*, *The Dark*, *The Leavetaking*, *The Pornographer* and *Amongst Women*. His *Collected Stories* were published in 1992.

Frank McGuinness's

plays include *Observe The Sons of Ulster Marching Towards the Somme*, for which he won the *London Evening Standard* Award for most Promising Playwright. His other plays include *Innocence*, *Carthiginians* and *The Breadman*. He has translated works by Lorca, Chekhov and Ibsen. His most recent play is *Someone Who'll Watch over Me* which was nominated for an Olivier Award in London and a Tony in New York.

Eoin McNamee

has published two short novels, *The Last of Deeds* and *Love in History*. His new novel *Resurrection Man* will appear in the spring of 1994.

Deirdre Madden

has written three novels, *Hidden Symptoms*, *The Birds of the Innocent Wood* and *Remembering Light and Stone*. She lives in London.

Derek Mahon

has published six books of poems, including *Night Crossing*, *Lines*, *The Snow Party*, and *Antarctica*. His *Selected Poems* were published in 1991, winning the *Irish Times/*Aer Lingus Poetry Prize. He has translated plays by Molière and poems by Nerval and Jacottet from the French.

Paula Meehan's

collections of poetry are *Return and No Blame*, *Reading the Sky* and *The Man who was Marked by Winter*.

Paul Muldoon

is the author of six collections of poetry including *New Weather*, *Quoof* and *Meeting The British*.

Aidan Murphy's

poetry collections include *The Restless Factor* and *The Way the Money Goes*.

Tom Murphy's

plays include *A Whistle in the Dark*, *Famine*, *The Sanctuary Lamp*, *The Gigli Concert* and *Bailegangaire*. He is completing a first novel.

Joseph O'Connor

is the author of a novel, *Cowboys and Indians* and a collection of stories, *True Believers*.

Edna O'Brien's

novels include *The Country Girls*, *Girls in Their Married Bliss*, *Night* and *Time and Tide*. She has also published several collections of short stories.

George O'Brien

is the author of two volumes of memoirs, *The Village of Longing* and *Dancehall Days*, and a study of the plays of Brian Friel. He lives in the United States.

Fintan O'Toole

is the author of *The Politics of Magic*, a study of the plays of Tom Murphy, *No More Heroes*, essays on Shakespeare's tragedies and *A Mass for Jesse James*, a journey through Ireland in the eighties. A journalist with *The Irish Times*, he is writing a biography of Richard Brinsley Sheridan.

Tom Paulin

has published four volumes of poetry including *A State of Justice* and *Fivemiletown*. His *Selected Poems* appeared in 1993. He has also published several volumes of criticism.

Billy Roche

is the author of *The Wexford Trilogy*, first performed at the Bush Theatre in London, for which he was nominated for an Olivier Award, a number of other plays and a novel *Tumbling Down*.

Francis Stuart

has written more than twenty novels, including *Redemption* and *Black List Section H*. His *We Have Kept The Faith: Poems 1918–1992* was published on the occasion of his ninetieth birthday.